Love
AND
Orgasm

Love
AND
Orgasm

*A Revolutionary Guide
to Sexual Fulfillment*

ALEXANDER LOWEN, M.D.

COLLIER BOOKS
Macmillan Publishing Company
NEW YORK

COLLIER MACMILLAN PUBLISHERS
LONDON

Macmillan Publishing Company
866 Third Avenue, New York, N.Y. 10022
Collier Macmillan Canada, Inc.

Library of Congress Cataloging in Publication Data

Lowen, Alexander.
    Love and orgasm.
    Reprint of the 1967 ed. published by the New American Library, New York, which was issued in series: Signet books.
    1. Sex   2. Sex (Psychology)   3. Orgasm.
I. Title.
HQ21.L6 1975   155.3   75-8652
ISBN 0-02-077320-X

First Collier Books Edition 1975
17 16

Printed in the United States of America

Acknowledgments

My thanks are due to a number of people who graciously gave their time and effort to the preparation of this book. I especially wish to acknowledge my indebtedness to Mrs. Adele Lewis, my editorial assistant, who read the manuscript with me and contributed many suggestions to the writing of it; to Mr. Walter Skalecki for preparing the drawings and diagrams; to Mr. Stephen Zoll, formerly senior editor at Macmillan Publishing Company, for his interest and support; and to my friends and colleagues with whom I discussed the ideas expressed in this book.

To Wilhelm Reich
whose discovery of the function of
the orgasm made this book possible

Contents

1

Sexual Sophistication
versus
Sexual Maturity

Fifty years of increasing freedom from the Victorian restrictions upon sexual expression and behavior have resulted in an attitude which can be described as sexual sophistication, but which can hardly be called sexual maturity. Although the average person of today seems more knowledgeable about sexual matters than were his forebears, there are many indications that he is confused about his sexual role and uncertain of his sexual goals. Psychoanalysis has provided the enlightened individual with many answers to sexual questions, but it has done little to resolve his guilts or relieve his frustration. This frustration is not owing to the lack of opportunities for sexual experiences, but to an inability to obtain the joy and satisfaction that sexual love promises. There is available to the public an extensive literature that describes the sexual techniques of different cultures, East and West. Unfortunately, it offers no insight or help for the problems of sexual unhappiness that are presented daily to physicians, psychiatrists, and marriage counselors. Sexual affairs are discussed with an openness unheard of fifty years ago, yet considerable ignorance and misinformation about the nature and function of the sexual orgasm still exist. One suspects that the current sexual sophistication is a cloak that covers and hides the sexual immaturity, conflicts, and anxieties of its wearer.

The popular response to books that offer the "secret" of sexual fulfillment in a few easy lessons betrays a widespread immaturity and naïveté. The "How to Do It" books and the "How to Be Happy" books would be ludicrous if the sexual situation were less desperate. As it is, they distort the problem and in the end confuse the reader. The plethora of sex manuals should be a warning that the difficulties will not yield to a facile solution. Sexual behavior cannot be divorced from the overall personality of an individual. Sexuality is a part or an aspect of personality, and it cannot be changed without corresponding modifications in the personality. In turn, as will be shown later, sexuality informs and shapes the personality. For this reason, sexual fulfillment cannot be achieved through the use or practice of special sexual techniques. Rather, it is the product of a way of life, the experience of a mature personality. There is a great need for an understanding of sexuality as an emotional expression. This book attempts to meet that need, as well as to provide some clarity about the nature of the sexual orgasm. This cannot be done without a consideration of the relationship of sexuality to personality. Once this relationship is explored, it will be possible to formulate some of the reasons for the lack of sexual fulfillment in men and women. Individual case studies from my psychiatric practice will be used to illustrate problems that are common to many people. The critique of current sexual attitudes that will emerge from this study may help to prevent the errors that perpetuate sexual unhappiness. The material to be presented in this study embodies the knowledge that I have acquired in fifteen years of active psychiatric work and twenty years of study of this subject. It is based upon the simple observation, repeatedly confirmed in practice, that a person's emotional problems and his sexual problems reflect the same disturbance in his personality. To think otherwise would imply that there are two compartments in a person's life: one compartment for his daytime activities (in the light, with his clothes on) and another for his activities in bed (in the dark, with his clothes off). My experience is that people are not so split, despite their efforts to convince others and themselves that they are. Despite a common attempt to create the impression that one can function differently on these two levels, the fact is that the compulsive housewife is not a gay little nighttime moth, nor is the responsible executive a dashing Lothario. When it comes to the sexual response, the compulsive housewife is afraid to let go, and the responsible executive is afraid to get involved.

It is my contention that the sexual behavior of a person reflects his personality, just as the personality of an individual is an expression of his sexual feelings. The point of view that underlies this study is that the sexual behavior of an individual can be understood only by reference to his personality. To define and establish this point of view it is necessary to distinguish sexual sophistication from sexual maturity, the pretended from the real. Sexual sophistication manifests itself most clearly in the attitude towards: (1) the sexual act, (2) masturbation, and (3) the body. Each of these attitudes will be analyzed and its implications described after a preliminary definition of the sophisticated position.

The sexual sophisticate regards the sexual act as a performance instead of an expression of feeling for the sexual partner. In the sophisticated view sexual intercourse is considered a victory for the ego while masturbation is seen as a defeat. This emphasis upon ego values in sexuality serves to rationalize sexual inadequacy and to eliminate the consciousness of sexual guilt. The repressed guilt can be made evident in the feelings about masturbation.

The sophisticated attitude regards the personality as identical with the ego or the mind and ignores the role of the body and its physical processes in determining behavior and response. This ignorance is shown by a lack of recognition of the effect of muscular tension upon sexual responsiveness. Chronic muscular spasticities inhibit normal respiration and motility and depress sexual feelings. The sophisticated individual assumes that his sexual difficulties are purely psychic and is therefore out of touch with the somatic aspects of his problem.

1. The sexually sophisticated person has apparently freed himself from all sexual guilt. He knows the varieties of sexual positions and the intricacies of sexual technique, and he has transcended the limits that formerly distinguished the normal from the perverse. He has accepted as a social value the lack of any inhibition or restraint in sexual behavior. He is a devotee of erotic literature and an exponent of the objective, scientific approach to sexuality. He is the sexually emancipated individual. However, sexual performance sometimes fails to measure up to par, and we find him, occasionally, in a psychiatrist's office for help. His anxieties, he assures us, stem from his fear of failure. He is not afraid of sex, he says, and he has no guilt about sexual activity. He is afraid that he will not perform adequately—specifically, that he may not be able to erect, that he may lose his erection, or that he may have a premature ejaculation. And he is well

aware that because of his fears and anxiety, the very thing that he is afraid of can easily happen. The sexually sophisticated woman worries that she will not reach a climax or have an orgasm.

I can understand the idea of failure in terms of a defeat of a man's masculine ego—that is, I can comprehend failure in terms of his inability to satisfy the woman; I can conceive of a woman's failure to reach a climax as a blow to her feminine pride; but a view of sexuality in which the success or failure of a performance is considered a valid criterion of sexual function is a specious one. Let us analyze the ideas embodied in this view, since they express the underlying attitude toward sexuality of the sexually sophisticated person.

The idea that sexual activity involves a performance, the skills of which can be learned from books or developed through practice, is expounded by numerous books on sexual love. We should take heed at the very mention of "performance" in relation to sex. A performance suggests the execution of an act in such a way as to call attention to the special skill or artistry of the performer. There is a public quality to a performance in the sense that the execution of the act is subject to the observation and criticism of another person or of an audience. A performance is gauged by standards that are external to the performer. These distinctions can be illustrated by the function of eating. Ordinarily, when one eats, one doesn't perform. But when one eats in public. the actions involved in eating take on some of the qualities of a performance. One's table manners are subject to observation, and one cannot avoid criticism if one's behavior does not measure up to the standards of good breeding. Pleasure in eating is of no importance when one's table etiquette is called into question. Writing a letter, to take another example, is certainly a personal and private action, but when its style or grammar is judged or evaluated, it takes on the aspect of a performance. The concept of performance distinguishes public actions from private ones. We can see, however, that any action can become a performance if it is executed with an eye to impressing others or, what is the same thing, if it is subject to evaluation by objective criteria rather than subjective ones.

Normally the sexual act is a private action, but it becomes a public one when it is exposed to observation. It becomes so exposed when the style or manner of its execution is questioned and discussed apart from the feelings that the action is intended to express. It becomes a performance if we lose sight of the feelings that give it validity. It loses its personal meaning when the criteria by which it is judged are other than subjective ones. The sexual act is a performance if it is used more to impress one's partner than to express an inner feeling. It is a performance if the partner's satisfaction takes precedence over one's own need. It is a performance if ego values are more important than feeling or sensation. The sexual sophisticate is a sexual performer. He is said to "perform well" if he can bring his partner to a climax regardless of his own subjective experience of the act. In fact, according to Albert Ellis, it may not even be necessary for him to penetrate the woman, "since it is easy for him to stimulate a woman's most sensitive parts with his fingers, lips, tongue or other parts of his anatomy, if his penis is not adequate for the job."*

Many men in this sophisticated age are sexual performers. Their sexual behavior has a compulsive element that is based upon their need to impress themselves and others with their sexual prowess. They are fixated upon their masculine egos, the symbol of which is the erect phallus. Where formerly such behavior belonged to the few (Casanova is a prime example), it now characterizes the sexual attitude of the many. So long as the compulsion exists, the sexual act will be a performance from which the risk of failure is never absent. When the compulsion is reduced or eliminated in the course of analytic therapy, the true feelings of the individual emerge. One of my patients related this observation recently:

> "For the first time in my life, I find that I am losing my erections. This may have happened once or twice before in special situations, but now it is different. I used to be able to screw and then go out and box a couple of rounds. I guess this was the result of a compulsive need to show how strong I was. On several occasions, I have had four or five women in a single day, running from one apartment to another. It was my pride. Now I feel that I have no great desire for love, and therefore the erection subsides. It is even better now when I am under the woman rather than on top."

*Albert Ellis, *The Art and Science of Love*. New York: Lyle Stuart, 1960, p. 117.

In this patient there was a deep conflict between oral, passive, and dependent needs and his ego ideal of a strong, aggressive, masculine personality. He puffed out his chest, overdeveloped his muscles, and tightened his jaw as a defense against the child within him. His compulsive erective potency was part of the same maneuver. But he was never sexually happy or sexually fulfilled. The pose had to be given up before the conflict could be resolved.

If one is not performing the sexual act for the benefit of oneself or one's partner, how is it possible to fail? If a person finds that he has no desire for food, he would hardly describe his lack of appetite as a failure. If this is not a failure, why is the loss of sexual desire so regarded? The answer to this question must be that we view the sexual act as a performance, in order to hide from ourselves and from others our true feelings. Otherwise, erective impotence would be taken to denote a lack of sexual interest in the partner. Lack of interest may result from fear, hostility, or the absence of any sexual excitation from the partner; but only in a neurotic sense is this to be considered a failure. A more honest attitude toward the self would enable one to discover one's true feelings and thereby avoid a situation that is embarrassing to the man, to say the least. Similarly, the loss of an erection may be owing to fear of penetrating the vagina, a repugnance toward the female genitals, or other reasons; but, again, it should not be regarded as a failure. When the man's sexual advances toward the woman are motivated largely by the desire to gain her approval or avoid her contempt, it is hardly likely that he will be able consistently to sustain his erection. If the loss of the erection represents a failure, that failure lies in his being untrue to himself.

The sexually sophisticated person covers up his anxieties, his hostilities, and his guilt by transposing them into a "fear of failure." It becomes necessary, therefore, to unmask the performer and to expose the fear of failure as a sophisticated rationalization of his true fears. Some of the fears, guilts, and hostilities that lie hidden under the cloak of sophistication are revealed in the following statement by a patient who had been tormented for many years by erective impotence and premature ejaculation:

"I once wanted to have sex with my mother, badly. ... I was so ashamed ... guess I still am. Christ, you don't admit things like this. I can see her ... naked ...

white ... beautiful ... tormenting me. It makes me uncomfortable to think of it. I feel tense and my throat is tight.

"I remember Mary, a cunning and vicious bitch who twists everything that's said and plays the role of a savior of drunks. I'd like to 'screw' her ... good and long and make her crawl to me because I could do it so good and hard and long. I'd want her to chase me, crying and pleading, and I'd 'groove' her and tease her and build and build until I'd make her come and almost scream with the feeling. I'm becoming excited but I'm afraid. She's such a strong wily bitch who would skin my balls. I'm afraid of her ... frightened ... and I could never do it to her. I've known many Marys and I've been afraid of them all because I wanted to do the same to all of them. The Great Lover, that's my bit, my role because I hate, because I fear a real woman, because I'm not a man."

Several things emerge from this pathetic statement that indicate why the patient was sexually impotent. First, there is so much fear and hostility expressed toward the woman that there is little room for any positive or tender feelings. Second, the patient's sexual feelings are so involved with the need to excite and satisfy the woman that there is very little feeling left for his own needs. He might be able to "perform well" in situations that approximate his fantasy, for these situations excite him greatly. However, such women as he describes also frighten him greatly, and he avoids them. Toward other women, including his wife, he is too ambivalent. Third, the origin of all fears and anxieties is in his almost overwhelming sexual feelings for his own mother. She is the source of the ambivalence that reduces him to impotence. He was orally dependent on her and genitally attracted to her, identified with her and was hostile to her. She is the Madonna and the bitch, the mother and sexual object. How could he not "fail," for to succeed would mean to possess his own mother sexually.

The oedipal problem is not unique to the sexually sophisticated individual. What is unique and characteristic of sexual sophistication is the distortion whereby the fear of the woman is changed into the desire to satisfy her, the fear of success (possession) into the fear of failure. This distortion must be recognized if we are to understand the confusions and contradictions that exist in our present-day sexual mores. In a recent magazine article, J. B. Priestley writes: "The encouragement and exploitation of eroticism, sometimes out of hatred of woman and fear of real sex and love, but mostly for commercial gain, now constitute one of the worst features of our Western civilization." The exploitation of eroticism in literature, the movies, and the entertainment world would not be quite so feasible if sexual sophistication were not confused with sexual maturity.

2. The distortion that underlies sexual sophistication includes another transposition of meaning. Formerly, failure meant the inability to inhibit or suppress overwhelming sexual feeling. It now refers to the inability to experience strong feeling. As we trace back the psychosexual development of the sophisticated individual, we almost invariably find that he had a rather severe masturbation problem in early adolescence. He struggled with anxieties and guilts that now, in adult life, he has rationally overcome. "Oh, yes," the patient says, "I thought it was harmful and wrong then; now I know better." He has learned that it was not the masturbation that was wrong, but the guilt that accompanied it. He is a sexually enlightened person. But if we accept his conscious attitude as representative of his unconscious feelings, we risk overlooking a major problem.

For the problem with which my patient struggled as a young man was not only his guilt about masturbation, but also his inability to control his masturbatory activities. Why couldn't he stop? Was there something wrong with his will power? Despite every resolve made again and again not to masturbate, he found himself subject to a practice that he could in no way, even if he was finally able to accept it as innocuous, consider a virtue. Thus each act of masturbation was viewed as a failure of self-discipline, a weakness of will power, a defeat for the ego. In the context of such experiences, the sexual act becomes associated with the idea of failure, an association that persists in the unconscious and subverts adult sexual activities. Thus the fear of failure is also the fear that one will not be able to control the sexual impulse. It is directly expressed by every individual who suffers from premature ejaculation. In his conscious fear that he will reach climax too quickly, he attempts to control the sexual impulse, not realizing that in the very attempt to control it, he will become tense, fearful, and unable to maintain the sexual charge to orgasm. The individual with prematurity of ejaculation is in a vicious circle: the more he attempts to control or delay the buildup of excitation, the faster will he reach climax. It is precisely in his fear of failure that the sexual sophisticate reveals the presence of basic guilts and anxieties about sexuality that have not been resolved but only glossed over.

What I have said about a man is equally applicable to a woman in her fear of sexual inadequacy, namely, that she will not have an orgasm. Whether or not a woman has an orgasm is no valid criterion of her adequacy or inadequacy as a female What kind of status symbol is orgastic potency in a woman or in a man, for that matter? Every woman is biologically capable of an orgastic response in the sexual act. If, therefore, she fails to achieve a climax in the sexual act, this may be owing to a variety of conditions over which she has no conscious control. It may reflect basic anxieties and guilts about sexuality that inhibit her surrender to her sexual feeling. It may reflect an unconscious hostility to her partner or to men that inhibits her full commitment during sexual union. Her response is certainly conditioned by the sexual potency of the man, and it may therefore reflect his sexual inadequacy. But unless she, too, is performing, her lack of full response expresses her true feelings and should be so interpreted. Nothing will prevent a woman from enjoying sex so much as her belief that the sexual act is a performance whose success or failure determines her adequacy or inadequacy as a female.

Sexual sophistication is such a barrier to sexual maturity that it must be eliminated if our sexual freedom is to lead to pleasure and joy in life and in love. Regrettably, it has become part of our sexual mores, and it has infiltrated into current sexological thinking. It is particularly manifest in the present-day attitude toward masturbation. It is a common clinical experience in psychiatry that patients report that they experience guilt during masturbation but not during sexual intercourse. Such a situation is accepted as quite normal by many analytic therapists and writers. Edrita Fried says:

I think that, in some measure, the shame and guilt following masturbation have a self-protective function, for they tell the adult person who can go out and try to find a partner but who settles for autoeroticism that something is wrong.*

*Edrita Fried, *The Ego in Love and Sexuality.* New York: Grune & Stratton, Inc., 1960, p. 159.

I believe that everyone is aware, including the masturbator, that the pleasure or satisfaction to be derived from intercourse is far greater than that which can be obtained through masturbation. When an individual turns to masturbation, it is usually because the pleasure of sexual intercourse is unavailable. This may be owing to lack of members of the opposite sex, to a neurotic inability to approach members of the opposite sex, or to a state of conflict between husband and wife, for example. In any case, I see nothing to justify the acceptance of the guilt or shame or anxiety. Naturally, as a psychotherapist, I would endeavor to help a patient to remove the obstacles to the full enjoyment of sexual intercourse. Every disturbed individual has guilt, shame, and anxiety that he will attach to masturbation. It is the function of doctors and therapists to remove these guilts, not to condone them. The act of masturbation itself is never self-destructive, and many times it has the positive effect of calming a state of anxiety. What is so damaging to the personality in masturbation is the presence of guilt, shame, and anxiety. Should therapists not find out why a patient needs to use an inferior method of obtaining sexual satisfaction rather than criticize his use of it? Why is more guilt associated with masturbation than with intercourse?

It has been my experience as a psychiatrist that the guilt of sexuality is masked in intercourse by the social acceptance of the act today. There are all kinds of rationalizations to justify the social acceptance of sexual intercourse by adult individuals. We speak of it as the deepest form of communication between two persons, as communion and sharing, as the expression of love, and so on. These descriptions are quite true, but the fact is that sexuality needs no justification. It is a biological function that derives its motive power from the pleasures and satisfactions it yields. Man is a placental mammal; if he cannot accept his animal nature as part of his biological heritage, he will struggle with guilt and shame about his sexual function.

Although it is easy to rationalize the value of sexual intercourse, it is difficult to justify masturbation for social reasons. And it is in reference to masturbation that the guilt about sexuality shows itself most clearly. One of my female patients expressed this clearly:

"Do you suppose my inability to masturbate with satisfaction goes hand in hand with guilt? It's something

I can't do for myself, so I want a man to do it for me. It's hard to admit these things." Then she added: "I was never able to masturbate until I started therapy. In fact, I never masturbated. I was so afraid of my private parts that I was afraid to use Tampax until I was twenty-two. I had intercourse for the first time when I was twenty-three, and I was scared. I was twenty-five when I first masturbated. Only last night was I able to masturbate with some pleasure, but it made me cry. I felt I wanted a man."

The crying that followed this patient's pleasurable masturbation cannot be understood in terms of her feeling of aloneness. She had never cried when her masturbation was unsatisfactory. In view of her pleasure, I pointed out that her crying was reminiscent of the crying of persons who are reunited with loved ones or relatives who have been away for a long time. Then she remarked, "I suppose you would say it's like me finding my body again." In masturbation, because of the absence of another person, one has the opportunity to fully encounter one's bodily self. When the masturbation is satisfactory, far from isolating one, it adds further incentive to find a partner to share the pleasure.

The girl who feels that her vagina is dirty and is repulsed when she touches it with her own hands, but permits a boy to caress her or to have relations with her is shifting the responsibility for her sexuality. Similarly the guilt that men feel about masturbation indicates their lack of self-acceptance. Intercourse, then, becomes a matter of ego satisfaction that hides the lack of fulfillment and pleasure in the act. In such cases, if one pierces the veil of sexual sophistication, one exposes the underlying sexual guilt. I was consulted by a married man of forty who was the father of several children. He had been in analysis for several years with some improvement, but without a resolution of his major problems. In our early discussions, I asked him about his sexual feelings and about masturbation. He admitted that he did masturbate and added that it was a source of considerable concern to him. I was surprised at this response in view of his previous therapy. When I assured him that there was nothing wrong or immoral about masturbation, he breathed an audible sigh of relief. "Doctor," he said, "you have removed a worry that haunted me for many years." I am always astonished when a patient who has been in analytic therapy tells me that the subject of masturbation had not been explored. It is one of the tasks of analysis to uncover and clear away the cloud of sexual guilt about masturbation that insidiously darkens all sexual pleasure. The physician's affirmation that masturbation is a natural activity helps greatly to counteract the harmful effects of this guilt.

Wilhelm Reich once said to me, "The patient who cannot masturbate with satisfaction has not completed his analytic therapy." This is not to encourage masturbation. It is to say that the inability to masturbate with satisfaction indicates the existence of sexual guilt that is frequently hidden by the sophisticated acceptance of sexual intercourse. Masturbation is an experience in self-perception and self-acceptance. As such, it has a legitimate role in the individual's life, as I shall show in a later chapter. In *Black Ship to Hell,* Brigid Brophy pointed out, quite correctly, I believe, that the fear of being alone is related to the fear and guilt about masturbation. Only when one is alone is one tempted to masturbate, but only when one is alone has one the opportunity for self-encounter.

3. The third area in which sophistication reveals its defensive function is in its attitude toward the body. The growth of sexual sophistication parallels the common acceptance of psychoanalytic ideas which in the lay mind denote the dominance of the mind over the body. The fact that psychic attitudes are structured in body posture and determined by physical tension is reluctantly admitted. The pseudo-intellectual can use his facility with psychological terms to hide his lack of body feeling. One can dispute the validity of a psychological interpretation but one cannot argue against an evident lack of harmony and grace in body movement.

Personality and sexuality are conditioned by the functions of the body and reflected in the physical expression of the body. The way a person holds his body and moves it tells us as much about his personality as what he says, often more. In our relations with other people we respond to their physical appearance and mannerisms without analyzing the basis for our response. Thus we are aware if someone holds himself stiff and rigid and we sense intuitively that this postural attitude represents a corresponding psychological attitude. We do not expect such a person to be warm and easy-going and, generally, we are not mistaken in our judgment. Similarly, as Gordon Allport points out, we rely heavily upon many motor signatures as indices of personality: the expression of the eyes, the shape of the mouth, the tone of voice, the quality of the handshake, and the manner of gestures, to mention a few.

The concept, formulated by W. Reich, that the character structure of a person is functionally identical with his body attitude is an important tool in our understanding of disturbances in personality and the sexual function. I have used it as a diagnostic technique in my psychiatric practice for many years. The principles which underlie this concept and the observations and conclusions to which it leads were elaborated in a previous book, *The Physical Dynamics of Character Structure.** Since this concept will be widely employed in this study of sex and personality, a short explanation of its basic thesis will be given here.

The repression of a feeling or the inhibition of an action is always associated with certain bodily changes which distort the form and motility of the body in a characteristic manner. An example will illustrate this point. I had a patient who had great difficulty in crying and in expressing any loud sound such as screaming or yelling. When an urge to cry arose in her, her throat became tight, her jaw became hard and set, and the urge disappeared. When this happened, her thought was, "What's the use?" A discussion of this attitude revealed that it went back to early infantile and childhood experiences. My patient was one of ten children. She had always felt that she could not assert her needs in the face of the large demands made upon her mother by the other children. In this situation, she had learned to repress her crying and to inhibit her desire for more attention and affection. The result was a rather grim-faced young lady whose throat was constricted, whose jaw was chronically set and immobile, and who tended to hold her breath. In the course of therapy, it became apparent that it was the impulse to suck that had been severely inhibited. She had considerable difficulty making sucking movements with her mouth. On one occasion when she put her knuckle into her mouth and tried to suck on it, she burst into deep sobs. This happened only after much time had been spent relaxing the muscles of her jaw, throat, and chest. Her grimness and her inability to express her feelings were responsible in part for her failure as an

*A. Lowen, *The Physical Dynamics of Character Structure*. New York: Grune & Stratton, 1958.

actress. Her case illustrates how an emotional problem becomes structured in a physical attitude.

Perhaps the most common disturbance in both sex and personality is caused by too early or too severe toilet-training practices. If the child is forced to become "clean" before voluntary control of the anal sphincter muscles is acquired, a chronic distortion of pelvic motility results. In such cases, the child uses the gluteal muscles and the muscles of the pelvic floor to establish some control over the anal function in place of the normal sphincter control. The result is that these muscles become chronically contracted as a safeguard against "soiling" or "dirtying." The effect is to bring the pelvis forward and to fix it in this position. At the same time, an outward rotation of the thighs occurs, which is characteristic of the problem. Also typical are small, hard buttocks that are tucked in and immobile. The natural swing of the pelvis is sharply reduced, so that sexual movements are forced instead of free. Such individuals also have a tendency to push their bowel movements out instead of evacuating in a natural, spontaneous way. This happens because repression of the anal conflict removes conscious control over the chronically contracted muscles. It is surprising how generalized this tendency becomes. One patient described himself as a "pusher." He said, "I make love like I do everything else. I push at it." And his sexual experiences, like his work function, were often unsatisfactory. The association of sex with anality because of the persistence of an unresolved anal conflict is responsible for the widespread feeling that sex is "dirty" or "filthy."

From the physical point of view, there are a number of factors that determine the sexual response of a person. The most obvious of these is the vitality of the individual. Sexuality is a biological process that depends upon the availability of excess energy for its proper functions. Conditions of fatigue and states of exhaustion greatly diminish an individual's sexual feeling; by contrast, the healthier, more energetic person will naturally have a stronger sexual response. Psychological factors can distort this relationship, but they cannot change it. Individuals who are physically tired may manifest a seemingly strong sexual desire. However, the lack of energy will markedly reduce the intensity of the final response or orgasm. Intercourse when one is in this condition may easily prove unsatisfactory. The sexually sophisticated person thinks of sexuality only in psychological terms and ignores the reality of the physical factors that determine the quality of the experience. It is a mark of sexual maturity to be aware of the state of one's health and one's body.

Since chronic fatigue is probably the most common medical complaint today, it is little wonder that there is so little real sexual satisfaction. Many persons are unaware of the low energetic state of their bodies. They move between states of elation and depression, unconscious of the relation of these psychic states to the underlying condition of chronic fatigue. The vital person has a well-balanced and stable psychic equilibrium.

There are many physical signs of a low energy level: the pale, pasty, or muddy complexion of the skin; the dullness of the eyes; the poor tonus of the body musculature; the lack of aliveness and spontaneity of gesture. These are some of the reliable criteria that I constantly use in making an evaluation. Despite some patients' statements to the contrary, I cannot conceive of a healthy and satisfactory sexual life associated with evidence of lowered vitality. It generally turns out that the patient does not know what a full and satisfactory sexual life really is.

Another physical factor that determines the quality of the sexual response is the motility of the body. Rigidities that limit motion reduce the intensity of sexual feeling and decrease the orgastic response. Rigidities are frequently encountered in the ankles, the knees, the hips, the shoulders, and the neck. These are always related to characterological rigidities that represent blocks in the expression of feeling. The stiff-necked person is obstinate, the unbending individual (speaking psychologically) cannot bend physically. It would be illogical to expect such a person to be able to yield to the feeling of love. To resolve such rigidities, I have found it necessary to analyze their psychological significance and at the same time to restore the motility of the body.

On the other hand, there are conditions of exaggerated motility that indicate the presence of pathological personality conditions. The patient who has the ability to bend backward almost in half may suffer from the lack of a strong "backbone" feeling. Such a lack may also be discovered by an analysis of the patient's behavior, and one diagnostic method can be used to confirm the observations of the other. I have invariably found that the absence of a strong "backbone" feeling is associated with a lack of ego strength and a loss of the sense of self, both of which are important, as I shall show, to healthy sexuality.

One further observation may be sufficient to establish the validity of this approach. During an initial interview with a female patient, I noticed that she stood with all her weight on her heels. A slight push almost toppled her backward. When I pointed out her lack of balance and its significance for the inability to stand up against pressure from others, she replied, "That's what the boys call 'round heels.' If you are a pushover for them, they say you have 'round heels.'" This was the very problem for which she was consulting me. Her complaint was that she could not resist the aggressive advances of men.

The body is the common ground upon which sex and personality meet. Not only is the body the physical reflection of the personality, it is the instrument of the sexual impulse. Every bodily disturbance is reflected equally in the personality and in the sexual function. As we study the relation of sex to love in the next two chapters, we shall see that the biological basis of man's emotions lies in the natural functions and needs of the body. The sexually sophisticated person is unaware of this relationship. To the degree of his sophistication it can be said that his "sex is in his head." This means that he functions with illusions instead of reality.

The sexually mature person, as I see him, is neither sophisticated nor burdened with sexual guilt. He is not a performer; his sexual behavior is a direct expression of his feelings. He is not an ideal, but neither is he a pretender. He is not sexually fulfilled in every experience, because the vicissitudes of life do not allow for perfection. Success or failure is not a criterion by which he judges his sexual behavior. He knows that sexual satisfaction cannot be divorced from overall satisfaction in living. Yet these satisfactions are his because his maturity represents a realistic and wholehearted commitment to life and love.

2

Sex and Love

It is illogical to write about sex without discussing its relationship to love. The sexually sophisticated person views sex and love as two distinct and separate feelings. Such a view is a characteristic attitude of neurotic individuals. It is based upon a superficial understanding of these emotions. This chapter will examine the relationship of sex to love to find the common functions that unite them.

Sex is an expression of love. In an article that I wrote for the *Encyclopedia of Sexual Behavior,* I went so far as to say that "there is no sex possible without love." A copy of the article was sent to the editor of a Catholic quarterly who had expressed an interest in my work. He wrote back that while he was impressed with the ideas in the article, he could not reconcile this statement with the behavior of men who visit prostitutes or of soldiers who rape women.

Before such a reconciliation can be attempted, it must be recognized that the average human being in our culture is not free from neurotic conflicts and ambivalent attitudes. Ambivalence means that opposite tendencies are present in the personality at the same time. Thus a wife may love her husband yet show a hostile attitude toward him. A mother may be devoted to her children yet express such anger against them that they are afraid of her. Ambivalence accounts for the presence of love and hate in the same relationship. It derives from a conflict in the personality that splits what should be unitary feelings into two opposing emotions. If sexual activity were not an expression of love, no mature person would speak of coitus as an act of love. Sex is a biological expression of love. If the sexual act is accompanied

27

by feelings of hostility or contempt for the sexual partner,
this ambivalence denotes the dissociation of the individual's
conscious feelings from his instinctive behavior. The intimate
connection between sex and love can be clearly shown.

The feeling of love inspires many relationships that are not
primarily sexual. We use the word "love" to describe our
feelings for a brother, for a friend, for our country, and for
God. All relationships in which love enters are characterized
by the desire for closeness, both spiritually and physically,
with the love object. "Closeness" may not be a strong enough
word. In its more intense forms, the feeling of love includes
the desire for fusion and union with the love object. As Erich
Fromm pointed out in *The Art of Loving,* the answer to the
problem of human existence "lies in the achievement of
interpersonal union, of fusion with another person, in *love.*"
This is true not only of the love of one person for another,
but also of the love that a person feels for the symbols and
material objects that he cherishes. Love impels one toward
closeness both in spirit (identification) and in body (physical
contact and penetration). We desire to be close to those we
love, and we love those toward whom we feel this desire.

In what way is sex different? Sex brings people together. It
might be said that sex brings people together physically, not
spiritually. This is not so. The spiritual side of life can be
separated from the physical only at the risk of destroying the
unity and integrity of the whole being. The physical act of
sex involves the spiritual experience of identification with and
knowledge of the partner. In ancient Hebrew and Greek, the
word "cohabit" is expressed by the verb "to know." The
Bible relates that "Adam knew Eve his wife, and she conceived and bore Cain." This choice of words is neither
fortuitous nor prudish. It denotes the intimate relation between knowledge and physical closeness, between knowing
and the primordial sense of touching. To know (love) an
object, one must be close to it. Viewed in this light, the
sexual act is the most intimate form of love.

The relation of sex to the desire for closeness is demonstrable. There are other phenomena that can be interpreted
to support the thesis that sex is an expression of love. The
erection of the penis depends upon the tumescence of that
organ with blood. And just as tumescence is necessary for the
male sexual function, congestion is necessary for the female's
sexual response. The feeling of fullness in the vagina and
clitoris, the flow of the lubricating secretions, and the sensa-

tion of heat result from the flow of blood into the pelvic area of the female's body. Biologically, genital excitation may be viewed as a function of the blood and the circulatory system. In the sexual act, two organs suffused with blood and so highly charged that they are often pulsatile come into the closest physical contact with each other. Erotogenic zones are characterized by the richness of their blood supply. Close contact between bloodrich organs occurs in kissing and in nursing, which are also regarded as expressions of love.

In dealing with feelings as opposed to ideas, it is valid to inquire into the physical localization of a feeling. If a person says, "I feel a pain," it is natural for the doctor to ask, "Where does it hurt?" Similarly it is possible to localize a feeling of anxiety such as a sensation of pressure in the chest, butterflies in the stomach, shaky legs, trembling hands, and so forth. On the other hand, there are generalized feelings of anxiety which are manifested in sweating, weakness, and chills. Love can also be experienced as a general or localized feeling. The feeling of love as opposed to the idea of love is often localized in or about the heart, although it also extends into the arms, when reaching out to a love object, and to other parts of the body, the lips, and the genitals.

The relation of the heart to love is expressed in common symbolism and everyday language. Cupid's arrow pierces the heart to indicate that love has been awakened. The heart is the symbol of St. Valentine's Day, the patron saint of love. We use such expressions as, "My heart is full of love," "My heart aches for love," "You have touched my heart," and so on, to express our unconscious sense of this relationship. Love songs are full of references to the heart as the symbol of love.

The symbolism of blood as the bearer of love is only slightly less known. Blood relationships are naturally assumed to be love relationships. Lovers pledge their troth in blood and may act this out by cutting each other and mixing the two bloods. One of my psychotic patients wrote a note to his girl friend in his own blood to show his love for her. To shed one's blood for another is a direct expression of love for the other. The color of love is red, as is the red rose, which symbolizes the blood and the heart. In *The Ego and the Id,* Sigmund Freud suggested "that some substance ought to be the principal representative of Eros," but he never did say what that substance might be. Yet a moment's consideration of the description of Eros as "the life force" leads to the thought that it could be associated with the blood.

These ideas do not constitute scientific proof that an erection is an expression of the desire for love, but, then, the phenomenon of love is a most difficult subject for scientific investigation. In the view of science represented by physiology, the heart is only a pump that drives the blood through the body. Such scientific thinking, however, gives us no understanding of human behavior or feelings. If the heart is only a pump, if the penis is only an organ to introduce sperm cells into the female body, then the human being is only a machine that requires no feelings of love or pleasure to motivate its functions. I reject the concept that a man is only a mechanism whose behavior is explained solely in terms of physiochemical laws. I believe some credence must be given to beliefs and ideas by which the human mind has attempted to understand its own feelings and actions.

A more serious objection to the view of the erection as an expression of love is the phenomenon of the so-called cold erection. Many men experience this kind of erection on waking in the morning. It is attributed to the stimulation of a full bladder, since it is not associated with the idea or feeling of sexual desire. Donald W. Hastings,* in discussing the "morning erection," states, "That a full bladder is not the explanation is seen in the fact that civilized man encounters many situations, mainly social, wherein his bladder becomes full but no erection occurs." Morning erections are proof to Wilhelm Stekel† that erective impotence is psychic in origin. If there is such a thing as a cold erection, it would disprove the thesis advanced above. The fact is that the penis is not cold but warm. What is cold is the mind, not the penis. This condition indicates a state of dissociation of the conscious mind and the unconscious biological processes. On the unconscious or body level, the individual is sexually excited, but his conscious mind is not "with it." He may be preoccupied with the practical affairs of the coming day, and he may be anxious to get going, so he urinates and the erection subsides. The so-called cold erection can be regarded as an unconscious manifestation of the desire for sexual love. It illustrates the degree to which a man can be dissociated from his

---

*Donald W. Hastings, *Impotence and Frigidity*. Boston: Little, Brown & Co., 1963, p. 57.

†Wilhelm Stekel, *Impotence in the Male*. New York: Boni & Liveright Inc., 1927.

physical functions. It raises the possibility that love and sex, which are normally united, can be dissociated in the mind and behavior of an individual.

The cold erection is characterized by a warm penis, not a hot one. While the cavernous sinuses of the erectile tissue are filled with blood, the superficial arterioles, capillaries, and venules are contracted. The result is a lack of surface heat. The penis is rigid and insensitive, a condition that also occurs in men whose sexual function lacks the heat of passion. In such men, too, the rigidity and insensitivity are characterologically structured both in the body and in the mind. Women have described such men by saying that the penis is not part of the man. It functions like a detached part of his being. And in these men, the conscious feeling of love is absent from the sexual act. In the presence of such dissociative tendencies, the sexual act tends to be unsatisfactory. While not erectively impotent, the rigid male is relatively orgastically impotent. I could describe this condition simply by saying that the love is not wholehearted and leave it to the reader to decide whether he wishes to take this remark literally or figuratively.

As indicated earlier, there are corresponding biological phenomena in the sexual makeup of the female. The nipples and the clitoris are erectile organs, the latter being, in fact, a miniature penis. Erection occurs as the blood flows into these organs. Of more importance, however, is the flow of blood into the pelvic area of the woman and especially into the uterine venous plexus and into the vaginal venous plexus. The vaginal venous plexus is a network of veins on either side of the vagina, so that this organ is surrounded with blood when the woman is sexually aroused. The suffusion of the pelvic area in the woman with blood makes the tissues of the genital apparatus full and firm. And it is the presence of the blood that accounts for the heat she experiences in sexual desire and response. In many ways, therefore, the female's sexual reactions parallel those of the male. She, too, is capable of dissociating her heart from her vaginal response in varying degrees.

An interesting example of this dissociation is the case of Suzie Wong. In the delightful picture *The World of Suzie Wong,* Suzie justified her activities as a prostitute by saying that while she gave men her body, she did not give them her heart. The sexual act became thereby emotionally meaningless to her. When she was in love, however, it was differ-

ent. She gave herself fully to her lover. The difference should
be obvious to any man, Suzie claimed, unless he had a small
heart. Our sexual mores make no such distinctions, but there
is merit in Suzie's argument.

The importance of Suzie's idea is illustrated in the following story told me by a patient:

> "My girl friend had expressed her intention to termi-
> nate our relationship," he said. "It hit me hard, because
> I really loved this girl. I began to cry deeply. You know
> how hard it is for me to cry. I then told her how much
> she meant to me. She was touched by my feelings, and
> she embraced me. One kiss led to another, and we had
> sexual relations. I never had such an experience in my
> life. My whole body reacted in the climax. It was
> ecstatic. The next day, I felt different. I felt so alive, I
> could feel my heart beating. It seemed that I could feel
> the pulse of all living things in my heart. It was a great
> sensation while it lasted."

The dissociation of sex from love is conditioned by all the
emotional disturbances with which the psychiatrist is familiar. I analyzed many of these problems in a previous study.*
Here, I shall examine two of the situations in the upbringing
of a child that may lead to this dissociation. The first is the
fixation of the child's psychosexual development at the oral
level owing to the lack of fulfillment of his infantile oral
needs. The second is parental prohibition of the expression of
infantile sexual feelings both in autoerotic activity and in
bodily play and contact with the parents.

Infantile oral needs include the needs for bodily contact,
food, affection, and care. The first two of these needs are
ideally fulfilled in the natural function of breast feeding. The
relation of mouth to nipple is the prototype of the later
genital relation of penis to vagina. In nursing, the child
expresses his love of the mother in his desire for physical
closeness and for the union of mouth and breast that makes
the two one. The mother's love is expressed in her response
to the child's needs. Just as the mouth-breast relationship sets
the pattern for the later genital function, so the quality of
love that the child experiences in its closeness to the mother
determines the form of his adult love responses.

---

*A. Lowen, *The Physical Dynamics of Character Structure.* New
York: Grune & Stratton, Inc., 1958.

An interesting experiment confirmed analytic findings about the effect of the deprivation of mother love upon adult sexual behavior. Newborn rhesus monkeys were separated from their mothers and raised upon two substitute mothers. The substitute mothers were wire figures; one was covered with terry cloth and heated by an electric bulb to provide warmth; the other had a bottle with a nipple to provide nourishment. It was discovered that the infant monkeys preferred the terry-cloth figure. From this observation, it was deduced that the infant monkey's need for physical contact and warmth exceeded its need for food. Harlow's* description of the infant monkeys' reactions in a strange environment to the presence or absence of the cloth mother is striking. "When the cloth mother was present, the infants would rush wildly to her, climb upon her, rub against her and cling to her tightly. ... However, when the cloth mother was absent, the infants would rush across the test room and throw themselves downward, clutching their heads and bodies and screaming their distress." All the experimental monkeys showed disturbances in emotional development and behavior. Completely unexpected, however, was the finding that none of the experimental monkeys could successfully perform the sexual act when they had reached maturity.

During the oral phase of his development, the child is on the receiving end, the mother on the giving end. In this phase, the child fills up with the supplies he needs for growth and maturation. These supplies include love, food, attention, play, and so on. Psychoanalysts describe them as narcissistic supplies. Since the pattern of growth and development in the child is from the head downward, any lack or deprivation of these supplies will most seriously affect the functions of the lower part of the body, that is, those functions associated with the legs and the genitals. These are the functions that determine the independence and maturity of the organism. They include the ability to stand on one's own feet, move about freely, and function as a sexually adequate adult. Psychiatrists have found that these are precisely the functions that are impaired in the orally deprived individual.

It is not generally recognized that these disturbances are manifested physically as well as psychologically. An examina-

---

*Harry F. Harlow, "The Development of Affectional Patterns in Infant Monkeys," *Determinants of Infant Behavior,* ed. B. M. Foss, New York: John Wiley & Sons, Inc., 1961. p. 78.

tion of the body of such an individual often reveals the
following characteristics. The legs are underdeveloped muscularly. The feet are flabby and have collapsed arches or they
are narrow, small and have high, tightly contracted arches.
The knees are locked backward to give the legs more rigidity
and to compensate for a feeling of weakness. Control of the
leg movements is poor, and coordination is inadequate. In
positions of stress, the legs tire very rapidly. In addition,
there is an overall muscular underdevelopment that is associated with a tall, thin body. William H. Sheldon described this
type of body constitution as ectomorphic. Severe muscle
tensions about the pelvic girdle severely limit the scope and
freedom of the sexual movements.

The deprivation of love (body contact, affection, care, and
food) during the early years of life results in an unfilled and
emotionally underdeveloped individual. The personality that
results from this deprivation is characterized by inner feelings
of emptiness, the dependent need to be taken care of, the
longing for contact and closeness. Such an individual is described as an immature person. His relations to other people
are conditioned by his lack of inner resources. Maturity, on
the other hand, depends on a feeling of fullness, an ability to
give and take, a desire for independence, and a sense of
responsibility. The oral character, as he is called in psychiatric language, has the same need, the same capacity, and the
same feeling of love as anyone else. In other words, he, too,
has a heart, and he, too, wants to be close to a loved person.
But the feeling of love does not move down into his genitals
strongly enough to enable them to function as an organ for
discharge. Instead, part of the feeling moves upward to his
head and mouth to complete a "taking in" that was unfin-
ished in infancy. In his relations to the opposite sex, part of
his love feelings go one way, part another. He is divided
between orality and genitality. This split occurs to some
degree in every individual in whom oral tendencies resulting
from deprivation persist into adulthood.

That there can be no sex without love holds true for the
oral character as well as any other. The dissociation in the
oral character is not between love and sex. Rather, it is a
splitting of the love impulse into the infantile longing for
contact and security and the adult desire for penetration and
discharge. In consequence, the genital charge is weakened,
and genital satisfaction is not attained. Genitality is subverted
in the interest of orality; that is, the oral character uses sex

as a way to gain love and affection. The loved person is divided into a mother and a sexual object, to neither of whom can he give his whole heart. As a result, the oral character is orgastically impotent.

The second situation that may produce a disturbance in the relation of sex to love is parental prohibition of the manifestations of infantile sexuality. These manifestations, which appear between the ages of two and six, take two forms in the child—autoerotic play and body contact of an erotic nature with the parent of the opposite sex. The severity of the prohibitions, which are frequently accompanied by some kind of punishment, is a direct reflection of the parents' guilt about their own sexuality. Frequently, prohibitions against exposure, against touching the genitals, and against sexual play are coupled with the threat of the withdrawal of parental love and approval.

Adults make the mistake of confusing the sexual activity of children, which is erotic play, with adult genital activity. The child's sexual feelings tend to be diffused over his whole body, with only a small degree of focus upon the genital organ. While the sexual activity of the small child is pleasurable and exciting, it serves the same purpose as other play activities; namely, it is his way of discovering the pleasure possibilities of his body. For the same reason, body contact with the parent of the opposite sex enhances the child's pleasure in and identification with his body. If this need were more clearly understood, much unnecessary harm could be avoided. For the child reacts with intense feelings of frustration and anger to the denial of this need. Unfortunately, owing to a misunderstanding of the child's nature, his anger is met with further threats and punishments.

The problem reaches a climax at the age of five or six, when the oedipal situation forces the child to choose between his love for his parents and his sexual feelings. Confronted with this problem, the average child suppresses his sexual feelings in favor of overt submission to parental authority. His love for his parents takes on a defensive function and a compulsive quality. He becomes a good child. But the suppression is not easily achieved. The frustration and its accompanying anger must be contained and repressed if the submission is to be effective. This is accomplished by the development of a rigid attitude, manifested both physically and psychologically. Rigidity enables the child to repress his sexual feelings and his anger, without surrendering his independ-

ence. It enables him to enter the next stage, the latency
period, without an overt sexual conflict. He divorces his
feeling of love from its sexual component. This split permits
him to express affection which has become abstracted from
its bodily and erotic meaning.

The resurgence of the sexual drive in puberty causes the
upheaval of this neurotic balance. The young adult again
faces the conflict between love and sexual feelings, now in
the form of strong genital urgings. The conflict is accentuated
by further parental prohibitions against genital activity in the
form of masturbation or sexual relations. Again the effort is
made to repress sexual feelings in the name of love and good
moral behavior. But with advancing years and more maturity, the problem changes. The same person as an adult is
expected to function sexually with a maturity that he never
had the opportunity to develop. In order to function sexually
at all, the response that was made in childhood to the conflict
between love and sex must be reversed; the conflict itself
cannot be eliminated. This time, love feelings are suppressed
in favor of sexual activity. Actually, it is only a matter of
turning over the coin. Nothing is really changed. The rigidity
that the child developed to cope with its original frustration
becomes the armor that imprisons the adult's tender feelings.

I have described the type of personality that emerges from
this background as the rigid character structure. The rigidity
is apparent in the functions of both the body and the mind.
Psychologically, the rigid character may be described as
affect blocked; that is, emotional expression is limited. For
example, a man with this personality structure finds it difficult to cry. His approach to life is rational and aggressive, but
the aggression is exaggerated and serves a defensive function.
Physically, the rigidity is manifested in a stiff backbone that
is relatively inflexible. The chest wall is hard and unyielding.
The jaw is set and has a determined expression. Both the
physical and the psychological rigidity protect the individual
from emotional hurts. For this reason, such an individual is
said to be armored.

The oral and the rigid character types are neurotic personalities. They are neurotic because unresolved conflicts have
split the unitary feelings of the organism. It is as natural to
love the person who is embraced sexually as it is to embrace
the person who is loved. Broadly speaking, sex and love are

two different modes of expressing the unitary desire for closeness and intimacy. They become opposing and conflicting values under the influence of a culture that regards the physical mode as degraded and the spiritual mode as exalted. Such a culture also splits the unity of being into body and mind, with the assignment of higher values to the latter and lower ones to the former. The conflict of the rigid character is a direct expression of the cultural tendency that dissociates sex from love. But the problem of the oral character has its roots in the same dissociative process. The abandonment by women of the basic function of breast feeding is largely responsible for the widespread prevalence of oral tendencies in our culture. The practice has not only been widely abandoned—the art has almost been lost. The rejection of breast feeding by mothers in our time is an expression of a cultural tendency that values the ego more than the body, eroticism more than sexuality, and science more than nature.

Another aspect of the same cultural tendency is the psychiatric practice of divorcing the physical aspect of the patient from the psychological in the treatment of emotional disturbances. In the discussion of the oral and rigid character types, I have indicated that emotional difficulty is structured in physical tensions as well as in mental attitudes. Valid as the idea of body-mind unity is, it is nevertheless usually ignored in analytic practice. Without such a concept and without an approach that treats a person holistically, physically as well as mentally, the emotional problems of neurotic patients will evade solution. Similarly, any view of sex that ignores its relation to love will prove sterile and unsatisfactory.

What are the exceptions to the statement that sex is impossible without love? Are the sexual relations of a man with a prostitute to be considered an expression of love? The answer must be yes. The sexual feelings of a man for a prostitute express his love for her in his desire for closeness and in the fact of erection. Unfortunately, sexual love in our culture is not free from secondary feelings of shame, disgust, guilt, and hostility. Their presence in a person distorts the significance of the sexual act and undermines its values. They may render the expression of sexual love impossible except under conditions that permit the release of these associated feelings. The man who can function sexually only with a prostitute indicates thereby that he is capable of loving only a prostitute, not a woman of his own class or standing. How-

ever, the love for the prostitute is real. Not infrequently it
has developed into a more abiding and respectable relationship. Both history and literature bear witness to the genuine
affection that a man can have for a mistress or a prostitute.
And not infrequently the feelings of the prostitute for her
lover is more sincere and affectionate than that which the
man had inspired in other women. In *The Great God Brown*,
Eugene O'Neill depicts such a relationship in sympathetic
terms.

How explain the rapist? Is not his sexuality an expression
of sadism rather than love? To analyze pathological sexual
behavior in detail would require more space than I can give
to it here. I shall have to limit my comments on this problem
to the observation that sadistic behavior is directed only at
those who are loved. It manifests the condition of ambivalence: love and hate directed toward the same object. The
element of love in a rape determines its sexual content; the
element of hate denies to the act its normal pleasure and
satisfaction. To the extent that the expression of sexual love
is inhibited, distorted, or encumbered with secondary feelings, the sexual function is limited in its capacity to yield
pleasure and satisfaction.

If love is conceived as being more than a "noble sentiment," it must be recognized that it contains a force that
impels to action and that seeks fulfillment and satisfaction in
all relationships in which it is present. A person is not happy
unless he can do something to express his feelings for a
friend. A mother is frustrated unless she feels that her efforts
for her child lead to its well-being. The lover is a giver. But
love is not unselfish. The need to love is as much a part of
our biological makeup as the need to breathe or to move.
The impulse of love aims to satisfy this need. The satisfaction
of love derives from the expression of love in some concrete,
material form or in some appropriate action. The universal
tendency to give gifts and presents to those we care for is a
manifestation of this need to give. Isn't this true of sex, too?
The act of sex is a giving of the self. Satisfaction results from
the full surrender of the self to the partner in the sexual
embrace. Without this surrender, sexual satisfaction cannot
be achieved. In other words, only when lovemaking is wholehearted, or not until the heart is joined to the genitals in the
act of sex, is it possible to attain orgastic fulfillment in sexual
love. If sexual happiness is relatively rare in our culture, it is

because individuals have lost the ability to give themselves fully to one another. The loss of this ability to love is both cause and result of the widespread neuroses of our time.

One of my patients made an observation that, I believe, clarifies the relation of sex to love. She said, "A man can't love a woman unless he loves women." The same could be said of a woman. She can love a man only if she loves all men. Love for the opposite sex determines the ability to respond sexually to that sex. It is very closely associated with the biological drive of sex, which on the unconscious level is nondiscriminating. It can be stated that the strength of the sexual feeling in a man is proportionate to the strength of his positive feelings for the feminine sex. The misogynist and the homosexual are relatively impotent males. What is true of the male is equally true of the female.

Love in the personal sense is a conscious feeling that results from the focus of this general affection upon a specific individual. Through this personal form of love, sex becomes discriminating. The same phenomenon can be observed in infants. A newborn or very young infant will nurse any breast. Once the baby has become conscious of his mother, he will focus his feelings and desires on her. Similarly, adolescent sexuality is dominated by the unconscious element in its broad responsiveness to the opposite sex. This explains why the Don Juan type of sexual behavior is described as adolescent. Mature sexuality is selective. It has a greater conscious component. This conscious component is superimposed upon the underlying generalized instinctual reaction.

This dissociation of sex and love can be described as a split between the conscious and the unconscious feeling of love. The man who can respond only to a prostitute is reacting to her on a nonpersonal level. As "woman," she is a legitimate object for his sexual desires. Her anonymity or her role as social outcast, which removes her from the society of persons, allows him to express his sexual feelings to her. His love is directed to the female in her, divorced from her personality. The rapist has a similar attitude. He can respond sexually to the feminine in a woman only if by his violence he can destroy the integrity of her personality. The degree of dissociation of the tender, affectionate feelings and the sexual feelings varies according to the severity of the neurotic disturbance. But to whatever degree it exists, it acts to decrease orgastic potency.

In this chapter, I have attempted to show that sex is an expression of love. But the relationship between sex and love has other aspects. Can it be shown that love is a manifestation of sexuality? I shall explore this idea in the next chapter.

3

Love and Sex

Freud made the statement that "love is aim-inhibited sexuality." The reaction which greeted this statement was almost as violent as that which followed his earlier assertion that children were sexual creatures. How dare he! The little innocents! To link love with sex was blasphemous. Love is divine. Sex is an animal passion. As I understand it, the expression "aim-inhibited" means that the need for erotic gratification is removed from the sexual impulse. What is left of the impulse is the feeling of affection and the desire for closeness with the love object. Freud called this love.

Theodor Reik, a neo-Freudian, categorically rejects Freud's concept. He maintains that love is a psychological phenomenon, sex a physical process. Love is cultural, sex biological. Love aims to possess the ego ideal, sex seeks only to discharge a physical tension. Reik's dissociation of behavior into psychological and physical ignores the basic unity of the living being. These categories can be used only as descriptive conveniences and do not refer to an actual split in the personality as Reik's statements imply.

Love is not sex any more than sex is love. This statement, however, does not reject the idea of an intimate relationship between these two feelings. Sex is an expression of love, but there are other ways to express love besides the sexual. Love is not sex, but it can be shown that it derives from the sexual function. Support for this idea can be found both in the evolutionary development of animals and in the personal development of the individual.

Love as a conscious sentiment is a relative newcomer in the field of emotions. By contrast, sex appeared early in the

41

evolutionary scheme of life. Sexual differentiation and sexual activity appear among the lower animals long before any behavior that can be recognized as motivated by feelings of affection or love. Even the basic feelings of mother love toward offspring are completely absent from most species of fish. Yet sex as it functions among fish in mating and reproduction is not so greatly different from the sexual functions of the higher animals, including man.

As one follows the sexual evolution of animals, it is interesting to note that signs of tenderness and affection appear as physical closeness and intimacy between the sexes increase in the course of mating. In the mating of fish, the male hovers over the spot where the female has extruded her eggs and discharges his sperm cells. In this activity, there is little physical contact between male and female. Contact during sexual activity is first noted in amphibians. The male frog, for example, clasps the female with special gripper pads on his forelegs as he covers her during the discharge of the sexual gametes. Both eggs and sperm cells are discharged freely into the water, where fertilization takes place. Amphibians have an advantage over fish in that the simultaneous discharge that occurs increases the chances of fertilization.

There was neither penetration nor deposits of sperm cells into the body of the female until the evolution of animals who spend their entire lives on dry land. Perhaps there was no need for sexual penetration among the water animals. The sea was the great repository, the great mother substance. Sandor Ferenczi expressed the idea that sexual penetration among land animals has the function of providing a fluid medium of approximately the same chemical composition as the ancient seas for the process of fertilization and embryonic development.* The human embryo develops and grows in a fluid medium exactly as do the fertilized eggs of fish and amphibians. In this sense, the saying that life began in the sea is true for all living creatures. But whatever the reason, the fact is that the evolutionary development of animals is characterized by closer and more intimate sexual contact.

With the increase in physical closeness and intimacy that characterizes the sexual act among birds and mammals, there is the appearance of behavior that reflects feelings of affection, tenderness, and love. Naturalists have described actions

*Sandor Ferenczi, *Thalassa: A Theory of Genitality*. New York: Psychoanalytic Quarterly, Inc., 1949.

among birds that can be understood only in terms of such feelings. Among many birds, it is customary for the female to preen the feathers of her mate as she perches beside him on a limb, an activity that he appears to relish highly. In return, he feeds her choice morsels of worms and other food as a token of his feelings.

I had occasion to watch and photograph a pair of collies who appeared to be attracted to each other at first sight and who were subsequently mated. The male ran beside the female as they romped along the sand, licking her at every moment. He was a large, handsome animal. Regularly, he placed his neck over hers, rubbing it to and fro. It was the first time I had seen true "necking." One evening when he heard her on the beach, he jumped out of a one-story window to be near her. He had been locked in his room because he had spent the whole of the previous night outside, close to the cottage where his "girl friend" was staying. It is important to add that the female was not in heat at this time. His behavior could not be explained, therefore, as sexual. In my opinion, it represented a real feeling of affection.

What I and others have observed in animals is behavior that parallels human behavior in similar circumstances. To ascribe feelings of love or affection to such behavior seems not beyond the realm of possibility. The point I wish to make is that behavior that can be described as affectionate is manifested only by the animals who are physically intimate in the reproductive process.

Among human beings, tenderness and affection between a man and a woman are commonly associated with sexual interest. One set of emotions involves the other. To argue that these feelings, love and sex, have no functional or organic relationship runs counter to common experience. Even in long-married couples in whom sexual attraction has abated, it seems unreasonable to separate the affection that remains from the sexual feelings that originally drew them together. The question is, does the feeling of affection or love derive from the sexual attraction? If the answer is yes, it is important to know how. Some understanding can be gained from the study of the maternal behavior of animals.

The evolution of animals is also characterized by increasing physical closeness and intimacy between mother and young. Among animals who deposit eggs to be fertilized in the sea or who deposit fertilized eggs to be hatched unattended in the ground, there are no signs of maternal care or affection. Only in the higher animals, where the biological processes impose a closer physical relationship between mother and offspring, does evidence of maternal love appear. Birds not only hatch their young with the heat of their bodies, but also feed them and protect them until they are ready to leave the nest. Among mammals, the dependence of the young upon the mother is greater, and her response is broader. She cleans them, protects them, plays with them, and teaches them. Her obvious distress when separated from her young is the basis for the assumption of maternal feeling. The amount of feeling among animal mothers seems to be proportionate to the helplessness of the offspring.

What has mother love to do with sexuality? What connection is there between nursing and coitus? Even if it is granted that maternal love stems from the biological need of the infant for contact with the mother's body, this would not prove that love derives from sexuality. To relate the two phenomena, it is necessary to show that there is a direct connection between nursing and the sexual act. Such a connection exists.

The function of nursing is found only among those animals whose method of reproduction involves the insertion of a penis into a vagina. I do not think that these two processes developed in the same animals purely by chance. The nipple and mouth have a functional relationship that resembles in many ways that of the penis and vagina. Like the penis, the nipple is an erectile organ. Like the vagina, the mouth is a cavity lined with a mucous membrane. All four organs are richly suffused with blood. In each situation, a secretion is expelled into a receptive cavity. In both cases, erotic pleasure and gratification are obtained from the contact and friction of two surfaces. Further, the close physical intimacy of nursing parallels that of the genital embrace. On the other hand, the nipple is passive as compared with the penis, while the mouth is more active than the vagina. However, the similarities are much more striking than the differences.

From another point of view, it appears that the nipple is more closely related to the penis than its physiology indicates. An examination of the mammary line in some animals reveals that it converges on the clitoris in the female and on the penis in the male. In the female, the teats are secretory, while the clitoris is inactive. In the male, the reverse is true of the nipples and penis.

It is a logical assumption that the two functions, nursing

and genital reproduction, developed from a common root: the use of a projection (penis and or nipple) on the ventral surface of the body, and a receptive cavity (vagina and mouth) to unite two organisms. It is a poetic conception to believe that nature adapted the mechanism of genitality to nurture the offspring of genital activity.

The homologous nature of the penis and the nipple, which can be deduced from their similar biology and spatial relationship as described above, clarifies the intimate connection between orality and genitality that is seen in psychiatric practice. Fellatio for many women is an oral desire for the nipple that has been displaced onto the penis. Even sexual intercourse has the connotation of an act of nursing for some individuals. I have heard male patients express the feeling that they were feeding the woman. The idea of the *vagina dentata*, the vagina with teeth, indicates the displacement that may occur from the mouth to the vagina. During a therapeutic session, one of my patients had the vision of her mother's breast being transformed into her father's penis. It was a shocking experience for her. The foregoing may explain why some sexologists, such as Havelock Ellis, believed that semen was a nourishing substance.

A biological chain of events leads from sexuality through conception, pregnancy, and birth to nursing. Psychologically, this sequence normally starts with the love of a woman for a man and culminates in her love for their child, expressed in nursing, care, affection, and attention. In view of the logical association of these events, several important questions can be posed. To what extent can one phenomenon be dissociated from its successor? Can a woman feel one way about the father of her child and another way about the child himself? Specifically, is a woman's hostility toward a man transferred to his child? Can a woman have one set of feelings about sexuality that starts the cycle and a different set of feelings about nursing that completes it? These questions are difficult to answer. It would be naïve to assume that there is no connection between the attitudes and feelings that surround the events at one end of the chain and those that are expressed at the other end. It has been said that "healthy children had parents who were happy in bed." I would agree with this proposition. Clinical experience repeatedly confirms the reverse of this statement. The problems of neurotic children can invariably be traced to the sexual maladjustments and conflicts of the parents. The following might be a

good general statement: a mother who is fulfilled in her
sexual life can easily fulfill the needs of her child from the
abundance of her love.

The psychosexual development of the child provides good
material for the study of the relationship of love to sex.
Biologically, it can be said that every child is conceived in
love. This follows logically from the premise that sex is an
expression of love on the body level. Unfortunately, ambiva-
lences and conflicts are present in most individuals. Sex and
pregnancy are often contaminated by what Wilhelm Reich
called "secondary drives." Sex may be a submissive act to
avoid conflict rather than a voluntary surrender to love.
Pregnancy may be motivated secondarily by a woman's desire to tie a man to her or to fill an emptiness in her life.
These secondary feelings limit a mother's love, but they do
not deny it. Every expression of love and attention that a
woman shows her child manifests her love for him. But she
may also hate him. Many mothers have told me that at times
they felt like murdering a difficult child. A harsh tone, a cold
glance, a humiliating remark may betray a hatred which the
mother may not consciously perceive, but to which the child
is sensitive. In his earliest days, the infant, like all mammalian babies, simply reacts with pleasure or pain to the satisfaction or denial of his needs. He cannot understand the emotional problems of his mother.

As he grows older, a development occurs in the child that
transforms love as a biological function into love as a conscious psychological experience. This development is the
emergence of self-consciousness, together with its corollary,
the consciousness of the other. Early in life, the child becomes aware of his mother as an object that can provide
pleasure and satisfaction. The recognition of the human face
manifested by the smiling response of the infant, which
usually occurs at about three months of age, indicates, according to René Spitz, that memory and anticipation are
present in the infant's psyche. At about eight months of age,
the infant shows anxiety at the approach of unfamiliar persons. Spitz interprets this reaction as a sign that the infant
can distinguish the libidinal object proper from other persons.
From other behavior of the child, Spitz concludes that at this
age, "the ego has come into its own." It cannot be said
definitely that an infant of eight months is conscious of his
love for his mother. This will come soon. He is conscious of
his mother, he recognizes her special role in relation to his

needs, and he can express his desire for closeness by appropriate actions.

Psychoanalysts have recognized that the child forms two images of his mother that correspond to her behavior. The "good mother" is the one who fulfills his needs and satisfies his erotic desires. The "bad mother" is the punishing or threatening figure who is responsible for feelings of anxiety or pain. All the child's good feelings are directed toward the image of the "good mother." Through this mechanism, the child avoids the problem of an internal conflict. The "good mother" is recognized by her positive attitude, the "bad mother" by her irritability and denial. So long as the images remain separate and distinct, the child is not ambivalent in his reactions. When they fuse later into one person, behavioral difficulties arise.

However, when speech is well developed, at about the age of three years, a child expresses his feelings of affection for the "good mother" in words of love. Anyone who has heard a child say, "I love you, Mommy," cannot fail to sense the sincerity and depth of the feeling. The words seem to come directly from the heart. What was originally a biological response of pleasure and joy at the approach of the "good mother" has become a psychological experience that the child has learned to express in language. The use of language enables the child to dissociate the feeling from its base in the action of reaching out his arms to his mother. Memory and anticipation combine to create a feeling of affection directed toward the image of the "good mother" that can be perceived consciously and expressed verbally. Marcel Proust defined beauty as the "promise of happiness." I would define love as the anticipation of pleasure and satisfaction.

The love object of adult life always embodies aspects of the image of the "good mother." To know love presupposes a knowledge of the "bad" or "rejecting mother." The same idea is expressed by Theodor Reik when he says that love is "a counter reaction to the activity of repressed envy and hostility." According to Reik, "the starting point is the feeling of ego-deficiency and the need for ego-completion or ego-improvement." These two views of love are not inconsistent. Both are based upon the idea of antitheses of feeling: hostility and tenderness, envy and selflessness, hate and love. But whereas Reik believes the original problem to be within the individual, I regard it as a result of the child's relationship to his mother. Romantic love reenacts the earlier infantile situa-

tion. There is an unreality to love based upon its denial of the
negative: hostility and the image of the "bad mother." The
love object is always seen as good, pure, noble, that is, as an
ideal.

Love as a psychological experience is an abstraction. By
this I mean that it is a feeling divorced from its appropriate
action, an anticipation that has not found its realization. It
has the same quality as a hope, a wish, or a dream. These
aspirations and sentiments are necessary to human existence.
The appreciation of love as a psychological phenomenon
must not blind one to the necessity of its fulfillment in action.
Love finds its reality in the pleasure and satisfaction of the
biological urge to embrace and unite. Romantic love is the
handmaiden of sexuality. It serves an important function.

Love increases the tension of sexual attraction. It does this
by placing a psychic distance between the lovers. This distance is the heightened consciousness of the loved person.
Such heightened awareness of the other actually separates
two people. It defines their differences and accents their
individuality. The loved person is unique, never generic. The
saying, "Absence [distance] makes the heart grow fonder,"
may be interpreted to mean that the greater the love, the
greater the separation. This is where sex comes in. Sex has a
pleasure mechanism. It aims to eliminate the distance and to
discharge the tension, thereby producing pleasure. Since the
amount of pleasure is in direct proportion to the amount of
tension, as Freud pointed out, the more the love, the greater
the distance and the fuller the pleasure of the sexual union.

The change in the coital position from the rear approach
used by most mammals to the frontal approach used by most
men is significant in terms of the relation of love to sex. In
the face-to-face position, the awareness of the sexual partner
as an individual is extended and deepened. Each person can
more easily perceive the other's feelings. In this position, the
frontal surfaces of the body, which are the more sensitive
areas, are brought into physical contact. It is an interesting
speculation that this change in position may have made man
more conscious of the feeling of love.

The relationship between love and sex may be set forth as
follows. Sex divorced from its conscious correlates, that is,
sex as an instinctual drive, obeys the pleasure principle. The
buildup of sexual tension leads in such conditions to an
immediate attempt to discharge the tension with the nearest
available object. But when love enters the scene, the reality

principle becomes operative. Knowing love, one is aware that the pleasure of the sexual discharge can be heightened by certain sexual objects and lowered by others. Knowing love, one tends to hold back the action, consciously restraining the discharge of the sexual tension until the most favorable situation is available, which is, of course, a loved person. The insistence upon selectivity and discrimination in the choice of a sexual object for greater sexual pleasure is one of the main functions of love. When one looks for a special object, one becomes more conscious of the object, more sensitive to love and to the love partner.

Love can be expressed spiritually or physically. One does not rule out the other. Normally the two modes of expression are complementary. In a healthy person, the spiritual expression of love creates a tension that is discharged in some physical act of love. The pleasure that the latter yields increases consciousness and spirituality. One leads to the other and makes the other a more significant experience.

In an unneurotic individual, spirituality contributes to sexuality and vice versa. In the absence of dissociative tendencies that split the unity of the personality, more spirituality means more sexuality. For this reason, I would say that, generally speaking, the sexuality of a civilized person is superior, qualitatively and quantitatively, to that of a primitive person. Qualitatively, it contains a greater tenderness, a keener sensitivity, and deeper respect for individuality. Quantitatively, there is a greater frequency of and intensity to the sexual impulse. But this is true only in the absence of neurosis. The neurotic individual looks with longing at the sexual freedom and pleasure enjoyed by some primitive peoples.

Formerly, the primitive person envied the civilized man's seeming sexual superiority. The civilized man's sense of individuality and egoism awed the primitive man and fascinated the primitive woman. Unfortunately, the primitive mind was unprepared for civilized man's neurotic behavior, his trickery and deceit.

In *Laughing Boy*, the story of a Navajo Indian, Oliver La Farge explores the effect of the white man's sexual practices upon Indian attitudes. Laughing Boy meets and is attracted to an Indian girl who has been raised by white people and seduced by one of them. She introduces him to the excitement of love play, with its kisses and caresses, and also to alcohol. Laughing Boy falls madly in love with this girl and finds that he cannot leave her to go back to his people. On the other hand, she will not be accepted by his family. Still he must try. His dilemma is resolved by her death on the return voyage. But Laughing Boy is then left with the insurmountable difficulty of accepting one of the drab Indian girls as his wife. He decides to live alone, but he is not lonely, for the memory of his love is bright in his heart.

I have painted a one-sided picture of civilized man's love. The promise it offers is not easily fulfilled. Culture brings problems as well as promises, conflicts as well as excitement. Although love is the ally of sex, it can also betray it. The danger in any dialectical relationship is that one member of the pair will turn against the other. It is in the name of love that infantile sexuality is suppressed. The mother believes that she is acting in the best interests of her child when she stops his masturbatory activity. It is in the name of love that adult sexuality is restricted and undermined. How many women have expressed the thought, "If you loved me, you would not want such a thing from me"? True, such attitudes are less common today, but they are by no means absent. The antagonism of love and sex is also expressed in the double standard that many men follow: one does not sleep with the girl one loves, and one cannot love the girl one sleeps with. To sophisticated ears, this sounds old-fashioned, but the distinction between love and sex is emphasized by many current writers on love. The distinction is there, but to emphasize it is to dissociate love from sex, as Theodor Reik does. "I believe that love and sex are different in origin and nature." Sex, he says, is a biological instinct that aims at the release of physical tension only. Love is a cultural phenomenon that aims at happiness through the establishment of a very personal relationship. Reik believes that there is sex without love, "straight sex."* The effect of such an attitude is to degrade sexuality. It is reduced to an animal passion, lust, which is inferior to the noble quality of love.

The dissociation of love from sex derives from the division of man's unitary nature into opposing categories—body and spirit, nature and culture, intelligent mind and animal body. These distinctions exist, but to ignore their essential unity in man's biological nature is to create a schizoid condition. Culture can oppose nature only at its peril. An intelligent mind acts to control the body in the interest of a better body

*Theodor Reik, *Of Love and Lust*. New York: Farrar, Straus & Co., 1957.

function and a richer experience of its passions. Man can be human only to the degree that he is also an animal. And sex is part of man's animal nature.

All this, however, is only the philosophical explanation of the antagonism of love to sex. As was stated before, the dynamic mechanism of this antagonism goes back to infancy. The infant or the child can experience two distinct feelings in relation to his mother. One is erotic pleasure at her breast or in closeness to her body. The other is the awareness of the mother as a love object, a person who promises pleasure and fulfillment through her being. Normally, these two feelings are fused in the image of the mother. But, often, the image of the mother is split into a "good mother" and a "bad mother." The "good mother" promises happiness, and the child transfers his love to this image. The "bad mother" is the frustrating figure, the one who denies the child's need for erotic satisfaction. The child focuses his hostility upon the image of the "bad mother." Love thus becomes associated in the mind of the child with the promise of happiness, but not with its fulfillment.

In proportion as the promise is greater, the chances of its fulfillment decrease. One cannot fail to be impressed by the fact that all great love stories end in tragedy and death. *Romeo and Juliet, Tristan und Isolde* are the classic examples; *Laughing Boy* is a modern version. The list is endless. Is love an illusion that fades in the harsh reality of day? Is the world so cruel a place that a great love cannot survive in it?

I had as a patient an intelligent young woman who was very much in love. This is the way she described her feeling to me: "I said to him [her lover], 'I love you so much that nothing can satisfy me. I want to devour you, to consume you; I want to have every part of you inside me.'" Her love may be described as neurotic, infantile, irrational, and so on, but the sincerity and genuineness of her feelings could not be denied. She observed that even after the most terrific sexual experience, she never felt satisfied. And she remarked, "When I am most in love, I feel most helpless, dependent, and weak." She was intelligent enough to realize that a marriage could not be founded on such feelings. Eventually, each married some other person, but the attraction between them never fully vanished.

Any analyst could easily recognize in the remarks of my patient the infantile desire to eat the mother, which is an

extension of the unfulfilled longing for the breast. Mother
means breast in the first weeks of life. The love of this
woman is an expression of her need to be filled up. When not
in love, she was depressed and felt empty inside. How could
she find satisfaction in sex? She wasn't looking for genital
release. Genitality functions only on the basis of excess energy, a full organism, something to discharge. She was looking
for oral fulfillment, and her unconscious identified the penis
with the nipple. The happiness she sought was not sexual
satisfaction, but the bliss of the contented infant asleep in her
mother's arms. Perhaps it would be more correct to say that
she wanted to return to the womb, where every need is
automatically fulfilled. Love is our search for paradise lost.

My patient was neurotic, but isn't there some element of
this search for paradise in all feelings of love? And isn't
paradise regained when we find our beloved? This is the
magic of love; it transforms the ordinary into the extraordi-
nary, earth into heaven. Is it neurotic, infantile, or irrational?
I don't think so. My patient was neurotic not because of her
deep love. This was the best in her. She was neurotic because
she was unable to fulfill her love in a sexually mature way.
Her fixation upon the oral level prevented her from obtaining
genital satisfaction. Her problem was *not* the inability to
love, but the inability to express the love as a mature woman. Love reflects the child in us. We all love as children, but
we express it as adults. This patient was helped not by
pointing out the inadequacy of her love, but by resolving the
sexual conflicts.

Love that has lost its connection with its biological outlets
becomes a "hang-up." This is clearly shown by the phenomenon of transference that occurs in psychoanalysis. Many
patients fall in love with their analysts. It is regarded, analytically, as a transference of their unconscious feelings for their
father or mother. But it frequently happens that this love
continues for years. The patient daydreams about the analyst
and lives from one analytic hour to the next. Under these
conditions, very little progress can be made in working out
the patient's problems. In my experience, this "hang-up"
happens when the analyst is an unapproachable figure whose
real personality is veiled from the patient. Since no physical
contact with the analyst is permissible, the love feeling becomes spiritualized. The analyst is idealized. The patient lives
in a state of illusion. The "hang-up" can be avoided if the
analyst is an approachable human being whom the patient

can touch, observe, and react to. Then the love feeling is quickly changed into a sexual feeling that the patient will express in a dream, a slip of the tongue, flirtatious behavior, or in a direct statement. In this form, the feeling can be analyzed and the transference resolved. Love that is biologically fulfilled is not illusory. It has substance that derives from the physical satisfactions that the relationship offers. It has depth, since it has been tested in reality and reinforced by pleasure. It is broad, since the good feelings that surround it extend to the whole world. To talk of love in the abstract is like discussing food with a hungry man. It is a valid idea, but it is powerless to change his physical condition. The lives and welfare of living beings are governed by biological actions, not abstracted feelings. Sex is satisfactory. Nursing is enjoyable. Touch is reassuring. Contact is warm. The body is dependable.

Divorced from its roots in man's biological function, love is tragic. If paradise is sought anywhere but on earth and in the reality of daily living, the result is death. The divine in human form is the ecstasy of orgasm. In any other form, it exists only in saints, angels, and martyrs. If we cannot be saints and do not wish to be martyrs, we can be human in the full sense of the term, which includes our animal nature. The sexual sophisticate advocates sex without love. To proclaim love without sex is to promise a kingdom that is not of this earth. The reality of our being is that life and love arose from sex, which in turn became the vehicle for the expression of love. The great mystery of life is sexual love. Love promises the fulfillment that sexuality offers.

4

Death, Sex,

and

Individuality

The consciousness of love implies the knowledge of paradise
lost. To know the meaning of love one must have experienced
the loss of love. This is one instance of the broad principle
that consciousness arises through the awareness of opposites:
light and dark, up and down, male and female, pleasure and
pain. Another example of this principle is the association in
consciousness of sex with its opposite, death. The intimate
psychological connection between sex and death is the symbol of the ground or the cave which represents both the womb
and the tomb. Orgasm anxiety—that is, fear of ego dissolution that overwhelms the neurotic individual at the approach
of the full sexual climax—is perceived as the fear of dying. Is
this association of sex with death the result of neurotic
anxieties or does it have roots in basic biological processes?

It is ordinarily assumed that death happens to all living
organisms. It happens, however, only to living organisms who
have developed a fixed body organization. So far as is
known, the amoeba does not die from natural causes. But,
then, the amoeba does not have a fixed body structure, that
is, it is not an individual in the sense in which we understand
that term, nor does it reproduce sexually. The phenomenon
of natural death occurs only in organisms that reproduce
sexually and manifest a degree of individuality of body structure. It can be said that death is inseparable from sex and
individuality.

The amoeba, perhaps the simplest single-cell animal, reproduces by a process known as cell division. When it reaches a
certain size or state of maturity, it divides into two daughter
cells, each of which is one-half of the mother cell. The

resulting two amoebas then proceed to grow and mature until they reach full size, when each divides in half, thus producing four daughter cells. This process, it is believed, can go on indefinitely so long as the conditions for life and growth of the amoebas are favorable.

The same thing is true of such lower forms of life as bacteria and yeast cells. At this stage of development of life, two properties stand out—growth and multiplication. It has been estimated that a single bacterium, if allowed to grow and multiply continuously, would cover the face of the earth in a month.

Why does the amoeba have to divide in the first place? Why doesn't the amoeba go on growing bigger and bigger? There is no scientific accord on the answers to this question. Several factors have been suggested, namely, "an imbalance between nuclear and cytoplasmic mass, or between volume of the organism and its surface,"* and the attainment of a "critical size." The growth of living organisms differs in an important respect from the growth of crystals in the inorganic world. A crystal in a solution of its salt will grow in size by the addition of molecules to its surface. The addition is to the outside by a process of accretion. In living forms, however, growth takes place on the inside, from the center outward. When the amoeba reaches a "critical size," any further growth would increase the internal pressure to a point where it would exceed the surface tension of the membrane. The amoeba must find some way to reduce the internal pressure, or it will burst. Cell division accomplishes this reduction of tension: the mass is divided by two at the same time that the surface area is increased.

Life is characterized by the production of excess energy, that is, energy greater than the needs of the organism for survival. The production of excess energy is abundantly shown by the facts of reproduction: a fish can produce a million eggs, a tree one thousand apples, and a cat one hundred kittens in a lifetime. This excess energy accounts for the function of growth which may be viewed as an investment of excess energy in the organism. Life is a process of growth, of multiplication, and of evolution with its increasing organization and complexity of structure.

It takes energy to keep life going, and this energy is obtained in the form of food and oxygen. But life is not

*Reginald D. Manwell, *Introduction to Protozoology*. New York: St. Martin's Press, 1961, p. 187.

content just to keep alive; it is an ongoing phenomenon, expanding, reaching out; it is not content with the *status quo*. An organism doesn't produce excess energy in order to grow; it grows because the production of excess energy is the nature of its existence. If growth is viewed functionally, not teleologically, then we can understand the role of sexuality in life. When growth has reached its natural limits, some other use must be made of the excess energy that is being produced. In the case of the amoeba, this takes the form of an asexual mode of reproduction, cell division. In the higher animals, the excess energy is discharged in the sexual function, as Wilhelm Reich showed.

It is interesting to note that the sexual function in the higher animals does not become fully operative until the organism has reached full growth. Maturity means that the energy that was formerly needed for the growth process is now available for discharge via the sexual function.

Through cell division, an amoeba is rejuvenated by becoming two younger amoebas and this process can be continued. One investigator followed the offspring of a single amoeba through 3,019 successive generations before he gave up. Seemingly, the amoeba is immortal if conditions for its survival are favorable. Since nothing is added or lost in the process of cell division, the original amoeba may be said to live on in the daughter cells. Freud pondered this question of the immortality of the amoeba in his discussion of the death instinct. He concluded that it did not disprove the existence of a death instinct in living beings, since the amoeba can be compared with the germ cells of higher animals, cells that also have this quality of immortality. Natural death is an attribute of the individual; life itself, so far as we know, is immortal.

The question of the immortality of the amoeba is undecided. In the experiment referred to above, each new generation was placed in a fresh nutrient fluid environment. Under laboratory conditions without such special provision, the amoeba dies when it has exhausted its food supply or when the accumulation of waste products renders its existence impossible. How it behaves in its natural habitat in stagnant pools and ponds, no one really knows. But the amoeba exhibits another phenomenon that serves to renew its vital force. From time to time, two amoebas will come together, fuse into one body, mix their protoplasm, divide, and separate. Conjugation, as this phenomenon is called, revitalizes

the amoeba. It manifests a renewed vigor that is passed on to
the following generations. Apart from the fact that the two
amoebas that conjugate show no sexual differences, this
phenomenon is the prototype of the sexuality of more highly
evolved animals. It involves mutual attraction, excitation,
fusion, and a convulsive reaction that results in two renewed
individuals.

Another protozoan, more developed in its body structure
than is the amoeba, took the first step in evolution toward
sexual differentiation. *Volvox*, as it is called, is also known as
the "roller" because of its spinning movement as it travels
through the water. Propelled along by the shiplike action of
its innumerable cilia, *Volvox* looks like a jeweled sphere
revolving on its axis as it moves on its way. *Volvox* is
interesting for a number of reasons. First, *Volvox* shows in
its body structure the transition to multicellular organization.
Second, *Volvox* shows the beginning of sexual differentiation
and sexual reproduction. And third, *Volvox* is a mortal
individual. When its life-span is completed, *Volvox* dies a
natural death. Is there any connection among these phenomena?

Reproduction in *Volvox* is by both asexual and sexual
means. Most generations are asexual ones produced by a
process of internal "budding." Within the body of *Volvox*,
there appears a group of special cells, the vegetative daughter
cells that in time will be extruded to become new organisms.
Each vegetative daughter cell is exactly like the parent cell of
which it was a part. But after several generations in which
reproduction follows this pattern, a sexual generation arises.
Some of the little organisms produce a group of cells that are
very much like the sperm cells of the higher animals. These
are the male gametes. Other organisms produce egg cells that
contain nutrient material. Sperm cells and eggs are extruded
from the body, but a new organism does not develop until a
male gamete finds and fuses with a female gamete, or egg.
The new organism that grows from the fertilized egg is not a
replica of its parents. It contains hereditary material from
both parents and thus is different from each of them. Sexual
reproduction adds something new, creates something that is
different.

The parent cell that has extruded the gametes from its
body has by this process completed its life. It drops to the
bottom, stops all movement, and dies. As one zoologist expressed it, "This is the first advent of natural death in the

animal kingdom, and all for the sake of sex." He questioned whether it was worth it. *Volvox* dies naturally; it comes to the end of a span of existence and ceases to be. In the sense that it has an existence limited in space and time, it is unique. For the same reasons, it can also be considered an individual. However, it would be a mistake to assume that death is the price that the organism pays for sex. It may be true that death enters the stage of life from one wing while sexuality enters from another. But the process that introduces sex and natural death is the process of life itself in the creation of individuality. With the death of *Volvox*, its offspring carry on the phenomenon of life. Life itself is immortal, only the individual is mortal. Death is the price we pay for individuality. And sex is the means whereby individuality develops and is conserved.

Death is related to the loss of sexual feeling or libido. So long as the life process produces the excess energy that supplies the drive for the sexual function, natural death does not occur. If death occurs at the end of a sexual life, it is because the organism cannot provide sufficient energy to maintain its living functions. If anything, sexuality is a life-promoting experience for the individual as well as for the species. It offers physical renewal and psychological rebirth similar to the revitalizing effect of conjugation in the protozoans. A one-hundred-and-four-year-old American Indian stated this succinctly when he was asked the explanation of his long life. His advice was "Plenty of hard physical work—and don't lose your interest in the opposite sex." He remarked that he fathered his last child when he was ninety-one years old.

Broadly speaking, one can say that death is the result of the inability of the organism to sustain and move the individual structure that life has created. Age is characterized by the loss of flexibility and elasticity. The experiences of living are structured into the tissues of the organism, reducing its motility and available energy. This is clearly shown in the growth of a tree from seedling to sapling to giant of the forest. Each year increases its structure and reduces its motility and vitality. Similarly, advancing age means increasing rigidity. To appreciate this simple fact, one has only to compare the body of a young person with that of an old one. Death is *rigor mortis*—structure but no energy.

We die because we are individuals. We are individuals because we have developed a unique and persistent structure that maintains its functioning through our span of existence. Sexuality aids us in maintaining the functional continuity of our being because it reverses the process of individuation. We lose the sense of self as we merge with another being in the sexual act, only to be reborn and renewed as individuals through the experience. Sexuality is the antithesis of structure. It is perceived as a melting, a flowing, and a fusion. It carries us back to the source of our being, the single cell from which we emerged.

These relationships can be viewed differently. Norman Brown, in his study *Life Against Death,* takes the position that individuality results from death. He bases this view upon Freud's concept of the death instinct, a concept that I have never been able to accept. Brown's view leads to inherent contradictions. He states, "If death gives life individuality and if man is the organism which represses death, then man is the organism which represses his own individuality." Death is the great leveler, reducing all individuals to their common denominator, dust. The knowledge of death heightens the consciousness of individuality; the fear of death depresses the sense of individuality. If man is the organism who represses his sexuality, then man is the organism who suppresses his individuality and increases his fear of death.

If both sex and structure are viewed as manifestations of the basic life force in an organism, the close connection of sex and death in some animals can be understood. The drone, or male bee, who mates with the queen dies immediately after mating. It would seem that his life is spent in the sexual act. But the other drones do not long survive him. Their span of existence is limited to one season; and whether they mate or not, their time is up. Mature salmon who spend themselves to get to their mating grounds and die soon after spawning are another example of a species whose life-span is limited to one mating. They do not die for sex; they live for it. It marks their maturity and the end of their individual existence. Among other animals, however, the life cycle may provide for multiple mating seasons. Each mating is not a partial death but a renewal of existence. Unlike Brigid Brophy, I do not believe that we die a little each time a child is born to us. On the contrary, the birth of a child is a fresh incentive to live, a spur to our energies.

And yet there is a connection between sex and death that is peculiarly human. The demise of the ego in orgasm can be equated with death if the personality is equated with the ego. Brophy views the orgasm as a "temporary castration, a little death." Similarly, the loss of erection following intercourse can be regarded as a death, but, again, only if the personality is identified with the penis. G. Rattray Taylor, in *Sex in History,* makes the statement, "Sexual detumescence is a little death, and the woman is always, in some sense, the castrator of the male." I believe that the fear of death underlies the fear of sex, but the identification of sex and death on the basis of this fear has its origin in the development of human consciousness, or what in psychoanalysis is called the ego. No animal shows the ambivalence toward sexuality that marks the neurotic human being. Have we any clues about the source of this ambivalence?

The story of Genesis, which relates the fall of man, is subject to an interpretation that can elucidate this mystery. There are two versions of the creation in Genesis. In the first chapter, "God created man in His own image, in the image of God He created him; male and female He created them." Both sexes come upon the scene simultaneously with the injunction, "Be fruitful and multiply." In the second chapter, the story is that God first created man and then, to give him a companion and helper, created woman by removing a rib from man and transforming it into woman. The presupposition of the priority of the man reflects his presumed superiority. But the second version also indicates some belief in the original bisexual nature of life, the androgynous condition before sexual differentiation was achieved. Nothing in the creation story indicates God's displeasure with the fact of sexuality. Adam and Eve lived in the Garden of Eden in bliss and ignorance, for it was paradise to them until the serpent tempted Eve to eat the fruit of the forbidden tree.

It is written that when Adam and Eve ate of the fruit of the Tree of Knowledge, "the eyes of both were opened, and they knew that they were naked; and they sewed fig leaves together and made themselves aprons." Prior to Adam's disobedience, "the man and his wife were both naked, and were not ashamed." But after the act, Adam hid from God, saying as an excuse for his hiding, "I was afraid, because I was naked." God's question reveals the key to the myth. "Who told you that you were naked? Have you eaten of the tree which I commanded you not to eat?"

It is significant that the knowledge that Adam and Eve gained as a result of eating the fruit of the forbidden tree was the knowledge of their nakedness. This seems like very little gain for the terrible punishment that God inflicted. Is it not strange that prior to their transgression, Adam and Eve did not see their own nakedness? By what manner did man become Godlike ("Behold, the man has become like one of us, knowing good and evil"), when all that Adam learned was the obvious fact of his nakedness? What is the relationship between nakedness and good and evil?

The words are that "the eyes of both were opened, and they knew that they were naked." The emphasis is upon knowing as a result of observation. Adam saw his body and understood the significance of its nakedness. In his earlier state of bliss and ignorance, Adam's relationship to his body was similar to that of the animal to its body. He wasn't conscious of it as an object of observation. He was one with his body and with nature. He was an animal. He did not know of *differences*, such as good and evil, male and female, I and me. The differences were there, and he functioned according to them, as the animals do, by instinct and not by conscious knowledge. Man did not become *Homo sapiens* until he became aware of his body and its nakedness.

How can one understand the threat of death attached to the fruit of the forbidden tree? Adam didn't die as a result of eating the forbidden fruit. He gained the knowledge of his nakedness, which implies the knowledge of the mortality of the body. Man, unlike the animal, *knows* that his existence is finite in time and space. He alone is aware of the physical changes in his body that result from existence; that is, he alone is conscious of youth, maturity, and old age. His nakedness reveals these changes in his physical structure, the meaning of which he can easily deduce. No wonder Adam was afraid when he saw his nakedness, for he knew that one day he would die.

The expression "they knew that they were naked" may also be interpreted to mean that they knew that they were alone, isolated, individuals apart. The unity with nature was broken. Man was no longer clothed or enveloped in nature; he was of it, yet above it. Fear and anxiety enter the experience of man.

There is more to be said for the idea that the primary knowledge was an awareness of the body. The term "nakedness" may refer only to the genital organs, for these are the parts of the body that were covered. The awareness of the body, then, may be related to the consciousness of sexual differences and sexual feelings. The close relationship between knowledge and sexual intercourse was pointed out in the second chapter with reference to the verb "to know," which in ancient Greek and Hebrew has this double meaning. But the fact that his knowledge made Adam ashamed as well as afraid (he covered his nakedness) indicates the intimate association between knowledge, sexuality, and death. After Adam left the Garden of Eden, he "knew Eve his wife, and she conceived and bore Cain." Sex and procreation were not strangers in the Garden of Eden; they were part of man's animal background. What was new was the knowledge of the act. Can it be assumed that the knowledge referred to is the understanding of the relationship between coitus and procreation? This relation exists in the entire mammalian kingdom, but no animal other than man is aware of it. If the consciousness of the body makes man afraid of death, it also makes him aware of the possibility of creating life. Man truly becomes *Homo sapiens*. The phenomenon of knowledge distinguishes man from the other animals. It is the existence of knowledge that creates a psyche as opposed to a soma, an ego as opposed to a body.

The emergence of the ego creates the fundamental antithesis of ego versus body. To the ego, the body is an object to be understood, controlled, and used. The body is also the abode and representative of those strong instinctual forces over which the ego can never fully gain control and which constantly threaten to overwhelm it, namely, the sexual forces. Since sexuality is identified with the body and the body with sexuality, the antithesis may also be stated as ego versus sexuality. Freud postulated this antithesis on the basis of the antagonism of the so-called ego instincts and the sexual instincts. It corresponds to the physical polarity of the organism, the opposition of head end and tail end.

One result of this situation is the derogation of the body to a lower value, while the psychic functions are accorded a higher position. This derogation of the body has its basis in the phenomenon of shame, in man's need to cover his body, to hide his genitals. The awareness of nakedness, the sense of shame, the fall from grace, and the curse "to earn thy bread by the sweat of thy brow" were the penalties that man incurred for the loss of his innocence. It cannot be assumed, however, that it was an unmitigated catastrophe. For as the serpent pointed out to Eve when he tempted her to eat the forbidden fruit, "You will not die. For . . . your eyes will be opened, and you will be like God, knowing good and evil." Was the serpent's inducement a lie and a deceit? It would seem so, for the serpent is regarded as a treacherous animal. How could he promise Eve immortality based upon a knowledge of good and evil? Despite his fall from grace, man has not gained a knowledge of good and evil. That knowledge must be acquired anew in every situation of life. What man gained was the concept of good and evil—that is, the knowledge of opposites. It was as if he were struck by a thunderbolt which illumined his consciousness and revealed his insignificance. Man acquired an ego and lost his innocence.

Observing his body, man becomes conscious of time and of the changes it produces in his body. Man knows not only that he will die, but also that he will grow old, become hungry, need shelter, feel sexual desire. And knowing these things, he will act consciously to provide for them. The consciousness of the passage of time implies a knowledge of its continuity and an awareness of past and future. When Adam's eyes were opened, he saw not only his nakedness, but he also could observe and understand (see) the interaction of cause and effect. To be like God is to know cause and effect in nature; for with that knowledge, man can impose his will upon nature as God is supposed to do. Knowing cause and effect, man can determine good and evil. Man thereby gains immortality, as the serpent foretold, but it is the *immortality of the spirit*, manifested in the continuity and transcendence of knowledge.

Man gains immortality of spirit by denying the body, which has become the symbol of man's finite, earthly, and animal existence. In the story of the Fall, we can discern the origin of the division of man's unity into higher and lower values, into immortal spirit and mortal body, into a cultured mind and an animal body. Thus man becomes human to the degree that he rises above his animal nature, thereby creating the categories of human being and beast. To the beast are assigned the passions and lusts, specifically aggression and sexuality, the lower values. Death and sexuality are connected in the mind because both are associated with the body, a thing of corruption. The life of the body is a life of corruption, only the spirit is incorruptible, eternal.

Although the story of man's expulsion from the Garden of

Eden is allegorical, it is reenacted, nevertheless, in symbolic form in the upbringing and education of every civilized child. The original condition of the human animal is one of unity. He is naked but not ashamed. Whether as the fetus in the womb or as the newborn infant, he lives in the bliss of ignorance. He has not yet become conscious of his body and its functions. This early condition is not paradisiacal as an adult might conceive of that state, but it resembles the Garden of Eden in its timelessness and in the absence of knowledge of cause and effect, of good and evil. It is also the animal state in nature, a condition in which the mind has not evolved to a point where it can dissociate itself from the body and dominate it. Psychologically, this state antedates the formation of the ego.

The ego, as Freud described it, embraces the functions of perception and consciousness. It reaches its apotheosis in the phenomenon of self-consciousness. It develops through consciousness of the body and the conscious control of its motor functions. The human ego includes the consciousness of death. On the biological level, death and sexuality are antithetical phenomena. To the animal, sexuality is life, and it knows nothing about death. The animal lives fully in the timelessness of the present and in the immediacy of its body. To the ego, however, sexuality and death are associated phenomena, since both assert the dominance of the body over the ego. The ego cannot counter its consciousness of death with sexuality, which is itself a corporeal or bodily function. It can oppose its consciousness of death only with its consciousness of timeless bliss, which is the memory of its original state. This memory exists in man as a residue of his animal heritage, reinforced by his experiences at his mother's breast. It is perceived as the consciousness of the other, the mother in whose arms the infant consciously experienced the bliss of fulfillment and repose. In the preceding chapter, love was defined as the consciousness of the other (mother or sexual object) who offers the fulfillment of the need for closeness and union. Love is the ego's answer to the consciousness of death. On the psychic level, love and death are diametrically opposed concepts.

History is replete with stories of individuals who have faced death with courage. The crucifixion of Christ is an example of the power of love to sustain the spirit in the face of death. The Christian martyrs are other examples of this power of love. Heroes such as Nathan Hale demonstrate that

the love of country may be a force strong enough to overcome the fear of death. Such actions may be understood in
terms of the dialectical formula. When the total ego is
invested in the love for the other (person, humanity, or
country), there is no psychic energy left to cathect the fear of
death. In other words, death is divorced from feeling, since all
feeling is transferred to the other. In love, the self is fully
identified with the other, as so many writers have emphasized.

The first person with whom one identifies is the mother.
The love of an infant for his mother is the prototype of all
later love relationships. All love relationships involve, therefore, elements of need and dependence. The lover cannot
exist without the love object. In this respect, he is very much
like an infant, who cannot survive without the mother or
mother substitute. What happens when both parties in a love
relationship have the same feelings of need for and dependence on each other? What happens when neither can exist
without the other? Each lives off the other in a symbiotic
relationship that can end only in their mutual death. But by
the same token, death holds no fear for such lovers. Some
such reasoning as this must be used to explain the fact of
tragedy in all great love stories.

If the primary love relationship of an individual, that is, his
relationship to his mother, allows for his self-expression and
self-realization, then love becomes one with its biological
fulfillment. The identification that develops under these conditions is limited to the biological need and fulfillment and
does not consume the ego, or self, of the lover. Self and
other remain two independent organisms that merge and then
separate, to merge again when the mutual need is imperative.
Love dissociated from its biological expression—that is, love
as a psychological phenomenon only—may remove one from
the fear of death. However, such love provides no basis for
life. Love in action expressed either as a biological response
or social response to the needs of others is life sustaining and
life renewing. Psychological love is an antidote to the fear of
death. Sexual love, or love in action, is the antagonist of death.

The phenomenon of human individuation, or self-
consciousness, gives rise to the problem of anxiety. It is the
overwhelming and destructive impact of anxiety on civilized
man that is responsible for the research and effort expended
to write books on sex, psychology, and related subjects.
Adam became afraid when he became aware of his naked-

ness. This was interpreted to mean that Adam became afraid when confronted with his mortality and his aloneness. It matters little which of these two aspects of nakedness is stressed. I believe that one implies the other. Death makes us feel our aloneness in the world, and being alone makes us conscious of our mortality.

One cannot dispute the observation that the feeling of being alone, apart, isolated is anxiety-producing. Many psychologists are of the opinion that the isolation from which modern man suffers is the underlying cause of the anxiety against which he struggles. But this isolation is—in part, at least—a function of uniqueness of personality, a concomitant of individuality. Where individuality is less developed, the sense of aloneness does not occur. Primitive man, whose identity was determined by his membership in a clan or in a tribe, was rarely conscious either of his individuality or of his isolation. An amoeba is never alone. It exists as part of a continuous flow of life from one amoeba to another. The lower organisms all show the phenomenon of being part of the natural order—one with their environment. But the lower animals have no feeling of individuality or, at most, very little feeling. The more individual we become, the more alone we sense ourselves, the more isolated we feel ourselves. Personality, by definition, creates uniqueness, difference, isolation. The more one merges with the herd or the crowd, the more one loses one's individual personality. It is a common way to escape anxiety. By contrast, the more highly developed the personality (the greater the individuality), the more separate is the individual from the mass. The functions that are associated with the growth and development of personality create in the individual a sense of uniqueness, a feeling of apartness, and the condition of aloneness.

What is the antidote to the aloneness of individuality? How can we avoid the destructive anxiety that it can produce? It is often said that love is the answer. Such an unqualified answer can be heard in every pulpit on every Sunday, but all it offers us is moral uplift. The answer *is* love, but it is love in action, the primary form of which is sex. The fact is that a man in bed with a woman whom he loves, cares for, or has strong desires for does not feel alone. So long as the sex drive is imperative, so long as it is conscious and free from guilt, the anxiety of aloneness is not experienced. One may be alone under these circumstances, but one is not anxious about it.

If it is correct to relate anxiety to the condition of isolation or aloneness, it is equally correct to relate it to the
inhibition of sexual feelings or the guilt associated with them.
In this sense, it can be seen that the Freudian view that
anxiety is related to sexual problems is as valid as the current
sociological view that relates anxiety to inter-personal difficulties. Life creates two forces—one tends to individuality and
structure, the other to merger and loss of unique structure.
These two forces can be recognized as personality and sex.
Personality is the expression of the unique structure of our
being. Sexuality is the force that leads to closeness, identification, and union with the other—always the representative of
the world.

Sexuality and personality are interdependent. Sexuality
conditions personality, since it determines the individual's
relationship to the other and to the world. Personality, on the
other hand, shapes and molds the sexual behavior of an individual. The sexual person is a loving person and a joyful
person. His sexuality provides the main source of his pleasure
and satisfaction in life. It also provides a positive orientation
toward others and toward the world. The sexually frustrated
person is invariably a bitter person. But personality modifies
and controls sexuality. The bitter person cannot enjoy the
sweetness of love. It turns sour in his mouth. The depressed
person is sexually depressed as well. If the personality is vital
and alive, the sexuality of the individual will show the same
qualities. A rigid person's sexual function is just as rigid and
mechanical as his personality. And a person whose behavior
is designed to impress others will act out the same need in his
sexual function.

Personality is not limited to the psychic functions of an
individual; it includes his physical aspects as well as his
psychic ones. Of course, there is nothing new in this idea.
What is new is the ability to understand the language of body
expression. Without this ability and knowledge, one can easily
be misled into confusing the symbol with the reality. Marilyn
Monroe, for example, was a symbol of sexuality, not the
embodiment of it. Her body showed a conspicuous lack of
unity and integration. A body without unity reveals the lack
of fusion of the pregenital libidinal drives into a strong,
focused genital urge.

The sexuality of a person is in his being. His sexual
fulfillment is reflected in his overall good feelings, his joyful-

ness, and his happiness. His sexual maturity is reflected in his physical appearance and movements. A body that is harmonious, integrated, coordinated, and alive—simply, a body that is beautiful and graceful in its normal and natural movements —characterizes the sexually mature person. These physical attributes are merely the external evidence of a spirit that is free, independent, and responsive to life. Sexuality is the expression of life and the antithesis of death.

5

Homosexuality

In the preceding chapters, I stressed the sexual nature of life. Homosexuality appears to be a contradiction of this view. It raises the question whether there are two sexes or three. It makes one question whether man is basically bisexual, since he can be either heterosexual or homosexual. Is the homosexual a freak of nature who merits the popular designation of "queer"? Is he merely a misguided person who has succumbed to temptation because of personal difficulties stemming from an unhappy home? Is he the product of a confused society that cannot accept the varieties of erotic experience possible in nature? The answers to these questions may yield information about disturbances of the sexual function in heterosexual individuals.

One interesting aspect of the homosexual problem is the intense reaction that the homosexual evokes in many so-called normal people. These people frequently express considerable antagonism and hostility toward homosexuals. I have heard a number of men say that when they see a homosexual they have an impulse to beat him up. The homosexual is often an object of scorn and contempt. At the same time, these so-called normal people manifest a certain interest in and fascination about the homosexual. The "gay" bars in Greenwich Village are crowded with tourists who are curious about this strange life. These people expose themselves to the homosexual atmosphere at the same time that they express horror at and repugnance to the idea of it. It can be shown analytically that this anxiety derives from a stratum of latent homosexuality which is severely repressed in the average individual. Such a person may consciously feel that he is safe from the danger of "infection" with this "disease." On the other hand, his behavior toward the homosexual reveals a fear that he may be susceptible to this form of sexual behavior. In their unconscious, many individuals doubt the integrity of their sexual orientation.

The social attitude toward homosexuality mirrors the same anxiety. It is significant that while male homosexuality is almost universally condemned in Western countries, female homosexuality is tolerated. Thus, while there are laws prohibiting male homosexuality, there are no such laws against female homosexuality. This attitude must have at its base the fear that homosexuality is contagious and that affliction with the "disease" results in a condition of weakness, of loss of strength, and of impotence. Such a strong condemnation can proceed only from the conviction of a society that its survival depends upon its aggressivity. The homosexual is regarded as a passive individual; he is viewed as one who cannot be counted on to uphold and fight for the institutions of his society; in other words, he is considered an inferior being.

Another facet of the problem is the fact, which can hardly be overlooked, that the homosexual is frequently found in the forefront of cultural activity—in the theater, in the arts, in design and decoration, and in other creative activities. Certainly this must have something to do with the social forces in a culture such as ours, one that places an exaggerated value on aggressiveness, virility, and competitiveness. The heterosexual is discouraged from pursuing activities which depend upon the expression of the tender emotions and which therefore seem passive and feminine. He is encouraged to be hard, tough, and aggressive. The homosexual who eschews the competitive struggle is only too happy to have the creative field as his personal domain. But surely this cannot be the whole answer. This situation must also be owing to the fact that the competitive struggle in our culture is so severe, so fierce, that it leaves the normal individual who engages in it with little energy or inclination for the pursuit of artistic interests.

Society's role in homosexuality is a complex one. To the degree that a social structure is a homogeneous one, that is, when most of its members share all the society's work, homosexuality will be found to be the rare situation. In such a culture, there is no antagonism between the aggressive pursuits and the artistic pursuits, no conflict between the tender emotions and the fierce emotions. The warrior is also the dancer, the artist is also a worker. There is little distinction between the man of action and the man of thought. These conditions, of course, characterize only the simpler or more primitive cultures. As a result, there is no occasion for the homosexual way of life. This does not mean that homosexuality cannot occur in such communities. History and anthropological investigation have shown that it is an almost universal phenomenon. It can also be found in the animal kingdom. But, generally, it is a sporadic occurrence, the recourse of an individual who is denied access to the opposite sex. In the more highly developed cultures, homosexuality becomes a way of life. The division of labor, the stratification of the social organization, and the conflict between aggressive and passive tendencies isolate the sensitive and unassertive person and provide a milieu in which these qualities are acceptable.

Another view of the relationship between society and sexual behavior is presented by G. R. Taylor. According to Taylor, if the social restriction of the sexual drive is too severe, three reactions can be anticipated: the stronger personalities will defy the taboo; the weaker ones will turn to indirect forms of expression, or perverted forms of sex; in others, symptoms of psychoneurotic disturbance will appear. This view, with which I am in accord, does not contradict the idea that I have advanced. It adds a psychological explanation that needs further elaboration. The existence of weak personalities who are not integrated into the normal life of the community creates a reservoir of individuals who will seek, necessarily, indirect modes of sexual expression. Is there a special weakness which characterizes the homosexual and which is the predisposition to this form of sexual behavior? The present chapter will seek an answer to this question.

A word of caution should be added. The logic of Taylor's argument should not mislead us into believing that the etiology of homosexuality is a simple one. Our own time can hardly be considered an age of sexual restriction. If we are not sexually mature, we are certainly sexually sophisticated. Yet according to some authorities, homosexuality is more prevalent today than at any other time in the past century. I believe that one must look for a further explanation of this phenomenon, and this explanation must be sought in the personality of the homosexual.

Although homosexual communities exist in most large cities

in our culture, this is a development of the past few decades. More commonly, the homosexual is an isolated individual in the larger community of heterosexual men and women. Without a partner, he is lonely, insecure, and troubled. Despite the protestations of some confirmed homosexuals that homosexuality is a "normal" way of life, the average invert is aware that his propensity amounts to an emotional illness.

John is a good case to illustrate this problem. He consulted me because of feelings of depression and anxiety. A homosexual relationship that had gone on for a number of years had recently ended. John had been rejected in favor of another lover. He was upset and distressed, and although the relationship had been terminated more than six months earlier, he had been unable to get over his feelings of jealousy and anger.

John was a professional dancer. For many years, he had been a member of a leading troupe of modern dancers and his homosexual involvement had been with the leading dancer. In the troupe, he felt that he had been exploited, working hard for very little financial reward. Since his income as a dancer hardly sufficed to keep him alive, he supplemented it with certain musical activities. His overall earnings could provide little more than a cold-water flat, a few meager possessions, and a most modest life. But John was content with this arrangement. He needed very little to live, he said, and that little he could always raise. His biggest problem was how to obtain the money for the therapy that he believed he needed. But John was not without some measure of ambition. He wanted to achieve some success with his music and looked forward to earning a better living.

Some years earlier, John had attempted an affair with a girl, but it had been so sexually unsatisfying that he had abandoned the idea. However, he was friendly with several women who took a motherly interest in him. During the course of his therapy, John experienced for the first time a feeling of sexual excitation at the sight of a girl, which surprised him very much. Despite this, a subsequent attempt at relations with a girl yielded no better results than his previous effort.

Obsessed by the loss of his lover and tormented by his need for sexual contact and release, John "cruised" the streets or dropped in at homosexual hangouts. When John was successful in finding a partner, it was a one-night stand.

Although temporarily relieved by this sexual activity, John was never satisfied, never free from the gnawing feeling of loneliness that haunts the unattached homosexual. It is difficult for me to understand how the homosexual can be called "gay." True, homosexual parties and gatherings have a superficial appearance of carefreeness and lack of restraint. At one party of homosexual men in New York, the hostess was an attractive girl who went about completely nude serving the men. No one paid any special attention to her, and no one made any move toward her. The carefreeness and gaiety reflect the lack of strong feelings. They are masks that cover the inner deadness of the homosexual personality. On closer acquaintance and under analysis, the homosexual proves to be one of the most tragic figures of our times.

John was not an unattractive person. He was well-built, with good muscular development that had been furthered by his career as a dancer. His face had a youthful quality and regular features that were pleasing to the eye. One could detect John's problem in his soft, effeminate manner, delicate bearing, and quiet speech. These qualities have been associated with the male homosexual, but they are only secondary characteristics. Certainly the opposite qualities would not constitute a "real man." Was there not a deeper disturbance that would account for such a severe distortion of John's personality?

A closer look at John showed that his body, which at first glance seemed normal, was stiff and immobile. He stood like a wooden statue, he moved like a toy soldier. If this seems surprising in view of the fact that John was a professional dancer, it can be explained. The movements that seem free and graceful onstage are studied and the result of special training. Offstage, John was awkward and restrained. His muscles were tight and hard. Actually, he was muscle-bound. When I first worked with him, his body had a musty, unpleasant odor. I had the impression that it was "dead," without sensation or feeling.

The deadness in John's body was also mirrored in his eyes. There was no expression in them. He rarely looked at me directly. When he did, there was no feeling of contact between us. On one occasion, I had John keep his eyes on mine, and I could see some warmth appear in them. He smiled as someone does who has revealed something and became embarrassed. His reserve had melted for a moment.

A further appreciation of John's condition can be gained from an analysis of the following figure drawings that he made. They are expressions of his body image, that is, of the way in which he perceives his own body and, necessarily, of the way in which he perceives other bodies. Figure 1 represents his concept of the male figure.

Asked to comment on the drawing, John said, "I felt self-conscious about the drawing—I *do* draw." As to the figure, he remarked, "He's pleased with himself or wants to see if you're pleased with what he's pleased about. He's very stiff and limited in movement. He's happy. Doesn't know he has any problems."

Figure 2 is that of a woman. John described her as a "patient mother. A bit disappointed, but she won't register any complaint. She is unable to show any feelings."

It doesn't take much imagination to see that both figures are puppets or dolls—not real human beings.

To bring out more of John's feelings about his body, I asked him to draw a nude male. (Most patients, when asked for a figure drawing, respond with a nude rather than a clothed figure. John said that a nude was more difficult to draw.) Figure 3 which he then drew, is quite revealing. It portrays a "stiff," that is, a corpse, with an erection, supported by four projections that keep it from being in contact with the ground. The deadness in John's body is well depicted in this drawing. All his feeling is concentrated in the erect penis. This is the homosexual problem: genital excitation in a body that is devoid of pleasurable feeling.

The unaliveness of the body and the overexcitation of the genitals were vividly exhibited in one therapeutic session. Lying on the couch, John extended his mouth in a gesture of reaching out to kiss or suck. As he did so, he developed an erection, which surprised him greatly. He looked just like his drawing. The interpretation of this reaction provides some understanding of the homosexual difficulty. The excitation of reaching out with his mouth was immediately transmitted to the genitals. The body acted like a rigid tube, transferring the excitation from one end to the other without experiencing the flow of sexual feeling. This is not normal sexuality. Such a response bypasses sexuality in being limited to the genital organ. Sexual feeling is the desire for closeness and union between two bodies. The genitals serve as the discharge mechanism. The excitation that builds up through the contact of the two bodies is discharged in the sexual act through the

FIGURE 1

FIGURE 2

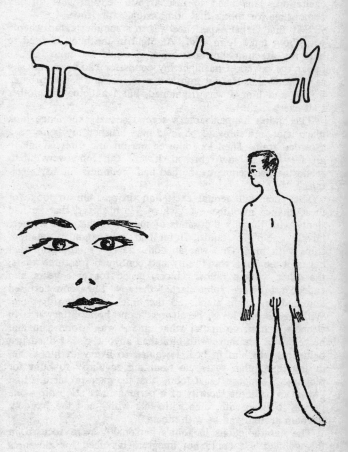

FIGURE 3

genital apparatus. Since John's body was relatively dead and unresponsive, he avoided closeness and intimacy of body contact, but sought only to eliminate a genital tension or excitation. This need to discharge a tension was directly responsible for John's first homosexual experience.

"My first sexual experience was in a summer camp when I was about ten," John said. "At night in the bunk, I tried to hide my erection, but sometimes it would be quite tentlike under the covers. One night my counselor came around and saw me awake. He got into bed with me, and I masturbated myself and him. I was frightened, but I anticipated another visit every night."

This didn't happen. John's second sexual experience took place later in a subway. "A lewd man brushed my penis on a crowded train. Then he followed me off and directed me to an alley. I was so frightened, I ran." But John went on to relate that, subsequently, he had had "countless subway meetings."

The persistent genital excitation drove John to look for these chance meetings everywhere. He observed that he had slept "with literally thousands of men, less than ten women. mostly one-night stands." John had two extended relationships with men. One was an "off and on" relationship that began when John was twenty and continued for three years; the other, with a fellow dancer, lasted for nine years and ended just before John started therapy. But John "cruised and had one-night stands all the time" he was with them. With his second lover, he always "came home afterwards to sleep with him, no matter what time it was." John said that he "enjoyed sex more with him than anyone else. I liked just being next to him in bed. I wanted to live with him." Yet during these nine years, he went out regularly to hunt for pickups. "I suppose," said John, "that the main problem is that I want to have the security of a permanent relationship—one person to sleep with, dine with, talk with—and the freedom to roam around and be with others."

The contradictions in John's personality were focused in this conflict. He could not integrate his need for closeness and companionship with his genital feelings, which had a strong sadistic component. On the other hand, John could not permit a decrease in his persistent genital excitation, since it was his lifeline. His rigid and unalive body forced him to seek the excitement of danger in the chance encounter. Immobility and restlessness pervaded his being and determined his behavior. John described his difficulty as "an inability to be where I am at the moment. The need to desire other things, places, and people than the ones I am involved with. My inability to say, 'No, that is not what I want, this is.' These are my problems." John's unresponsive body represented his unconscious rejection of the need for closeness despite a strong desire for it. John remarked that he wanted his lover back, but he added, "Perhaps so I can reject him again?"

What factors determined that John would be a homosexual with problems rather than a heterosexual with problems? John had no lack of feeling for women. At the beginning of his therapy, he said, "I am currently having sex with three men—an advance from the one-night stands, but it is still confusing and frustrating—and I am deeply involved emotionally with a girl, although I am not sleeping with her."

Analysis showed that John had strong but repressed feelings of hostility toward and fear of the female, which blocked any possibility of sexual gratification with women. To entrust his "precious organ" to a woman was to risk losing it and his life. Women represent orgastic discharge and the loss of genital feeling. The subsidence of the erection after intercourse has been described as a "little death." This is true only where all the feeling of life is concentrated in the genitals. In the normal person, the loss of feeling in the genitals after intercourse is compensated for by a wonderful feeling of glow and warmth in the body. This did not happen to John because his body could not participate in the sexual experience. His homosexual encounters relieved his tension only momentarily. The excitation returned soon afterward, and John could go around secure in the feeling that he had not lost his genitals, that he had not been castrated, that he had not died.

Nothing explains the homosexual so much as this preoccupation with the genitals, if not his own, then those of other males. The tight trousers that emphasize the buttocks and the genitals are one expression of this preoccupation. Current homosexuality is the modern version of the ancient phallic-worship religions, distorted so that what was once a fertility symbol is now its opposite. It has become the means of "acting out" all the negative feelings that the homosexual has toward his parents, toward society, and toward himself. This was evident in the chance relationships that John sought.

He described one such relationship as follows:

"I was wandering through the streets about 2:30 A.M. looking for a friend. I saw a fellow outside the bar who made a lascivious remark to me. I went home with him to his place, and I was very cold. I realized that he wanted to be beaten. I knew that he would service me. I tried to think of my feelings, and I realized that I didn't want to be there.

"He lay down and asked me to come all over him. I tried to masturbate on him. Then he asked me to spit on him. I did, but I got out of there as quickly as possible.

"It shattered me, because I realized that I allow myself to get into these situations. I can see what it is that I want: to be degraded, to be humiliated, and to be castrated."

In this encounter, John experienced the masochistic element in his personality while "acting out" sadistically upon his partner. His expression of contempt for his partner was a projection of his inner feeling of contempt for himself. This feeling lies at the core of the homosexual way of life. The homosexual often has contempt for all the values that the average person accepts. John admitted that he had a terrible work problem. He said, "I think, 'What for? Why work?'" His very mode of existence was an expression of contempt for the struggle men engage in to provide a home and a living for their wives and families. And his contempt for the men who engage in this struggle was reflected in his feelings of superiority to them. On what grounds can the homosexual feel superior? His attitude is based on his sensitivity, his intelligence, and his cultivation of aesthetic interests. The homosexual is a keen critic of our culture, though his criticism is often expressed in satirical and cynical terms. The perspicacity of observation and the sharpness of wit of Oscar Wilde are a case in point.

Charles Berg in *The Problem of Homosexuality*, quotes Mayer Gross as saying, "'As a matter of clinical experience it is remarkable how often homosexuals are of more than average intelligence.'" Indeed, Berg feels that on the basis of the "illustrious names" who were homosexuals, "there is some excuse for the invert's ridiculous claim of a monopoly of culture and genius."

The homosexual's fear and hostility toward women are repressed. What is expressed, not always openly, but "acted out," is contempt for women. It is "acted out" by hairdressers and fashion designers whose creations often distort the femininity of the female. It is expressed in plays in which the woman is often pictured as insensitive, domineering, and cruel. It is reflected in the superiority that the homosexual feels over women in feminine matters such as cooking, decorating, and designing. For the homosexual's problem is primarily a problem with respect to women, and only secondarily does it involve the homosexual's feelings about men.

Until now, I have avoided any discussion of John's background in order to present a picture of homosexual behavior and feeling. However, we cannot fully understand John without some knowledge of his relationship to his mother and father. He described his mother as a "loving, intelligent, and long-suffering [woman] who died of leukemia at about the age of fifty. She knew she was dying, but worked in the family store until it was absolutely urgent that she be put in a hospital." His father was an alcoholic who died of delirium tremens in a dirty room at the age of fifty-five. "My father," John said, "used to beat me when drunk, until one day I said, 'If you touch me again, I will beat you up.' He stopped." John recalls hating his father not so much for the beatings as for the humiliation of having to take care of him in his drunken stupors. John's feelings toward his father were not repressed. In his homosexual behavior, he acted out much of his hostility and contempt for his father. But his relation to his mother was very confused.

Analytic experience suggests that the combination of a seductive, close-binding mother and a rejecting father is often responsible for a homosexual son. John lacked an acceptable male image upon which to pattern his masculinity. But, more significantly, he overidentified with his mother and was unconsciously sexually involved with her. The result was an exaggeration of the oedipal situation to the point where the child could not resolve his incestuous feelings for his mother. If, in addition, the mother is self-sacrificing to the point of death, the sexual guilt, as in John's case, is enormous. In such situations, to reduce the guilt, the child must cut off his sexual feelings. The only way to do this is to deaden the body. Deadening the body reduces feelings and eliminates conflicts. But one cannot live with a dead body. Some safety valve must be provided. In the homosexual, it takes the form of an excited genital organ. Sexuality is abandoned, but castration is avoided.

John recognized early in the therapy the truth of my observation that his body was unalive. He also became aware that the bodies of his homosexual friends were equally dead. Of his former lover, John said, "He only feels his body when he is with me or with Peter." And then he realized, too, that his mother's body was dead—actually, dying—when he was a young man. John spontaneously remarked, "I want to fuck my dead mother to make her come alive." John now knew that his sexual activity was a compulsion—that he, too, used sex as a way to feel, to come alive; he recalled that he used to masturbate in the morning in order to wake up.

As part of the therapy, I had John do exercises designed to mobilize his breathing and increase the feeling of his body. Together with the analysis of his feelings, attitudes, and dreams, the body work made John feel more alive. One day some feeling appeared in his eyes, and his face looked softer, less masklike. John remarked, "I feel great. I feel different." But this feeling also coincided with the departure of his former lover for Europe. Temporarily, at least, the chains that had bound him in this relationship were broken. And at this time, a sexual feeling for the female broke through. He related, "Yesterday I saw a voluptuous woman and I got an erection. This was the first time I got an erection from a woman."

John also became aware of his lack of involvement with people. He said, "I get them stirred up and react to their stirrings. I don't participate. It is as if I play doctor." This detachment was most evident in relation to women. He had attempted to resume a former liaison with a girl to whom he felt attached. But this sexual experience, as mentioned earlier, was not satisfactory. He couldn't give in to his feelings. He couldn't control her movements as he did a man's. And he was afraid of the involvement. "I am afraid she will make demands on me that I cannot fulfill—that she will want me to continue the relationship—that I will become dependent on her."

One fantasy from childhood bears special relevance to this fear. John recalled, "When I was small, I remember this distinctly. I dreamed that I would open the door of the bathroom and find my mother sitting there dead. Then I really became afraid of opening the door for fear of finding her dead. Later I transferred this fantasy to my boyfriend."

John's therapy lasted about one year. I saw him once a week. He had improved in many ways, but the homosexual problem had not been resolved. Toward the end, John experienced warm and tender feelings for former girl friends and acquaintances. But these led immediately to the need for a homosexual encounter. John also noted that he sought these homosexual experiences the night before his therapeutic session. Fortunately, these encounters were becoming less and less satisfactory. Or was it that John was becoming more aware of how unsatisfactory they really were? Toward the end of his therapy, he admitted, "When it was over, I felt unsatisfied, as I always do after sex." Every case is different, but the essential features of John's problem are seen in all other homosexual cases.

Max was another homosexual whom I treated. He was referred to me following his arrest in a railroad lavatory for making a sexual advance to a male who turned out to be a detective. Max was a married man with three grown children, but sexual contact between Max and his wife was almost nil. This was not the first time that he had been apprehended for sexual misconduct. Several years earlier, he had gotten into trouble for trying to seduce two young boys.

Physically, Max showed many of the disturbances that characterized John's condition. Max's body was hard and tight; all his muscles were severely contracted and tense, like tightly coiled springs. Bending backward or forward was difficult for him. He had no flexibility in his pelvis whatsoever. The physical tightness extended to his face, the features of which were sharp and angular. His voice was high-pitched and thin. It lacked resonance and warmth. Max wore glasses because of his myopia, but he also did not look at me directly. Without the glasses, Max's eyes were lifeless and empty of expression.

Generally, Max tried to keep his homosexual impulses under restraint. He masturbated occasionally, without much satisfaction. Max tried to reduce his sexual feelings to a minimum. He did this by two mechanisms: the first was the extreme tightness of his body, which decreased all body sensation; the other was hyperactivity, manifested in constant change of position and compulsive busyness. Unfortunately, these means failed to work under conditions of unusual stress. Such a situation had developed at the time of Max's apprehension. He had become greatly excited over an impending change in his career, and he couldn't handle this increased feeling of excitation. As in John's case, Max's excitation was immediately transferred to his genitals. His need to discharge the sexual tension was so strong that Max approached a stranger, fully aware of the fact that detectives are often planted in public lavatories to trap the invert.

I have suggested that sexuality is a function of the entire body. Normally, the body holds the excitation until an appropriate situation is available for its release in sexual activity. But where the body is dead, as in John's condition, or so severely tensed that it cannot contain the excitation, as in Max's case, the genitals become charged with an urgency that impels to immediate action. All homosexual activity has a compulsive quality that is, unfortunately, not always absent from heterosexual functioning. Given genital excitation with a compulsive quality, intense fear of approaching a woman, and the inability to achieve a satisfactory release through masturbation, the homosexual is placed in a desperate position. He is driven to a homosexual encounter that is fraught with danger and fated to end in dissatisfaction.

It may be questioned whether what I have described is a true picture of homosexuality. Are there not homosexuals who maintain a relationship for many years with a fair amount of satisfaction for both parties? That homosexual relationships can last many years is conceded. John himself had one for nine years. But that it can yield sufficient satisfaction to both parties to make it a meaningful way of life is doubtful. The very nature of the homosexual personality makes this almost impossible to achieve. One of the partners generally feels trapped in the relationship and sees no way out. The jealousies, resentments, and hostilities that pervade these relationships are well known. Clifford Allen in *The Problem of Homosexuality* points out that "homosexual murder is common" and makes the statement that the "greatest importance of homosexuality is that it causes so much unhappiness." Among psychiatrists, it is generally accepted that at his best, the homosexual is an immature person; at his worst, he is either schizophrenic or paranoid. It is my experience that some degree of homosexuality can be found in every schizoid or schizophrenic individual. The reverse is also true. All homosexuals manifest certain schizophrenic mechanisms, even if they are not schizophrenics in the clinical sense.

If my analysis of the homosexual dilemma is correct, the

problem requires a twofold approach, the physical and the psychological. On the physical level, the phenomenon of the unalive or unresponsive body, which is the tangible aspect of the disturbance, must be recognized and remedied. I have described this condition in only two cases. However, it was present in every case of homosexuality, male or female, that I have seen or treated. To attack this aspect of the problem it is necessary to increase the patient's feeling of his body. This is done by mobilizing his respiration, creating more physical sensation in the body, and reducing its state of muscular tension. Since sexuality is a biological function, its physical correlates should be known.*

On the psychological level, the relation of the patient to the opposite sex must be examined analytically within the context of his total personality. The fear, the hostility, and the contempt for the opposite sex must be brought to consciousness and abreacted. This means that the patient must express these feelings in the analytic session and not act them out unconsciously on the outside. The patient's relation to his father and mother must be explored to uncover the source of his feelings about the opposite sex. It is also important that the ability to achieve self-gratification be developed by the patient. The importance of this ability is clearly shown by John's statement, "Why can't I do it for myself? I can do it for others, and they can do it for me."

In our culture, the guilt over sexuality attaches more to the act of masturbation than it does to any other sexual activity. This may be owing to the fact that the child first becomes aware of parental disapproval of sexual feeling when he engages in autoerotic activities. Dig deep under the sexual sophistication of the homosexual and you will find a broad vein of sexual guilt over masturbation. This guilt links up with the childhood guilt over incestuous feelings for the mother, since she is frequently the sexual object in the fantasies that accompany early masturbatory experiences.

In the first section of this study, it was shown that affectionate feelings and affectionate behavior derive from the biology of the organism. It follows that distortions in the feeling and expression of love have their roots in disturbances

---

*The rationale for this type of therapy was first set forth by Wilhelm Reich in *The Function of the Orgasm*. New York: Orgone Institute Press, Inc., 1942. It is further elaborated in A. Lowen, *The Physical Dynamics of Character Structure*. New York: Grune & Stratton, Inc., 1958.

of basic biological functions. This, I believe, is true of the
homosexual. The main biological disturbance in the homosexual is the lack of motility and feeling in his body. But there
are secondary disturbances, such as the restriction of respiration, the immobilization of aggressive impulses to kick and
hit, and the conflicting tendencies to suck and bite. In addition, the homosexual has severe inhibitions about anal functions. The restriction of respiration reduces body feeling and
limits the energy available for aggressive actions. The conflict
between the strong desire for and hostility against the mother
on the oral level operates to paralyze the homosexual. Early
and severe toilet training, in which the mother played the
dominant role, may lead to a submissive and passive attitude
in the homosexual that covers an underlying anal spite. A
patient's inability to kick rhythmically and forcefully can
often be traced to muscular tensions in the buttocks and
thighs, resulting from infantile anal anxieties.

On every level, oral, anal, and genital, the homosexual was
in conflict about his mother, a conflict which had to be
repressed in the interest of survival. The repression of this
conflict makes it almost impossible for the homosexual to
relate to a woman, since any significant relationship would
tend to evoke the original problems. In turning to a man, the
homosexual can avoid this dilemma and "act out" in symbolic
form his relationship to his mother. Clifford Allen makes the
interesting observation that the homosexual "tends to regard
other men as symbolizing a mother in some manner." In
homosexuality, according to Allen, the forbidden parts of the
mother's body are transmuted into male features and organs.
The buttocks bound by tight trousers symbolize the breast,
the penis stands for the nipple, and anus and mouth are
representative of the vagina.

The homosexual is fixated at the oral stage of development
because he suffered a deprivation at this stage. Yet it can be
shown in many cases that the homosexual was indulged by
his mother. From the behavior and attitude of the homosexual, it can be deduced that he was deprived of the erotic
pleasure that the child normally obtains from the breast and
from contact with the mother's body. Let me emphasize that
the deprivation was not always of the breast or of contact,
but of the erotic pleasure that these offer. How is this
possible?

A clue to the answer to this question may be gained from
Freud's study of Leonardo da Vinci, who was a homosexual.

It is presumed that Leonardo was the illegitimate child of a servant girl and her noble lord. At any event, he was raised without a father. His mother adored him, and he was very involved with her. Da Vinci's *Madonna of the Rocks* must be a representation of his mother. In Leonardo's time, children were normally breast fed for three years or longer. It is therefore unlikely that Leonardo was deprived of the breast or of contact with his mother's body.

In his study of Da Vinci, Freud relates a recurrent fantasy that Da Vinci recorded in his notebooks: a vulture descends to Leonardo and puts his tail feathers between Leonardo's lips. If this is interpreted as a homosexual fantasy, the tail feathers would symbolize a penis. But it can also be interpreted as an oral fantasy, the tail feathers symbolizing the nipple. In this case, the vulture would represent the mother. These interpretations do not contradict each other. If his mother used the breast and nipple to gain a sexual thrill from the child's nursing, both interpretations would be correct. It is a fact that women can get sexually excited by the nursing experience. Such a reaction is normal and does no harm to the child. But the mother who exploits this situation for her own needs turns the child into a sexual object. If Leonardo's mother was without a man, that is, deprived of a love object, it is conceivable that such an exploitation could have happened. The enigmatic smile of the *Mona Lisa*, which has long puzzled students of this painting, may express secret guilt and pleasure. Was this the vision that the child had of his mother as he lay in her arms?

When a relationship is thus twisted, two possible results may ensue. Instead of being the active participant in the relationship, the child is forced into a passive position. It is not his erotic pleasure that is important, but the mother's. The breast is not his to enjoy (his first little world), but hers. He is deprived for her benefit. The second result is the sexual excitation of the child. The sexual excitement of the mother passes into the child. This is no mystical theory. A child is almost part of his mother—he was actually part of her body a short time earlier. Every child is attuned to his mother's feelings. He senses her responses, her moods, her disappointments, her joys. A depressed mother will make a child depressed. A mother who is sexually excited by the child will excite the child. But the child has no mechanism to release this excitation. And the mother who uses a child in this way will unconsciously, out of her guilt, prohibit any sexual activi-

ty by the child, such as masturbation. The result is to increase the incestuous fixation upon her to the point where it
cannot be resolved.

If my hypothesis is correct, then for Leonardo to sleep
with a woman would be tantamount to incest. He had no
recourse but to become a homosexual, thereby reversing the
roles of infancy: by putting his penis (nipple) into a male's
mouth for his own erotic pleasure, he became the mother
who exploited the child (young boy or man).

One word about the anal fixation. When a mother gives a
child an enema, she is carrying out a symbolic sexual act. She
may be acting in the best faith, even upon the advice of a
doctor, but one cannot overlook the psychological symbolism
of this act. One enema can do no harm, especially if it is
really indicated. But the practice of giving enemas for every
bowel upset is fairly widespread in some segments of our
culture. And I cannot help but believe that some mothers
take advantage of this situation to act out upon the child
their own resentment at being females.

It is necessary to distinguish between a homosexual experience and the homosexual attitude or personality. The homosexual experience is engaged in for convenience, that is, in
the absence of an opportunity for relations with the opposite
sex, and is found in the animal kingdom, in all cultures, and
at all times. Those who engage in this relationship do not
deny their preference for the opposite sex. Such activity
indicates that the sex drive can be so potent, so imperative,
that it overrides the exigencies of reality. It is known that a
cow in heat will mount another cow. Sexuality is not limited
to the attraction and excitation experienced by male and
female for each other, although these responses are its
highest form of expression, its most evolved mode. The
contact of any two bodies is exciting and erotically pleasurable. However, heterosexuality is a more adequate, more satisfying way to release sexual excitation. The homosexual personality must be defined therefore as one that chooses an
inadequate mode of sexual experience because of an inability
to function on the superior level of heterosexuality.

It makes little sense to argue, as some homosexuals do,
that Socrates was a homosexual and that the Greeks approved or tolerated this form of sexual relationship. There
were many special conditions in Greek culture that could
account for this distortion in the sexual attitudes of the
ancient Greeks. For example, Greek society was built upon

the institution of slavery. For another, woman occupied an inferior position. Despite its democracy, Greek society was class structured. Work was a menial occupation that devolved upon the slaves or the women. Such a social situation, as I pointed out earlier, furthers the homosexual way of life. The aesthete or man of culture may hold himself above the need for a woman, but this is never true of the lower classes or of slaves.

I have suggested that the sexual drive can be viewed as the biological force that functions to overcome the sense of aloneness and of isolation that the process of individuation produces. Individuality is not only associated with a feeling of aloneness, it is also accompanied by a vague sense of incompleteness. The sexual impulse to union is not only an urge for closeness with another organism, it is also an urge for self-completion. It is as if the self is fully realized only in the sexual union, through which the isolation of individuality is overcome.

This concept is similar to a myth credited to Plato but probably of more ancient origin. According to this myth, man and woman were originally one being, one creature, whom God split asunder to create the sexes. Ever since then, the two halves have been struggling to come together again to become the whole being. The biblical story that Eve was created from Adam supports this concept. It is also reflected in other creation stories in which the heavens and earth were originally one. Or the myth may be interpreted as an awareness that life once functioned on an asexual level.

The feeling of incompleteness as related to sexuality is dramatically illustrated in certain recurrent dreams and fantasies. In one dream or fantasy, the man attempts to take his own penis into his mouth and thereby satisfy and fulfill himself. This desire to be self-sufficient, complete in oneself, and independent of the need for a woman is found in neurotic males who have an unconscious fear of the female. I have heard several male patients to exclaim: "I wish there was no such thing as sex!" But this fantasy also represents a "primitive" state in the history of the individual, when such self-sufficiency seemed to exist. Actually, this "primitive" state can be interpreted as representing two different periods, one in the history of the species, a phylogenetic phenomenon, the other in the history of the specific individual, an ontogenetic phenomenon.

The first period would correspond to the time in man's

evolutionary development before the consciousness of self appeared. In this period of his evolution, man felt himself to be part of the universe, as the animal does, and neither incomplete nor isolated. It is the story of the Garden of Eden before the Fall, the paradisiacal state. This early period is represented on stone tablets and other artifacts by the serpent with its tail in its mouth. Erich Neumann in *The Origins and History of Consciousness* describes this symbol as "the circular snake, the primal dragon that bites its own tail, the self-begetting uroboros." As the heavenly serpent, the uroboros "slays, weds and impregnates itself. It is man and woman, begetting and conceiving and giving birth, active and passive, above and below, at once." It is, in short, the symbol of the universe, including life that continually reproduces itself out of itself.

The second period would correspond to the time in man's ontogenetic development when he existed in the "round," of which the circle is the symbol. In this state, the organism felt complete and self-contained, unconscious of any need for effort. The symbol of the round, or of the uroboros, represents the organism's early life in the egg or the womb as much as it represents man's early state of unconsciousness of self. Neumann writes: "The uroboros appears as the round 'container,' i.e., the maternal womb, but also as the union of masculine and feminine opposites. In the womb, the organism is curled up into itself, unaware of any lack in itself."

It is obvious that once a person is born, once he is out in the world, it is impossible to get back either to the womb or to the primal state of unconsciousness in which one is unaware of one's needs or of one's isolation. The nearest the newborn infant can come to it is through contact with that other "round," the maternal breast. But even here, consciousness soon intrudes to inform the infant that the breast is not part of him but belongs to another. There is no alternative but union with another individual; and in this need, the homosexual is no different from anyone else. He, too, needs union with another, both to complete his feeling of self and to gain the feeling of belonging, of being part of the whole; in other words, he needs the feeling of loving and being loved. His pattern of behavior differs from the normal in that his love object is a person of the same sex.

Infantile sexuality as opposed to adult sexuality is characterized by the search for uroboric completion, that is, for fulfillment through self-love. This takes the form of masturbation, in which the circle is completed through the contact of the hands with the genitals. The love object of the homosexual is, on one level of consciousness, an image of himself. How frequently one sees homosexual partners who look almost alike! Even in the relationship of an older man with a boy, the young boy is the image of the youth in the older man who never grew up. On this level, homosexuality has many of the features of masturbation, especially the aspect of self-love. Each homosexual loves himself in the other. On another level, however, the homosexual is joining with another person in an attempt at a mature relationship.

Homosexuality can be viewed as a hybrid combining the self-love of infancy and the attempt at the adult love of heterosexuality. Similar relationships, some involving sexual contact, can be found frequently among preadolescent or young adolescent boys. Whether this relationship of young boys with each other involves sexual activity or not, it is a common stage in the process of development that leads to adult heterosexual love patterns. Homosexuality may be regarded, therefore, as development arrested at this stage. In his features, appearance, and actions, the homosexual often reminds one of a preadolescent or adolescent boy.

In terms of the other, homosexuality is also an unconscious attempt to establish a heterosexual relationship. Theodor Reik made the comment, which I believe is valid, that in a homosexual relationship, one of the partners unconsciously imagines that the other is of the opposite sex, even though he is conscious of the fact that he is not. In the homosexual relationship, one of the partners takes the role of the opposite sex, although this may be reversed later. And analysis of the homosexual's fantasies about the relationship reveals that the homosexual partner is often treated as if he were the symbol and representative of the woman and the mother. Even the act of masturbation reflects, on either the conscious or the unconscious level, an awareness of the opposite sex. For the man, the hand represents a vagina; for the woman, it is a penis.

If the homosexual acts out the heterosexual love act in symbolic form, why is he unable to do so in reality? I have suggested a number of answers to this question earlier, based upon information gathered from clinical and analytic investigations. One of the things these studies reveal is that the homosexual is afraid of the opposite sex. Related to this fear, but on a deeper level, are feelings of hostility toward women. Since the fear is uppermost, it blocks off the possibilities of expressing love or tender feelings toward a woman. If the feelings of hostility were uppermost, some sexual relationship would be possible with a woman. In this case, sufficient aggression would be available to permit the carrying out of the heterosexual love act.

I have stated that homosexuality has its origin in the child's incestuous feelings for his mother, feelings that the child cannot resolve. Clinical experience confirms the observation that the mother of such a child is usually an emotionally disturbed and immature individual. Often, the cause for the mother's incestuous attachment to the son is a lack of satisfaction and fulfillment in her sexual life with her husband. The mature parent would cope with this problem directly. The emotionally disturbed and immature mother transfers her sexual longing to her son. This is not done consciously but is acted out in a number of ways. The boy is frequently kept in his mother's company, exposed to her feelings, seduced into some seemingly innocuous physical intimacy such as helping her dress or undress, and discouraged from contact with other boys and girls. The mother of the homosexual has been described as CBI—close-binding-intimate. She ties the boy to her. Consciously, the importance of the boy to the mother is reflected in her feeling that "this boy of mine will fulfill me." This desire is interpreted by the mother as her wish that the boy will be a great man, an outstanding individual, and that people will point to his mother as the responsible agent. One cannot overlook, however, the unconscious sexual significance of such a feeling: the boy is the mother's lover.

Invariably, in these cases, the boy takes the father's place in the mother's affections. Not infrequently he is seduced into sharing the same bed with her. The result of this behavior is to create a sexual excitement in the boy with which he cannot cope. On the one hand, he cannot reject his mother; on the other, he cannot express his sexual feelings toward her. He is left with no choice but to cut off these feelings at the expense of deadening his body.

The father in these family situations is usually as neurotically disturbed as the mother. This is constantly being proved in analytic studies of the family background of emotionally ill persons. Frequently, the father's reaction to the mother's attitude is one of hostility toward the boy. He regards the boy as a competitor who threatens his own position. And it is difficult to see how he can avoid this feeling, since the mother has forced the boy into this role.

The father may also be negative and critical of the boy (partly in self-defense), calling him a "sissy." And, in truth, the mother is making a "sissy" of the boy by alienating him from his father. But the odds are that the father is also inadequate as a male figure with whom the boy can consciously identify and upon whom he can pattern his attitudes. The father's hostility makes it even more difficult for the boy to reject his mother. She becomes his protection against the hostile father.

Just as homosexuality may result from the parents' unconscious "acting out" of feelings upon children, so homosexual activity is the "acting out" upon another of the repressed feelings that the homosexual had toward his parents. No homosexual relationship is free from this tendency. It is invariably characterized by ambivalence—love and hate, fear and hostility, dependency and resentment, submission and dominance. It is frequently marked by the sadistic behavior of one partner and the masochistic submission of the other.

There is clinical evidence to indicate that on the psychological level, the homosexual feels himself to be a partially castrated individual. This is manifested, as noted earlier, in his preoccupation with his genitals, thereby betraying his fear and anxiety over the loss of genital sensation. This castration anxiety is reflected in dress and behavior that call attention to the genitals. In view of the sadistic tendencies of many homosexuals, I wondered why John wasn't afraid that one of his homosexual partners might bite off his penis. It later became obvious that his partners were chosen subconsciously for their masochistic submissiveness. But John became afraid when faced with a person who was not masochistically submissive. Whenever, in the course of therapy, I worked on the tense muscles of his pelvic girdle he shrank, afraid that I might hurt his penis. The homosexual doesn't bite: in childhood, he didn't dare bite the breast; in adulthood he won't bite the penis. But John didn't trust me. He projected his repressed oral, biting impulses upon me because I had the necessary aggression to carry them out.

In analysis, one finds that, usually, the homosexual is emotionally deadened. He may not lack creative intelligence or creative ideas, but there is a severe limitation in his range of emotional expression. Neither anger nor sadness are easily expressed, and such feelings as enthusiasm, excitement, and joy are often absent. The homosexual who is as alive and vibrant in his personality as Leonardo da Vinci must have been is the rare exception. Occasionally, one does turn out to be a great man, fulfilling his mother's conscious wish; generally, the homosexual is imprisoned in the armor that he wears to protect himself against his sexual feelings. The only two areas alive are his brain and his genitals.

The emotional deadness is paralleled on the somatic level by the unaliveness of the body. Skin tone and color are poor. Spontaneity in gesture and movement are usually absent. The motility of the body is markedly decreased. The bioenergetic charge of the organism, that is, its vitality, is noticeably reduced. This has been true of every homosexual I have seen.

In view of these observations, we must revise our ideas about homosexual behavior. His sexual activity is less an expression of a strong sexual drive than a need for sensual feeling (aliveness and excitement). Strangely enough, the homosexual gets the feeling and excitement that he needs through the same mechanism that was originally responsible for his problem, that is, by identification. The homosexual identifies with his partner and derives much of his excitement vicariously. He is both actor and acted on, subject and object of the same experience. What he does to the other, he once experienced himself at the hands of his mother or father. His sexual excitement is a recall phenomenon, an evocation of childhood feeling, the repression of which caused his deadness. By the homosexual maneuver, that is, by inverting the sex, the guilt that is attached to his incestuous and hostile feelings toward his mother is bypassed. The homosexual feels alive only in the homosexual relationship.

The homosexual is like a lost, frightened child who does not cry simply because he is too shocked by his feeling of abandonment and isolation to cry. He clings to the homosexual partner just as a lost child clings to a mother substitute. At the same time, he wants an emotional reaction from the partner-mother that shows that the latter feels his need and will respond to it. These feelings are transposed to the sexual level, where they are "acted out" in combination with genital desire and longing. Homosexual behavior is determined by a mixture of uroboric (infantile) elements and adult sexual feeling. The homosexual's actions attempt to combine the need for self-completion with the need for union with another person. It is said that in a homosexual relationship, two halves make one person.

One cannot approach the opposite sex with an inadequate sexual concept or a weak sexual charge. To do so would lead only to failure and to a deeper fear of castration. In the sexual experience with the same sex, the danger of failure is eliminated, as is the fear of success. In the homosexual experience, the genitals do not lose feeling. Quite the contrary. The homosexual contact leaves the genital organs with more feeling than before; the homosexual is more conscious of his genital organ and is therefore less anxious about it. But the body is unaffected by the experience. The heart is not touched, and it is this fact that creates the inner (bodily) feeling of dissatisfaction with which the homosexual struggles.

In a recent study* of homosexuality by a group of psychoanalytic doctors, the authors made an interesting observation about a group of adolescent homosexuals studied at Bellevue Hospital:

> The effeminate adolescents related comfortably to other effeminate homosexuals and to lesbians and women considered as asexual, but became very anxious in the presence of a woman perceived as "sexual." ... One such patient spent the night in the home of his girl friend when her parents were away. She came to his bed dressed only in pajamas and lay down next to him. He became "numb," "without feeling," "paralyzed." Within a few days he yielded to a compulsive urge to go to a Greenwich Village bar and pick up a homosexual.

The body of the homosexual individual cannot tolerate strong heterosexual feelings. It fights them by "going dead," that is, becoming numb and paralyzed, without feeling. The homosexual act is a reaction to this paralysis and deadness; it is an attempt to regain genital sensation.

*Irving Bieber, *et al., Homosexuality: A Psychoanalytic Study.* New York: Basic Books, 1962.

6

The Lesbian Personality

The term "female homosexual" conjures up the image of a woman who is trying to be a man. She is pictured as wearing mannish clothes and a mannish haircut, as having a large, muscular body and sharp, angular features. She may be regarded as a "man-eater." These ideas may be owing to the fact that the female homosexual is often in a position of dominance, frequently the head of a department or organization. However, such characteristics are found primarily in the masculine lesbian. In appearance, the typical masculine female is quite imposing. She has a large body, broad shoulders, a short neck, and a rather big head with strong features. She tends to be brusque and hard. She knows her business, and she knows what she wants. In manner and attitude, she is the successful executive. Behind her back, she is called a "butch" or a "dyke" in the vulgar language of the street. The masculine female usually attracts a soft, dependent, feminine type of homosexual in lesbian relationships.

The mannish female is a puzzle to the average person. He wonders what kind of feelings would lead a woman to turn away from her feminine nature. What special satisfaction does the lesbian derive from her abnormal relationships? What strange power does she possess that enables her to be so successful in the world of men? Is she as tough as her appearance suggests?

The problem of the "butch" became clear to me in the treatment of a young woman who in physical appearance impressed me as resembling a gorilla. In fact, the impression Debora gave of strength and toughness was almost frightening. Some time later, my patient expressed surprise that anyone could be frightened by her. In the course of analysis, she revealed an inner sensitivity that belied her outward appearance. She was easily hurt and quite defenseless in her relations with other people. Underneath the mask of the gorilla was not a little girl (this is so often found), but a "premie," as she described herself. By "premie," she meant a premature baby who had come into the world unprepared and unwilling. This case was a striking example of the contradiction between the outward appearance and inner feeling that is found in some individuals.

Debora faced the task of uniting these two opposite aspects of her personality. But before she could unite them, she had to understand them. She identified with the "premie" and had no idea of where the gorilla appearance came from. Simple as this insight was, it didn't occur to either of us for some time that the gorilla aspect was a device to protect the "premie," to scare off any hostile aggressors. But this insight depended upon a knowledge of the double personality that was Debora. As an observer, I saw only the gorilla. Subjectively, Debora knew only that she was frightened, alone, and desperately in need of warmth. She felt her prematurity.

Although her outward appearance was described as a mask, this does not mean that it was without an effective function. Debora was physically strong. As a preadolescent girl, she played football with boys. It was not a question, therefore, of shedding a costume. The feelings that supported the gorilla had to be reinvested in the infant. The "premie" had to become a mature person before the necessity for the neurotic defense could be discarded.

Under analysis, appearances prove to have a double meaning, one for the observer and another for the observed. Debora's big body served also as an incubator in which the "premie" slumbered and felt secure. But the need for mother love that would nurture the "premie" was sought by Debora in homosexual relationships. Unfortunately, these homosexual relationships maintained the *status quo*. Finally, Debora found her mother substitute in the form of a male therapist.

Another patient, Mary, presented a good example of this masculinizing tendency in the female. When she came for treatment, Mary prided herself upon being the best female lover in the city. This meant that she could take a girl away from any other lesbian. She moved within a wide circle of lesbians who knew and slept with one another. In her lesbian activities, Mary was always the active partner. In response to my inquiry about her sexual feelings, she said that she experienced a dozen orgasms in the course of each sexual act, which consisted in her performing cunnilingus on another woman. I let her remark pass, even though it sounded completely unrealistic. Mary had come to me for help, and I was not a prosecuting attorney. For about seven months, she maintained the fiction of multiple orgasms. Then as she came into better contact with her body as a result of the therapy, she admitted that she had never known a real orgasm. Mary had not been lying. She just didn't know. She was sexually sophisticated, and every minor flutter of excitement in the vaginal area was thought to be an orgasm. This is the true nature of sexual sophistication: the surface sensation is mistaken for the real thing. Only when Mary truly experienced her body did she realize how inadequate were her previous sexual experiences.

On the surface, Mary appeared to be a vibrant, alive person. She moved with determination and acted with decision. But this proved to be only a surface phenomenon. It broke down in the course of therapy, and for months Mary was exhausted. Her body ached. It was all she could do to get through a day, although she did nothing more than take care of herself. This could be anticipated from the way her body looked. It was rigid and immobile. Her shoulders were held high and were as square as those of a football player. Her chest seemed enormous, and her body tapered down to rather narrow hips. She had shaved off her pubic hair. The muscles of her legs were like steel bands. She could dance all night on them. At one time, Mary had been a teacher of ballroom dancing, but this fact could not account for the extreme tension of leg and calf muscles.

Mary gave one the impression that she was a strong, capable person. Square shoulders, strong legs, big body all contributed to this appearance. But it was only an appearance. As I got to know her, I discovered under this mask a little girl who was afraid of men and who tried to impress and frighten other women. Her whole homosexual orientation was based upon the need to prove what a great big strong "man" she was and how loving and protective she could be to other frightened little girls. Unfortunately, these feelings were not recognized, since they were all "acted out" in the guise of sex—"counterfeit sex," as Edmund Bergler calls it. Functioning in this way, Mary could gain some small sexual thrill vicariously. When her lovers became excited by her caresses, Mary reacted with some feeling.

Mary's body, like John's, was relatively dead. Her muscles were tense and contracted, her skin color was poor—muddy, not bright—her respiration was shallow. She had large eyes, and she kept them wide open in innocence as she looked at me. Nothing, however, passed between our eyes. She was afraid of any contact with me; instinctively, I did not force it. During the first few months of therapy (I saw her once a week), she wore slacks and made no effort to appear feminine. There was absolutely no sex appeal about her. There was so little softness in her body that her masseuse complained that she was tired out after working on her.

Mary's figure drawings and her comments on them reveal how much her problem was tied up with her perception of her own body. Figure 4 is her conception of the female body. When I asked for her reaction to the sketch, she replied: "For some strange reason, all my women look like men. I have never been able to get the feeling [of a woman's body]. I don't find a woman's body appealing aesthetically. She looks more like a hermaphrodite. Her expression is very sardonic, as if she were saying, 'I challenge you, I dare you.' There is some resemblance to myself from the shoulders to the waist." The wide shoulders, big breasts, and boyish lower half of the drawing did resemble Mary's own body.

The male figure, which she drew next (Figure 5), had the same characteristics (and the same expression) as the female figure—broad shoulders, no hips, indefinite legs, no feet. When she had completed only the bust and shoulders she stopped, and I had to ask her to finish it, to which she remarked: "I find it difficult to draw a penis on a man." Mary described herself as follows: "I am a very sensuous woman. I could hold my lover's hand and have an orgasm. Just looking at her would excite me. I am very interested in the body and in anatomy."

I then asked Mary if she liked to look at herself in the mirror: "Yes," she said, "when I am in good shape, but I can't stand my belly. When it is out, I can't stand it. When I was a child, they admired my broad shoulders. I was very boylike. My mother did want a boy when I was born." And she added: "I could have an orgasm kissing. When women love me, I have to pretend that they love me as a man. I am a man with a penis forty yards long." The extent of Mary's wishful thinking and fantasy life betrayed the infant in her.

FIGURE 4

FIGURE 5

Her perception of male and female was based not on sexual differences, but on the infantile notion that masculine means strong and feminine weak. Mary's orgasms were obviously not much more than infantile reactions to any pleasurable stimulation, like the child who wants to be tickled because it is exciting.

Like so many other homosexuals, Mary used sex, lesbian sexual activity, compulsively to keep some feeling alive in her body. Contrary to my expectations, she responded immediately to my analysis of her physical condition, and she worked hard to bring some feeling back into her body. She began to accept it as a feminine body and to invest her interest in it. As her body became more alive and responsive in the course of therapy, her sexual compulsivity decreased. She found that she could gain feeling and some pleasure in her body through nonsexual physical activities such as swimming. Slowly she lost the need for the vicarious excitation that her homosexual activity offered. Mary was quite surprised to find that she was no longer as sexually excited by her former lovers.

Mary's mother was an emigrant Polish woman who left her husband and came to this country with a daughter. Mary was born many years later, an illegitimate child. She grew up without a father figure who might have counteracted the effects of such hostility as the mother felt toward her. This means that Mary's orientation to homosexuality had to be explained in terms of her relations to her mother.

Mary described her mother as a strong, aggressive woman who was also patient and long-suffering. In the course of therapy, Mary remembered how frightened she had been of her mother. She knew that as a child she was given many enemas by her mother. She recalled that at the age of six, she developed a vaginal discharge, which her mother treated by inserting swabs into her vagina. Mary had the very strong feeling that her mother was always probing her orifices, even in such minor ways as using Q-Tips to clean her ears and nose. Mary's greatest fear, of which she became aware only gradually in the course of the analysis, was her fear of being penetrated. At the same time, she was frightened at the prospect of letting anything out of her body. She had great difficulty in crying, and she suffered from constipation. These fears were physically structured in deep tensions around the orifices of her body. Her throat closed in spasm if she tried to gag herself to relieve a feeling of nausea.

Although Mary was frightened of her mother, she closely identified with her through sympathy and understanding. She often referred to the struggle her mother had made to provide a home for her children. She admired her mother's courage in leaving the native land alone to start a new life here. But she also became aware that as a young child, she was left alone at home when her mother went to work. Mary's need for oral gratification as well as her need for body contact with her mother, had never been fulfilled, which left her with strong oral desires.

In her lesbian activities, Mary "acted out" her infantile relationship to her mother. In her role as the dominant and active partner, she was a mother substitute to the frightened little girls who were the passive recipients of her caresses. And by taking this role, she expressed her superiority to these girls, thus reversing her early relationship with her mother. But Mary was also a frightened little girl, and she was doing for others what she wanted for herself. Her lovers were substitute mothers whose approval she sought by her efforts to fulfill them sexually. The lesbian relationship thus involves a duality of roles for each partner. The active one, such as Mary, is the mother, but in her unconscious identification with her lover, she is also the passive sexual object who is being gratified. The same is true of her partner: the submissive role is compensated for by an unconscious identification with the dominant, active partner. Cunnilingus serves a double function. The tongue is used as a sexual organ to satisfy the partner, while the mouth is used as a sucking organ to satisfy the need for oral gratification.

Mary's body reflected the double aspect of her personality. Her square, broad shoulders, inflated chest, and tight, narrow pelvis expressed her conscious identification with the masculine. I would interpret this aspect of her appearance not so much as a desire to be a man, but as a fear of being a woman. To be a woman meant to be penetrated, and to Mary this signified the violation of her personality and unconsciously terrified her. In shaving off her pubic hair, Mary proclaimed that she was only a little girl who had not yet reached puberty and therefore should not be penetrated as a woman. The contradictions in the personality of the homosexual are so complex as to be almost beyond imagination. Every aspect, psychological or physical, is subject always to a double interpretation.

Mary posed as a masculine female to protect the vulnerable little girl within. However, her broad shoulders had another meaning. They expressed or suggested her ability to carry responsibility, that is, to shoulder the burden, a trait commonly associated with masculinity. Actually, the normal masculine shoulder is neither square nor broad. In a relaxed position, the male shoulder has a natural slope. What burden was Mary shouldering? In the course of analysis, it became clear that she was carrying the burden of her mother's struggle and suffering. It is important to know why Mary shouldered this burden, that is, why she identified with her mother on this level. Psychoanalytic theory has made it clear that the unconscious identification of the child is always with the parent who is the threatening figure. Mary was afraid of her mother, and this fear was also manifested in the square, raised shoulders.

Several physical reactions occur in the experience of fear: the breath is sucked in, the belly is pulled in, and the shoulders are raised. In addition, the eyes open wide, and the jaw becomes frozen. This is the picture that Mary presented at the beginning of her therapy. Without voicing her problem, she conveyed the impression of a frightened little girl who was desperately trying to conceal that fact from herself. The change in her personality noted earlier was accompanied by structural changes in her body. Her shoulders relaxed and dropped to a more normal slope. The reduction of tension in her shoulders was related to a deflation of her chest, produced by a better respiratory function. The quality of the respiratory act is a clear indication of the emotional state. When one is frightened, the breath is sucked in and held, inflating the chest; thus, the chronic inflation of the chest is a sign of repressed fear. In anxiety, the breathing is rapid and shallow. In the relaxed state, breathing is slow and deep. The changes in breathing during the sexual act reflect the increase in excitement as climax approaches and the subsidence of excitement following orgasm.

Many women fail to achieve a satisfactory sexual release because they hold their breath as the excitement mounts, out of fear of sexual surrender. Holding the breath also depresses all feeling. Getting Mary to breathe more deeply and more easily increased her bodily sensation. It was especially important to develop her abdominal respiration, since this increases pelvic sensation. Abdominal respiration is the natural type of breathing in the relaxed state. But this was accomplished with

Mary only after her sexual anxieties and guilts were released in the analytic procedure.

Concomitantly with the changes in the upper half of her body, the tensions in her pelvic musculature relaxed somewhat. Her hips broadened, and she developed a small belly. With these changes in Mary's figure, her clothes looked better on her, which pleased her greatly. As her fear of penetration diminished, Mary found herself able to respond with pleasure to the sexual advances of men. She developed a heterosexual relationship that, for the first time in her life, made her accept and enjoy being a woman.

There is another way of understanding Mary's psychosexual development. The fatherless girl and the husbandless mother developed a relationship in which each complemented and fulfilled the other's needs. Psychologically speaking, Mary became the husband to her mother in that she shouldered the burdens and adopted a masculine attitude. Her mother also acted as a father to Mary. She was the good father who provided for the daughter, but at the same time she was also the bad father who seduced the daughter by symbolic sexual acts in the form of bodily penetrations.

No single factor creates homosexuality in the male or the female. In the analysis of a homosexual personality, each of the neurotic forces that distort and limit the personality must be carefully elucidated. However, it can be said that the masculinization of the female is a defense against the feeling of being exploited as a sexual object. The degree of masculinity is a measure of the severity of the underlying anxiety. But a girl's rejection of her feminine nature is also related to the oedipal situation that exists in the home. To be feminine in some situations is to face two enemies: a rejecting father and a competitive mother. On the one hand, the girl risks her mother's hostility if she competes for her father's affections as a female. On the other hand, she risks her father's contempt for the female and the hostility arising from his insecurity in relation to women. The family constellation that is commonly responsible for a girl's abandonment of her femininity is a critical, sarcastic, and authoritarian father and a weak, helpless, and submissive mother. Frequently, the father is aggressive and ambitious and strongly desirous of having a son. To such a man, the birth of a daughter is a disappointment. The mother is usually self-sacrificing, but her submissive attitude hides her resentment and vindictiveness toward her husband. Unable to identify with her mother and feeling rejected by her father, the girl does not become masculine so much as she loses her sense of self. Her muscular development is an expression of her need to be strong, independent, and asexual. In the service of this defense, her body loses its personal meaning. It becomes a stronghold, a fortress, within which is imprisoned longing, sexual love, and fulfillment. But one cannot live in society like a prisoner. The lesbian relationship, like its homosexual counterpart, is an attempt to escape this neurotically structured confinement and isolation. Unfortunately, as many homosexuals have discovered, their inversion is the exchange of one prison for another.

The lesbian personality does not always manifest itself in the form of the masculine female. The "dyke" is only one of the character structures that develop as the result of the dissociation in the personality produced by a rejecting environment. In psychiatric language, the "dyke" can be considered a double personality in the sense that her being comprises the outer aspect of the monster and the inner feeling of the frightened child. The dissociative tendency also produces the split, or schizoid, personality. The form that this takes is an immaturity of physical development combined with a sophisticated intelligence. This personality type is often characteristic of the feminine member in the lesbian relationship. In contrast to the "dyke," the schizoid personality manifests its childlike nature in the physical appearance of the body. Its pathology consists in the denial of the body and the dissociation of conscious behavior and feeling from body sensation. Joan illustrates this aspect of the lesbian problem.

Joan consulted me because of her feeling that she was a failure in life. She suffered from depressions, as every homosexual I have seen does. She had trained as a dancer in both modern and ballet but was unable to do anything with it. She remarked that as a little girl, she had danced all the time. Joan also studied acting for many years, and she felt that once onstage she could adequately portray all feelings, but offstage she made a poor impression. Joan worked as a waitress and lived in a homosexual relationship, that had lasted for eight years.

About ten years before she consulted me, Joan had had a heterosexual relationship that proved "disastrous." She was alone and frightened in a strange city. It was while she was in this difficult and confused state that she met her female lover, who was somewhat older than Joan. Both were alone and lonely. Their relationship began as companionship. Only slowly did it grow more intimate. Then one night as they lay together in bed, Joan's friend caressed her. Joan felt herself get excited and allowed it to proceed. At the end, she experienced a sense of satisfaction that she had not known before. How could she give up this new feeling? What could she replace it with? She had no confidence that she could experience a similar satisfaction with a man.

The element of homosexual seduction cannot be ignored in this problem. True, the incipient homosexual is open to and willing for the experience. But without the experience of the homosexual encounter, with its resulting release and satisfaction, the homosexual would struggle to form a heterosexual relationship, difficult though that might be. Many lesbians have told me that their first homosexual encounter occurred directly after a disastrous experience with a man.

Homosexuality is a last choice. Joan would have preferred a normal life with a husband and children. It eluded her. Mary simply wanted to end her confusion and to find herself. The homosexual encounter, as someone once said, occurs *faute de mieux*. Everyone knows that heterosexual love is better and can be more satisfying. What the homosexual doesn't know is that even masturbation is better than the homosexual experience—if he can do it for himself! But he can't, and that is the root of his trouble. For satisfactory masturbation requires self-acceptance, and this is what is lacking in the homosexual personality. Self-acceptance is closely tied to the feeling of one's body. It is hard to accept yourself if you don't like your body, and it is hard to like your body if it is unalive and lacking in good feelings. Joan became aware of this aspect of her problem. She told me: "I have gotten to like my body a little. Ten years ago I negated my body. I never looked at it. I used to have a jerky walk, which I improved by dancing. It was like a doll on strings."

Joan introduces us to the second type of lesbian personality, one in which the masculine features are not so evident. Where Mary showed determination and aggressiveness, Joan appeared more confused and dependent. She needed the seeming strength of the apparently stronger personality to direct her and to sustain her. Appearances can be so deceptive. The more exaggerated the outside appearance is, the more suspect the inner person is of being just the opposite. It's not the appearance but the body that counts. "Body" denotes the quality of substance—substantial, as in "full-bodied." But "body" also refers to the fullness of feeling. In this sense, I have never seen a lesbian who was a full-bodied woman.

Despite her improvement, Joan's body revealed her difficulties. The lower half of her body was like that of an adolescent boy. Her pelvis had a definite android configuration. It contained no feminine curves and had no fat. It was also immobile and rigidly held in the retracted position, that is, held backward. When she bent her knees, her legs began to shake. Her balance, as she noted, was precarious. While her shoulders were tense, they were not square. However, her arms hung like alien appendages rather than extensions of her own body. She had a square face with a tight, grim mouth that drooped. Her eyes appeared blank and somewhat frightened. Joan commented about her jaw. She said, "I have felt my jaw as setting, getting tight. I felt my face get a tight, set feeling like holding on."

The psychiatric diagnosis in Joan's case was that of schizoid personality. I use the term to refer to a loss of self—more particularly, to a loss of the bodily self. The masculine female has a self-concept that holds the personality together. This concept is based on her conscious identification with masculine values. The schizoid individual lacks an effective self-concept. Her self-image is confused, and her sexual identity is not clear. Her personality manifests the bisexuality of the child, and in her lesbian relationships she is capable of alternating her roles. Her outstanding quality is her extreme sensitivity.

The point I want to make is that many passive lesbians tend to be schizoid. They are individuals in need of warmth and human contact, like deprived children, which they are, and the lesbian relationship offers this. Within its limits, they can experience some security and a partial fulfillment of their sexual drive. But it also becomes a prison for them, barring the way to self-realization. Having rebelled against the neurotic sexual roles of their parents they are in no position to overthrow this self-imposed bondage.

Lesbianism has been found to be a common phenomenon among prostitutes. Frank S. Caprio states that he has observed it in all the brothels of Europe. Harold Greenwald, who has made an analytic study of prostitution, has also found it to be a frequent form of relationship among call girls. The question is often asked whether prostitution leads to homosexuality or whether homosexuality leads to prostitution. The association, however, should not surprise us. If the foregoing analyses of the lesbian personality are correct, that is, if the lesbian is a person who lacks a sense of self and the feeling of identification with her body, the prostitution of the body amounts to no more than an affirmation of dissociation from it and an expression of contempt for it. The denial of the body that is characteristic of the passive lesbian is not far removed from the sale of the body by the prostitute.

The tight, set quality of Joan's jaw expressed her determination not to cry. "What's the use?" Joan said. "No one cares. No one comes." Actually, Joan was unable to cry. The rigidity of her jaw and the tension in her throat made crying too painful and too difficult. It also interfered with her respiration, for it constituted a constriction of the air passages. In consequence, her chest was inflated and her breathing shallow. The first breakthrough in crying came when Joan attempted to make sucking movements with her mouth. Feeling her frustration and limitation, Joan began to sob in a pitiful way. Her inability to cry, the restriction of her respiration, and her difficulty in reaching out with her mouth were expressions of her inability to assert her need for love and fulfillment. Her lesbian relationship offered her only companionship and some sexual gratification.

Joan claimed that her relationship with her father had been devoid of all feeling. She insisted that he ignored her existence. On another occasion, however, she remarked that she was regarded as her father's favorite by the family. And she admitted that her father had called her "the princess." I suspected that her denial of feeling represented the repression of her sexual feelings toward her father. It explained why father and daughter were embarrassed in each other's company. On one occasion, Joan experienced a feeling of longing to be held by her father, and she became very angry. She turned on me with a threatening gesture, as if I were responsible not only for this feeling, but also for her frustration. This episode made Joan realize that her lesbian orientation was a defense against the fear of disappointment and rejection by the male. But her hostility toward the male, based on her feeling of being rejected by her father, made subsequent rejections and disappointments inevitable. If this hostility was to be released, its nature had to be understood. Joan's hostility against the male was shown to have a significant relation to her tight, set jaw.

A clue was provided in a dream that Joan had about this

time: "I dreamt that I was in bed with a woman who had a penis that I was sucking. It felt very pleasurable. Then the scene changed and she no longer had a penis. I felt frustrated and angry." The interpretation of this dream showed the complexity of this problem. The woman with a penis is a uroboric symbol, the Great Mother, who combines masculine and feminine aspects and who is, therefore, a representative of the preconscious condition before the separation of opposites occurred. The first scene refers to the pleasure experienced in the womb and in the early postnatal state and expresses Joan's wish to return to that situation. In the second scene, reality in the form of a consciousness of differences (woman without a penis) is associated with frustration and anger because of the loss of the desired object (penis = nipple). The feeling of anger suggests the presence of hostile impulses directed at the penis that, in view of its disappearance, can be interpreted as impulses to bite it off.

Since the dream ended on a note of frustration and anger, it can be assumed that these emotions characterized Joan's unconscious attitude during this period of her life. In her lesbian relationship, Joan was frustrated and angry because the woman had no penis. She could not, however, relate to a man sexually, since the fact that he does have a penis might tempt her to bite it off. In the lesbian personality, the repression of hostile impulses toward the penis blocks off any erotic desire for that organ. By picturing the woman without a penis, Joan could deny both her impulse to bite it off and her guilt for wanting to do so. Cunnilingus symbolically satisfies the desire to bite and swallow the penis; at the same time, it reassures the lesbian that she need have no fear of such a desire, since there is no penis. Of course, all this goes on in unconscious fantasy.

Joan's tight, set jaw represented a defense against her impulse to bite as well as against the desire to suck and the need to cry. Joan confirmed this interpretation of the meaning of the tension in her jaw. She said, "I know I have strong feelings to bite, but I didn't realize that I wanted to bite the penis." The fear of biting plays an important role in the genesis of orgastic impotence in the female. The significance of biting is revealed in many expressions: "sink your teeth into it," "take a bite out of life," and so on. The inability to bite must represent an inability to commit oneself aggressively to a situation. In a sense, a woman "bites" the penis; that is, she makes contact with it and gets a grip on it. It is difficult to conceive how orgasm can be achieved if a woman is afraid of her gripping or biting impulses.

Joan's relationship with her father was burdened by the transfer of her unfulfilled oral needs to him. Her sexual feelings for her father were complicated and intensified by her longing for oral fulfillment. The oedipal problem becomes insurmountable when it is compounded of oral and genital feelings. The dilemma of the homosexual, male or female, is the inability to renounce the former in favor of the latter, infantile in favor of adult functioning. Joan related another dream that expressed this conflict: "My friend B. invited me to a *menage à trois*. The girl is masturbating while standing up and also sucking her thumb. She comes closer to me, but I tell her, 'I'm not interested.'" In this dream, the homosexual attitude is rejected.

Homosexuality in all forms manifests relationships of dominance and submission. It is true that "active" and "passive" are misleading expressions. Homosexuals or lesbians who are active at one time may be passive with the same or other partners at another time, or their roles may be reciprocal during one sexual experience. But in every homosexual relationship, one partner is dominant and the other submissive. This describes the interaction of their total personalities. One can say that often this is also true of heterosexual partners. To the degree of its existence in a heterosexual relationship, it distorts that relationship. My contention is that homosexuality is not the union of equals. Equality belongs to heterosexuality, for only in that relationship can one partner fully respect the other.

Does the lesbian have the same feeling of contempt for men that the homosexual has for women? The answer, broadly speaking, is yes. The lesbian's contempt for men stems from her experience of their impotence, their egotism, and their fears. It reflects her mother's conscious or unconscious attitude toward her father. In this respect, she identifies with her mother. The lesbian "acts out" her mother's unconscious fantasies. The mother who unconsciously wishes that she were a man and who has no respect for her own feminine nature is a force pushing her daughter into homosexuality. But the contempt for men has its exceptions. It fades away in the face of a sexual man, one who has no pretenses and is secure in his manhood. I treated a lesbian some years ago who was an editor for one of the leading national magazines. She had earned a PhD in psychology, which, together with a sharp intelligence and a literary background, supported her feeling of superiority over me. I didn't challenge this attitude at the beginning of the treatment, and the result was the failure of the therapy.

Toward women, the lesbian has mixed feelings. She feels inadequate and inferior compared with normal women, but at the same time she feels superior to them. Without this feeling of superiority, she could not tolerate a homosexual relationship. It would be too humiliating. This feeling of superiority over women, which amounts to a feeling of contempt, stems from her experience of her mother's failure as a woman. Separated as they are from the strivings of the average individual to whom status and appearance are important, the homosexual and the lesbian see through the pretenses that highlight the social scene for the normal person. But the contempt and feeling of superiority vanish in the presence of a genuinely sexual woman.

Homosexuality is a form of compulsive sex. Compulsiveness also exists in some form in many heterosexual relationships. The compulsive quality of homosexuality arises from the need to stimulate the body, that is, to recover suppressed sexual feelings. We do not describe a hungry person as compulsive because he eats with relish or gusto. The compulsive eater is one whose eating satisfies some need other than hunger. Similarly, the homosexual doesn't seek sexual contact because he is sexually excited; rather, he seeks the contact for the sexual excitement. Homosexuality is a sensual phenomenon that results from the suppression of sexual feelings.

If the sexual feeling is suppressed in childhood, the awareness of sexuality persists. The homosexual does not go through a normal latency period. As a boy, he shows more than normal curiosity about adult sexuality, which ends in the strange preoccupation with sexuality that characterizes homosexual behavior and thinking. It is as if the sexual feelings that were lost in the body become resurrected in imagery and fantasy. Stories by homosexuals are vivid in their sexual imagery. The normal person is more concerned with his body feelings than with symbolism and fantasy. This is so because he has body feelings. The reverse is true in homosexuals.

When one analyzes lesbian relationships, one is impressed with the amount of sadomasochistic behavior that dominates them. Edmund Bergler, who makes this factor the central point of his attack upon the homosexual problem, is quite correct in stressing its importance. All homosexuals and lesbians have a major component of masochism in their personalities. Sadism is the reverse side of the coin. How does this masochism arise? Bergler's contention is that it has its base in the condition of infantile megalomania. The infant, who regards himself as the center of the universe, reacts with fury to any frustration or denial of his needs. But since his muscular system is not sufficiently developed to express this fury in aggressive behavior, the child reacts with crying, screaming, spitting, thrashing, and so on. This kind of behavior will ordinarily provoke his mother's displeasure and may lead to further deprivations or punishments. The result is a conflict in which the child can only lose. Eventually, his hostility and aggression are turned inward, creating the condition called psychic masochism.

A masochist is one who seems to derive pleasure from pain or suffering. The classic masochist is the individual who wants to be beaten during his sexual activity. His sexual pleasure is contingent upon his being beaten. It was believed, prior to Wilhelm Reich, that the masochist actually derived pleasure from pain. Reich showed, however, that the masochist did not seek pain but sexual excitation. His pleasure was obtained from the sexual excitation accompanying the beating, not from the beating itself. The psychic mechanism that creates this strange association of pain and pleasure can be stated simply: "If you beat me, you accept my sexually naughty nature, and you will only beat me for it, not castrate me." The punishment the masochist seeks is always in lieu of the more dreaded punishment—castration. In view of the clinical observation that all homosexuals, male and female, suffer from severe castration anxiety, it is not surprising that one finds so much actual masochism among them.

The psychic masochist differs from the above picture in that his pain and suffering are derived from psychic insults rather than physical ones. Humiliation, not beating, serves as the stimulus for the release of sexual excitation. The mechanism, however, is the same: "If you humiliate and degrade me, you accept my sexual nature, and you will not otherwise punish me for it—you will not castrate me." In both conditions, the essence of the masochistic problem is the inability to express the sexual feeling except under conditions of humiliation, degradation, pain, and suffering, conditions in which the self-respect of the individual is lost. Masochism can be described as the psychic state in which self-respect is missing. It is accompanied, therefore, by strong feelings of inferiority, compensated for by an inner attitude of superiority. This may seem to state the problem in its simplest terms, but the loss of self-respect can be documented in every clinical case of masochism.

In *Homosexuality: Disease or Way of Life?*, Bergler seems to imply that some degree of masochism is inevitable in social living: "Objective reality clashes with subjective magical notions. In the inevitable outcome reality wins." If all children do not become masochists, this is because some "succeed in the diplomatic adaption to a stronger reality." But why some succeed in this adaptation while others fail is a "moot question" to Bergler. My criticism of this view is that it regards the outcome as somewhat independent of parental behavior. This is contrary to my clinical experience. It can be shown that every case of masochism has its roots in the parents' disregard of the personality of the child.

To describe an infant as "megalomanic," as Bergler does, is to distort reality. An infant does not think magically. He hardly thinks at all. He responds with his feelings to every situation, whether of pleasure or pain, fulfillment or frustration. In this respect, the human infant is like the young of all mammals. He is born an animal organism with an innate sense of what is right for himself. If his rights are respected, as Margaretha Ribble has shown in her book *The Rights of Infants*, he will grow up to be a happy, well-adjusted child and adult. The difficulty, as Freud pointed out, is that the child is a sexual being. One cannot accept the child if one rejects this essential quality of his being. And one cannot accept this quality in a child if one rejects it in oneself.

The sexuality of a child is manifested in all his bodily functions. It is a diffused body sexuality, not a genital one. Nursing is the prime example of the relationship between bodily function and erotic pleasure, but every other bodily function has a pleasurable component that can be described as erotic. Isn't all bodily pleasure erotic in a sense? Any loss of this bodily pleasure is experienced as a physical deprivation or injury, to which the child reacts by whatever means he has available. The issue should not be confused by applying adult psychology to infantile behavior. At this stage, the deprivation is not experienced by the child as an injury to its narcissistic pride. Pride is a later development, the product of a strong ego, which only comes into being in the course of experience. The masochist is without pride simply because he never had the opportunity to develop a feeling of pride in himself and in his body.

Sexuality cannot be divorced from the body nor the body from the personality. The body of the homosexual has lost its good pleasurable feelings, that is, its sexual feelings; correspondingly, the homosexual is an individual without pride. On the personality level, he becomes a masochist. But this is not inevitable in the upbringing of a child. The conflict between culture and nature can be handled by parents in ways that will guard against the child's loss of self-respect. It can be avoided if the parents can handle their own problems with self-respect and dignity. I am amazed at the absence of these terms from studies of sexuality. Self-respect is the one quality that distinguishes mature sexuality from sexual sophistication. It includes pride in oneself and in one's body. It is an element necessary to the experience of sexual orgasm.

Psychology is limited in its study of masochistic behavior; it overlooks the bodily condition that is the foundation of this disturbance. The masochistic body structure is characterized by severe muscle tensions that inhibit the expression of feeling. These tensions are particularly marked in the pelvic area, where they have the function of suppressing the strong sexual excitation that the masochist fears. The suppression of sexual feeling extends to all pleasurable feeling and eventually includes all body sensation. The masochist is caught in a web of tension from which there is no release. If he wants to be beaten, it is so that he can feel body sensation again, albeit only pain. If one can feel pain, then one can feel pleasure. The two are inseparable. The former is sought as a way to the latter.

One has only to observe the appeal of the soap opera, the sob story, and the sentimental film to appreciate the need that many people have for emotional stimulation of a sorrowful kind. The need to awaken the body, to make it feel and come alive, is so imperative that some people will go to any lengths to achieve it. Nothing is worse than deadness and its accompanying psychic feeling of depression and emptiness. We cannot be too critical, therefore, of the homosexual. His is a condition that merits our sympathy and calls for our help. It is a condition that, as Bergler and others have shown, can be "cured." This means that the homosexual tendency can be greatly reduced, even eliminated, but the physical marks of the disturbance cannot be fully eradicated from the body.

Improvement and cure are inversely related to the severity of the disturbance. The depth of the suppression of feeling is a factor that will influence the outcome. Where the loss of body feeling is as marked as it was in John's case, the problem will be more difficult. In other cases, a favorable outcome will be more easily achieved. Much depends, too, upon the skill and understanding of the therapist. Warmth and empathic comprehension are important therapeutic qualities. The homosexual is not a monster but an emotionally ill person. Viewing his behavior objectively, we have been critical of his actions, questioning of his motives, and distrustful of his rationalizations. Subjectively, however, the homosexual does not always experience his behavior as we have described it.

Is there any love in a homosexual relation? Is the homosexual act an expression of love? To answer these questions in the negative would be to deny my own assertion that sex is an expression of love. Further, the homosexual often describes his feelings for his partner in terms of love. John constantly spoke of his love for his friend, and I had no reason to doubt that the feeling was genuine, as genuine as any feeling John could have. It was an ambivalent feeling, a confused mixture of love and hate, desire and rejection. John had some insight into his feelings, but he was powerless to do anything about them. He described them as follows:

"Staying with M. and finally convincing myself that this is the way it's going to be, that it's not so bad, really. Secretly hating him for my loss of freedom (yet wanting him to be there and wanting to be there myself), and loving him and preparing him for his freedom. Am I making myself miserable now in return for making my mother miserable? Do I love M. in a motherly way? Giving him things? I guess he is really a part of me, and that part is where I am not. But many parts of me are dispersed. Go on to the next, dispersing, leave off now when through, and go on to the next involvement."

This confession makes sense only in terms of its contradictions: to hate those whom one loves, to reject those whom one desires, to resent those who are like oneself. This is

homosexuality, a twisted way of life. Yet it is the only life
the homosexual knows. We must accept the homosexual if we
are to help him. This does not mean that we should approve
of his behavior. It does mean that we should try to understand his desperate need to find somone to love. His desire
for physical closeness to another in no way differs from that
of the normal person. However, his ability to express these
feelings is severely limited. For love can be fully expressed
only in a heterosexual relationship, which for the homosexual
is so charged with guilt that it is a closed door. But the need
to love and be loved must find some outlet in the homosexual. It does, but through back doors and side doors, under
cover of darkness, with the homosexual despising the person
he needs and hating himself for the need. What a tragic way
to live! What a limitation of the potential of the human
personality!

Unfortunately, the tragedy is not limited to the homosexual. If his sexuality has been sacrificed in expiation of someone else's sexual guilt, others have not been left untouched.
The problems of masochism and homosexuality haunt the
unconscious of many normal persons, as we shall see in the
next chapter.

7

Latent Homosexuality

Every psychiatrist is familiar with the patient who in the course of analysis discovers that he has latent homosexual tendencies. Such a patient's sexual activities have always involved the opposite sex, he has never engaged in any homosexual act, he has never felt an attraction to members of his own sex, until some event or dream reveals a hidden homosexual feeling. This experience is often very shocking. The patient doubts his masculinity, and the psychiatrist has to allay his anxiety in this regard. I shall illustrate this problem.

William was a patient of mine for several years. At the time he consulted me, he was involved in a sexual affair with an older woman. He was twenty-eight years old and still lived with his father, who opposed the relationship strenuously. William was in a quandary. His father wanted him to break off the relationship, the woman wanted it to deepen into a more enduring form, and William wanted only to be free. He felt guilty toward the woman, but he was unable to oppose his father. William was an architect who, while competent in his work, was unable to achieve the success to which he aspired. He felt trapped, bogged down, unable to move. There was no complaint, however, about his sexual potency, nor was there any feeling of dissatisfaction with the sexual function.

The main feature of William's personality was its masochistic component, psychic masochism as distinguished from physical masochism. It manifested itself in strong feelings of inferiority, in a preoccupation with his lack of success, and in an inability to make decisions. On the physical side, William's body was muscularly overdeveloped, although he was no athlete. He looked muscle-bound, and his muscles were very tense and contracted. His body was large and rather hairy, which, together with a poor skin tone, made it appear heavy. Movement for William required an effort. Another physical feature that related to his problem was a relative underdevelopment of the buttocks and pelvis. In addition, the pelvis was carried too far forward. William lacked the quality of cockiness that one expects from a lively young man.

In the course of therapy, his body relaxed, his pelvis filled out somewhat, and he developed greater motility in his pelvic movements. He gained self-confidence as his ability to assert himself increased. Analysis helped him to resolve many of his problems with his father and brought to the surface repressed feelings about his mother. He left both his father's home and his girl friend and set up his own apartment. He made new friends and undertook new activities.

Then William fell in love with another woman, who was also several years older than he. She was in a social position that he considered superior to his own. It began as a casual affair, but the sexual feelings between them were so strong that it developed into a more intense relationship. It seemed promising, but personal difficulties arose to complicate the relationship. Besides the differences in age, social position, and background, there was a difference of religion. Emotionally, William was still unprepared for marriage, and when the girl became pregnant, William found himself under a pressure to which he could react only by withdrawing.

It is said that there are three women in every man's life—the woman he loves, the woman who loves him, and the woman he marries. I suppose this is true of the woman, too. It points up the fact that marriage is often a compromise. The great romance, the exciting sexual relationship, frequently ends in a breakup. Is it the undercurrent of sexual guilt that deprives one of the happiness one dreams about? In this case, neither William nor the woman was mature enough to accept the relationship for the positive values it offered. William was reluctant to get married; he feared that he would be trapped. His commitment to the woman was half-hearted, and the guilt he had experienced in the previous relationship returned to torment him. He felt that all he could give the woman was sexual pleasure, and he felt inferior to men of her acquaintance who could offer her marriage and social position. In any event, the relationship deteriorated into fights, jealousies, recriminations, and blame. And the sexual feelings deteriorated correspondingly. As the sexual excitement between them diminished, their need for each other appeared to increase. Without his girl friend, William felt desperate. He sat in his room, morose and brooding. The relationship persisted for some time, with momentary flashes of good feeling and pleasure, although each one knew that it could not work out. The fear of rejection dragged it on.

The homosexual incident happened after William realized that he was clinging to his girl friend as though she were his mother. He knew that he had to build his own life and that it had to have enough meaning to sustain him as an individual alone. He was aware that he could not achieve a secure sense of self through another person. He tried to make new friends, especially men, of whom he had few.

Among William's friends were two men who lived together. William knew that they were homosexuals, yet he accepted an invitation to visit them. When they asked him to stay overnight, William sensed that it would leave him open to a homosexual advance, but he stayed. During the night, both men made sexual overtures to William, which he rejected. Nevertheless, William felt that he had deliberately exposed himself to a homosexual situation and that it had some attraction for him despite his conscious rejection of it.

What interpretation explains William's action in terms of his personality? Could he be seduced into homosexuality if he didn't resist it actively? On the basis of Bergler's contention that psychic masochism and homosexuality go together, one could expect to find homosexual tendencies in William. Obviously they were there. This didn't make William a homosexual. It indicated that his sexual feelings were confused and ambivalent, and it revealed a conflict about sexuality that was not clearly apparent before.

William was not the exceptional patient. Most patients reveal a homosexual component in their personality makeup, which means that some degree of latent homosexuality can be expected in every neurotic individual. The extent of this problem can be gauged by the prevailing opinion that neurosis is widespread and affects to some degree nearly every person in our culture. The presence of these latent homosexual feelings in the so-called normal person is the obvious explanation for the fascination with and the repugnance to the overt homosexual. The existence of these tendencies cannot be used logically to support the contention of writers like Albert Ellis that homosexuality is on a par with heterosexuality and that the male who prefers the former to the latter is merely expressing a difference of taste, "as a man may prefer blondes to brunettes."

The specific meaning of the homosexual tendency in William's personality can be learned from a study of his relations to his parents. William was afraid of his father, and while inwardly defiant, he was outwardly submissive to him. He had placed his mother on a pedestal as one whose love and devotion for him could not be questioned. William's mother was a self-sacrificing woman who had died when William was fourteen. His image of her was vague. As a young child, he was very close to his mother, who overprotected him. His rebellion against her took the form of frequent temper tantrums, for which he later felt very guilty. Weaning had been difficult for William. He could not accept the idea that he had to give up his mother and stand on his own feet. He reacted to weaning with a feeling of being rejected and abandoned. He experienced the threat of a breakup with his girl friend as a similar rejection and abandonment.

Between mother and son, there was an anal attachment that undermined William's individuality and selfhood. His training in excremental cleanliness and bowel control started early and left its mark in the tightly contracted and held-in buttocks. In addition, he had received numerous enemas from his mother, which placed him in a passive, feminine position with respect to her. It also laid the basis for the feeling of being trapped by a woman. The incestuous feelings between mother and son could have been responsible for William's repeated attempts to seduce an older sister when he reached puberty.

These experiences encumbered and limited William's adult sexual function. They made it difficult for him to approach a girl with any feeling of ease and assurance. When the necessity for a new sexual relationship became evident after the breakup of his love affair, William became desperate. His symptoms were markedly aggravated; he felt morose, discouraged, and frightened. It was while he was in this frame of mind that the abortive homosexual encounter to which I referred happened. Unconsciously, the homosexual way must have appeared to be an easy solution—he would have overcome his need for a woman and gotten physically closer to a man. Letting himself be seduced would have allowed him to avoid the guilt about his sexual feelings, and he could have "acted out" his sexual impulses without fear of rejection. Anal intercourse with a man could satisfy his desire for revenge in two ways at once. The man as a symbol of his father would be placed in a submissive, humiliating situation to make up for the many humiliations that William felt he experienced at the hands of his father. As a symbol of William's mother, the man would be the means whereby William "gave it back" to her as she had "given it" to him. Some men can act this out with a woman (anal intercourse); but, generally, the implications of such actions are too clear for most conscious minds to accept. Homosexuality is the easy way out. If William had taken this path, it would have led to a further loss of self-respect and further destruction of his integrity as a man. Obviously, William had too much self-respect to choose this direction. The incident, however, served as a warning and enabled William to face his feelings more directly.

Some patients reveal their latent homosexual feelings readily. Others, however, erect strong defenses against any such feelings, and the latter have to be inferred from behavior or from chance remarks. For example, Ted came into my office walking like a West Point cadet. He was a tall man; his chest was stuck out, his belly was sucked in, his backbone was as straight as a board. He was thirty years old. Ted's problem was that he was involved with two women and couldn't decide between them. When he was with one, he wanted the other. When he was sure of one, she lost her appeal. Both women exploited the situation to keep Ted on the hook. Ted was raised by his grandmother, to whom he was so attached that when he left for preparatory school and had to be separated from her, he suffered a nervous breakdown.

His grandmother overindulged and overprotected him. She accompanied him to school every day and called for him when school was over. The male members of his family felt that Ted was growing up to be a "sissy" and exhorted him to "be a man." Their appeals made no impression on Ted. Yet here he was grown up, to all appearances a man and fully acting the part.

I detected a weakness in Ted's personality that was masked by this manly bearing. The exaggeration of the bodily posture was one clue. But he had other problems, which he did not conceal. He had spells of anxiety that centered about the idea

of traveling. When he first consulted me, he could not face
spending one evening alone. He was terribly afraid of failure
in sex. The thought of fighting or physical aggression frightened him.

Ted had never had any homosexual experiences or any
fantasies of homosexuality. But neither did he ever have any
close male friends. He considered a man who was involved
with men in manly pursuits to be suspect. Ted's personal life
was completely taken up by his involvement with these two
women just as his earlier life had revolved around his relations to his mother and grandmother. He felt that he was a
man because he was interested in women.

In the course of therapy, his homosexual fears revealed
themselves on several occasions. Once when bending down to
pick up something, with his back to me, he had the sudden
fear that I would make an anal attack on him. At another
time, while sucking his knuckle, he said that it reminded him
of sucking a penis or a pacifier, then he stiffened up. These
indications plus his physical attitude were enough to convince
both of us that Ted was afraid of latent homosexual tendencies in himself.

What value is there in unearthing latent homosexual feelings in a patient? Admittedly, Ted had never been a homosexual and most likely would never be one. His real
problem seemed to be his inability to accept himself, to find
personal meaning in his life, and to gain some pleasure and
satisfaction from the living of it. But Ted could not do this,
since a large part of his psychic and physical energy was
invested in the effort to suppress his homosexual feelings.
And the homosexual tendency is directly related and propor-
tional to the fear of castration. Ted could not accept this
definition of the problem because all he could feel was his
anxiety at being alone, his fear of being abandoned. Anxiety
at being alone is connected, as Brigid Brophy suggests, to
guilt over masturbation. She points out that masturbation
occurs when one is alone and that being alone gives rise to
the temptation to masturbate. Ted suffered from severe masturbation anxiety. As a young man, he had believed that
masturbation would weaken him, destroy his sexual potency,
cripple him, even make him insane. At thirty, he still believed
that it had a deleterious effect on him. He claimed that it
made him feel tired, weak, and nervous the next day. It was
a job to convince him that this reaction was the result of his

anxiety and could not be attributed to the act of masturbation.

In Ted's case the fear of abandonment stemmed from the
childhood fear of being rejected because of his sexual activity. Psychic castration results from the threat that if the child
does not give up his sexual feelings, his mother will leave.
Ted's grandmother used this means of controlling the boy. "If
you are not a good boy, I will go away." It was unfortunate
that his father died when he was five years old and was not
available as a figure with whom he could identify. He had an
older sister who often threatened to "penalize" him. Until
quite late, Ted thought this meant that his penis would be cut
off. Ted's childhood situation was one that could have resulted in a homosexual personality. His previous analyst had
expressed surprise that this had not happened.

Burdened with severe castration anxiety, Ted could not
work out a satisfactory relationship to any woman. Any
threat to leave by a woman with whom he was involved
immobilized and panicked him. I hoped to overcome this
problem by freeing him from his unconscious fear of castration by the woman. However, it is likely that he was really
more afraid of anal penetration by a man than he was of
being abandoned by a woman and that his fear of being
alone was a defense against his latent homosexual feelings. It
was suggested earlier that to be a "good boy" under the
threat of abandonment meant to desist from any erotic
self-gratification, but it also had another meaning. Ted was a
"good boy" when he allowed his mother to give him an
enema to relieve his constipation. These enemas, he told me,
were a weekly occurrence. He was as firmly convinced that
they were necessary and helpful as he was that masturbation
was harmful and dangerous. To regard submission to anal
penetration in any form as an ordinary procedure betrays the
degree to which Ted had surrendered his manhood to his
mother early in his life.

Ted was, in a sense, constantly being castrated by the two
women with whom he was involved; that is, they humiliated
him, criticized him, and made him feel guilty. He submitted
masochistically to the degradation of his personality in order
to avoid what he thought was the more dangerous threat—to
be left alone. At the time that he consulted me, he was
repeating the pattern of childhood. Ted did not realize that
his passive submission to the women represented a repetition
of his acceptance of the enema. He felt guilty because he was

well aware that he used one woman as a defense against the
other. He understood them, and he accepted the validity of
their complaints. He had done the same thing as a child. He
could rationalize his behavior to a point that was frightening,
for his inability to see his dilemma imprisoned him in a
hopeless situation.

If Ted were an overt homosexual with the same problems,
their relation to his sexual anxiety would be apparent, but he
believed that on the sexual level he was functioning like a
man. This illusion maintained his neurosis. Ted presented the
difficult problem of a brainwashed individual. The one element that didn't fit into his picture of himself was his homosexual fear of anal attack. As long as he could block this
fear from conscious perception, he could maintain the *status
quo*, one that would be tolerable only to a person with a
homosexual personality.

Ted's behavior can be understood only in terms of the
sadomasochistic tendencies that underlie homosexuality. He
manipulated the situation with the two women so that each
was bound to him financially. He violated their privacy by
constant telephone calls. Psychologically, he "acted out" upon
them the insults and injuries that he had suffered at the hands
of his mother and grandmother. In fact, Ted was a latent
homosexual in the sense that his behavior had all the aspects
of the homosexual attitude, "acted out" in a heterosexual
relationship. It is evident, therefore, that the uncovering of
latent homosexuality in a neurotic personality sheds light on
the meaning of disturbances in the heterosexual function. For
William, the homosexual temptation denoted a deep desire to
give up the struggle for mature sexuality and regress to the
infantile pattern of being cared for and protected. It expressed his longing for the easy way out. For Ted, his fear of
homosexual attack represented his unconscious perception of
his true problem. In such cases, the homosexual fantasy,
wish, fear, or impulse lies at the core of the individual's
sexual problem. It is not surprising therefore that these tendencies are so severely repressed. The exposure of latent
homosexual feeling and the analysis of its elements open the
way to a resolution of the heterosexual difficulty.

Rose was a patient who accepted her homosexual feelings
without anxiety, although she was not an overt homosexual.
She had much more difficulty in accepting her sexual relations with her husband. About the latter situation, she remarked, "I feel like a board lying there and being submissive

to him." Then she remarked about her relations to a girl friend whom she had known since she was sixteen: "she is a pretty girl with masculine tendencies who is a lesbian. When I was younger, I wanted contact with her. One night about a year ago, we kissed each other. It felt very good to me, and right because of my feeling, but also not right because I realized it could go no further."

The contrast between Rose's feeling about her homosexual experience and her feeling in the heterosexual relationship revealed her unconscious conflicts. In kissing her lesbian friend, Rose felt herself to be a free agent and regarded her participation as having the dignity of a voluntary act. The sexual act with a man was viewed as a masochistic submission. The difference between these responses must be attributed to Rose's fear of the penis. For her, this organ was a symbol of power and authority to which she could not surrender. Her conflict arose from an unconscious need to control the sexual situation and her feeling that sexual relations with a man reduced her to an impersonal sexual object. The analysis of her homosexual tendency enabled her to understand the meaning of her difficulty, and she said, "My mother always impressed on me that I should be the best. So in bed I've always been good—putting on a good performance. The few times I was relaxed, I really enjoyed sex. After my last visit, my husband and I had relations. I found that I wasn't conscious of my body, so I gave up my control. I had a fine orgasm, and I realized with a flood of feeling that I was like my mother—having to control everything."

Rose's statement indicated that her need to control the sexual situation stemmed from an unconscious attitude toward her body. She had to control her body lest she give way to her sexual impulses. Analysis revealed that the impulses she feared were directed toward self-gratification. In our discussions, Rose described her sexual activity as "screwing," but she felt that masturbation was objectionable. The sexual sophistication that accepts a vulgar connotation of normal intercourse but rejects the natural function of self-pleasure is typical of the modern neurotic individual. Rose could relax in the lesbian situation because it did not involve vaginal penetration. Her homosexual tendency expressed her rejection of her own feminine body. It was this insight that enabled Rose to achieve a better response to her husband.

The homosexual tendency in Rose was consciously recognized and experienced. In other cases, the homosexual ele-

ment has to be deduced from the fear of close contact with a
person of the same sex. A woman's repugnance to being
touched by another woman can indicate the presence of a
latent homosexual tendency. The observations of another
patient, Anna, revealed some aspects of this problem. I asked
Anna to discuss any homosexual feelings she might have had.
Her answer:

> "Whatever repressed desire I might have to love or be
> loved by a woman, there is so much distrust of women
> and competitive jealousy that the other seems so out of
> the question. I think I also feel undesirable basically,
> and more so with women than with men. I feel that I
> am both afraid of not being seduced as well as afraid of
> the temptation of being seduced. For instance, when a
> woman doctor touches me, I find it so comforting that I
> think maybe I would like her to love me and desire me.
> Yet I know she won't, because no woman has, really—
> or maybe if they did, that is, at camp, it was as an
> innocent, loving little girl. But if ever I feel even a
> shadow that maybe she could desire me, I am frozen
> with awkwardness and fear. I can see wanting to touch
> another woman's breast but nothing else. I might like
> another woman touching me, but only rubbing my back,
> for instance, not touching my breasts, because that
> brings up my feeling of inadequacy."

The confusion of feeling that was evident in Anna's remarks revealed the extent of her emotional illness. It mirrored her conflicts and difficulties on the heterosexual level
and provided the key to the understanding of those difficulties. Without a knowledge of the latent homosexual tendencies in a person such as Anna, the disturbances in her
heterosexual function would be less comprehensible. On the
surface, Anna was a lively, vivacious, and bright young
woman. She was twenty-four years old, had been married
and divorced, and had a child of five years. Under her gay,
excited appearance was a little girl, terribly sad, angry, and
confused. She suffered from severe feelings of depression
verging on melancholia. These feelings would vanish, however, in the presence of a new man. She observed: "I feel so
exhausted and depressed. I know it's not Tom's fault. But I
know that if I am with another man or a group, the tiredness
would disappear instantly. I would perform." In this situation, Anna would become the "life of the party," outshining

every other girl present. If she failed to do this, she would become depressed and deflated. She had acted this role of the "gay little princess" for her father when she was younger to brighten his despondency and to gain his affection. "With a new person there is a new experience, a new discovery that picks you up," she said. "Proust says of every new relationship: 'Maybe this is the key to open the door to the golden treasure.' Hope." Proust himself was a homosexual. In this statement, he expresses the hope and the failure of the homosexual way.

Anna responded strongly to the feeling of being sexually desired or needed. This was clearly evidenced in the masochistic fantasies that she used to reach a climax. In a typical fantasy, her partner became "lover-husband who is tyrannical but adoring. I am irresistibly beautiful, especially my body. The lover-husband wishes to keep me always in his power. He excites me, then stops before we go out anywhere. Then when we are out, he decides to make love to me there, sometimes as a punishment for my having looked or been looked at by someone else. His ability to excite and make me come is a sign of his mastery."

The second part of this fantasy varied. One scene was described as follows:

> "We were in the dressing room of a department store. He decides to do it there. I am partially undressed, just a slip, perhaps, and made to stand back against the mirror, with my arms stretched out or behind me. My legs are always spread somewhat. Sometimes he orders someone to hold them open. In this fantasy and some others, it is a woman who does this, perhaps the saleswoman. Then he titillates me genitally with his hands, fast and lightly. Then at the last moment, he inserts his penis. But somehow I associate the penis entering with the idea of hurting me, as if it were too big, so that this part of the fantasy is not often used."

In another variation of this fantasy, the lover-husband "titillates my breasts, too, often through a covering, such as a slip, then at the climax, puts his hand inside the slip or bra. Sometimes he excites my breasts until I bare them myself."

Many elements in this fantasy revealed Anna's personality problems. First, she was evidently exhibitionistic. At the beginning of her therapy, Anna was studying to be an ac-

tress. She discovered that onstage, while performing, she
came to life. Second, much of her excitement stemmed from
the man's desire and passion. She was the delectable morsel
whom the man would devour with his lust. The vicarious
nature of her experience gave it a homosexual flavor. Third,
her fear of the penis was clearly expressed. Since the penis
was usually subordinate to the hands and to the role of
exposure in her fantasy, and since the fantasy did not always
end in coitus, it could be duplicated in a homosexual experience.

In view of Anna's feelings about a woman touching her
breast, her fantasies can be better understood in terms of
homosexuality. The lover-husband who titillated her breasts
and excited them until she bared them voluntarily was a
female figure who could be no one other than the mother.
This follows because every homosexual relationship is on one
level a repetition of the infantile experience with the mother.
Anna identified with this mother-lover and derived her excitement from the pleasure the mother-lover had in caressing
her breasts. This identification made it clear that the roles
could be reversed. Anna was also the mother whose breasts
were being fondled, and she was the child who would love to
fondle her mother's breasts. In other words, this fantasy
expressed Anna's repressed infantile desire for her mother's
breast. This interpretation was made easier by the knowledge
of her homosexual anxiety.

It might seem that the other parts of the fantasy had a
heterosexual orientation. Such an interpretation, however, is
out of line with her oral character structure. Anna's relation
to her lover-husband in the fantasy depicted the experience
of a child with a mother. Her passivity expressed the helplessness of the infant. The power and control that Anna
placed in the man originally belonged to the mother. The
penis signified the breast, and Anna was the infant who was
teased and exploited by her mother-husband. This exploitation of the child by the mother for the mother's sexual
pleasure has been present in every case so far discussed. In
real life, Anna functioned as an adult woman, but her fantasy
life and her fear of homosexuality revealed the longing of the
unfulfilled infant.

The split in Anna's personality was reflected in a dissociation from her body. She manifested a lack of body feeling,
which is characteristic of the schizoid personality, but her
personality also contained a major oral component, which

appeared in the expressiveness and aliveness of her face and mouth. Anna oscillated between schizoid withdrawal and oral longing. If her reaching for pleasure and excitement met with no response, she retreated into depression and nonexistence. She began to understand her moods as she gained a stronger sense of herself as a person. She said, "Earlier I used to feel nonexistent unless I was in touch with another body. I used to lie in contact with my husband. Now I don't feel nonexistent. If I feel sad or lose contact with myself, I want to touch Tom. But I can also think more of myself—what I can do. This is an improvement on the feeling of being left alone. I can cope with the feeling now."

Anna harbored a fury that was related to the lack of fulfillment in her being. It was always directed at the mother-husband-lover if he failed to satisfy her. Her description of her feeling is almost frightening: "The other night when Tom failed to maintain an erection, I felt myself turning into a panther. It was like in the movies where one sees a person changing into a werewolf. I felt as if my hands were turning into claws, and I wanted to scratch him. I actually did scratch his back. I felt evil and powerful."

There is a latent fierceness in all human beings related to the extent of their deprivation. And Anna was a hungry child, hungry for love, whose fantasy exceeded her grasp. If it became cannibalistic, as the following shows, it merely reflected the longing of an infant for a fat breast and a full belly. One day she reported: "I had a horrible fantasy while I was masturbating. I felt my legs were very huge and extended above me like the legs of a monster insect. My vagina was like a trap into which I wanted to suck the man to his destruction. Once he got in, he would be lost, devoured."

The displacement from the mouth to the vagina could not be more clearly expressed. In the face of such a fantasy, it is not surprising that some men would show a fear of the vagina. But the male is vulnerable only to the extent of his own anxieties. His genital organ is not so easily destroyed. Anna could frighten only a man whose fear of castration at the hands of a woman was already established.

Despite the strength of her latent homosexual feelings, Anna retained a heterosexual orientation because of an important influence in her life—her father's positive response to her femininity. This enabled her to make a transference of her oral feelings from her mother to her father, although it subsequently involved the male in all her problems. It also gave her a positive image of herself as a sexually desirable female, to which she clung desperately.

As Anna gained more self-awareness through therapy, the use of fantasy during the sexual act made her feel guilty. For, as she said, "I have really not been making love with him and, therefore, can never express my love and desire for him." Much as the fantasy seemed to be necessary to intensify her feeling, in another sense, it served to limit Anna's response. "If Tom is moving too fast, I completely withdraw, as if I can't let my feelings take over. I have to control the whole thing in my imagination, so that I, and not Tom or my body, decide when I am going to let go."

Anna's problem was so focused on the male that it made one question whether her heterosexuality was not a defensive maneuver. Her inability to identify with her mother consciously accounted for her lack of satisfaction with her own role as mother and housewife. The fear and mistrust of women were projections of her own repressed oral-homosexual impulses. Anna accepted herself as a woman when she realized that she was "acting out" upon her child the rejection she had experienced from her mother. The integration of her function as a mother into her personality allowed her to abandon the infantile position of sexual object and hungry child.

The relationship between homosexuality and the psychic and physical traumas that lead to neuroses is generally deduced through the interpretation of dreams, fantasies, and attitudes. In the following case, this relationship is vividly demonstrated in a fantasy and a dream that the patient reported:

"After last session, I felt very good. We had done a lot of physical work. My legs were shaking, and I had a good perception of my body. I felt very erotic. I wanted a woman very much, but I couldn't reach my girl friend. I went home and masturbated. I wanted to put something in my anus while I masturbated, like a candle. The thought occurred to me that I might enjoy a homosexual relationship through the anus. That night I had a dream.

"In the dream, I was helping another person to cover himself with a salve which would make him invisible so he could kill some old enemies. I asked him whom he

would attack first. He said, 'I would kill my mother.'
Later, I saw him plunge a knife into a man's throat.
When I woke up, I realized he was *me*."

A candle in the anus leads to a knife in the throat, the
desire to kill the mother ends as an attack on a man—the
transpositions and transformations that produce the homosexual feeling are incredible! The representation of a mother by
a man in a dream or fantasy is owing to the presence of a
strong masculine component in the mother's personality.
(This transposition was a striking feature of Anna's case.)
The masculine mother is the mother with a penis, who is a
familiar figure in mythology and psychiatry. I shall discuss
her significance later. In this case, she was a mother who
excited the child anally by inserting an enema nozzle into his
rectum. This is one way in which an anal fixation develops.
The effect is to focus libidinal or erotic feelings on the anus
and to make them unavailable for genital satisfaction. The
desire for a homosexual penetration to release these erotic
feelings is counteracted by anger at the violation which is
projected upon the homosexual. This may be one of the main
causes of murder in the world of homosexuals.

It was suggested in Paul's case that exaggerated masculinity may be a defense against latent homosexual feelings. The
exaggeration is achieved by postural rigidities and muscular
tensions. These tensions also have the opposite effect. They
circumscribe movement and limit motility, thereby producing
gestures and mannerisms that appear effeminate. Another
sign of effeminacy in a man that is easily recognized is a soft,
rolling tone of voice that verges on the sibilant. This is
produced by a rigidity of the thoracic and abdominal musculature and by muscle tensions in the neck and larynx that
decrease the flow of air and reduce vocal resonance. Sometimes the effect is to raise the pitch of the voice. The overall
rigidity of the body reduces the normal aggressiveness of the
individual and produces a character structure that can be
described as passive-feminine. The homosexual tendency in
the passive-feminine character is directly related to the
dynamics of his body.

Similarly, the presence of signs of masculinity in a female
are suggestive of latent homosexual feelings. The most common of these signs is an overdevelopment of the musculature.
These overdeveloped muscles are tense and contracted. Their
overdevelopment serves not only to give the girl the appear-

ance and illusion of strength, but to control and decrease
sexual feeling. Other signs of masculinity in a woman are
broad shoulders, narrow hips, straight body lines, hirsutism,
and so on. In a pronounced form, these features often characterize the masculine partner in a lesbian relationship. But
exaggerated femininity, especially exaggeration of the sexual
aspects of the personality, is also suggestive of latent homosexuality. Analytically, it can be shown that the sexual
exaggeration is designed to seduce the female as well as the
male. There is a psychological principle that states that every
exaggeration of attitude develops as a compensation for the
opposite condition. I have never known this principle to be
wrong. It is supported by the repeated observation that
exaggerated masculinity in the male covers repressed homosexual tendencies. It is equally true of the female—
exaggerated feminine characteristics, such as those of the
"sex pot," must likewise be viewed as a cover-up of latent
masculine tendencies of a homosexual nature.

Who is free of the taint of homosexuality? I would say
that very few people in our culture are completely free. Does
this mean, then, that the human being is fundamentally
bisexual? Have we not supported the contention that the
average person would engage in some degree of homosexual
practice if he were not restrained by social forces? Kinsey's
figures on homosexuality, which purport to show that 37
percent of American males and 28 percent of American
females have had one or more homosexual experiences in the
course of their lives, are usually cited to support the idea of
bisexuality. Are there individuals who are naturally bisexual,
who can derive full satisfaction from sexual relations with
either gender? Frank S. Caprio makes the statement that
"since every human being is primarily bisexual it follows that
latent homosexuality exists in all of us." He bases this assertion on Wilhelm Stekel's writings, which he quotes to the
effect that "all persons are originally bisexual in their predis-
positions . . . the heterosexual then represses his homosexuality. He also sublimates a portion of homosexual cravings in
friendship, nationalism, social endeavor, gatherings, etc. If
this sublimation fails him, he becomes neurotic.' " This line of
thinking is said to be the logical extension of Freud's
views.

To assert that neurosis results from a failure to sublimate
the homosexual craving is to put the cart before the horse. It
is my contention that homosexuality is the result of the

neurosis, not the other way around. Each case history I have presented shows that the same etiologic factors that produced neurosis are responsible for homosexuality. The sublimation of the homosexual desire in friendship results in a neurotic friendship that becomes corrupted by the repressed (sublimated) homosexual attitudes. The argument that human beings are primarily bisexual should be supported by evidence that the so-called bisexual individual achieves full satisfaction in his sexual activities. I have never known one who did. In every case of bisexual behavior that I have studied, the individual proved to be confused about his sexual role, immature in his personality, and inadequate as a sexual being. The problems of the bisexual are clearly illustrated in the following short case studies.

Jim was a rather good-looking young man of twenty-eight who had frequent relations with girls, supplemented with homosexual adventures. Jim knew that he was confused and disturbed and needed help, but he had never taken any situation seriously, and therapy proved to be no different. He had a very youthful appearance, so much so that I called him "baby face." His body was superficially soft; his deeper muscles, however, were tense and contracted. He drew a figure of himself, spontaneously to show me where his body problems were located (see Figure 6). The arrows indicate areas of disturbance.

His feet, he said, lacked feeling. He was not "grounded." He pictured himself as "flighty," running away from situations. In the drawing, his knees are locked. The "knee action," or elasticity, is missing from the legs. The pelvis is in a pulled back position, and the buttocks protrude. In actuality, his pelvis had a very feminine appearance. An arrow points to the stooped shoulders, with their evident lack of manliness. With its swollen belly, the figure gives the impression of a hungry child. The second figure shows Jim in flight; the third shows him without a head (ego).

With these pictures of Jim in mind, let us look at some details of his personal history. He said that by the age of four or five, it was necessary to use devices (unspecified) to stop him from sucking his thumb. He recalled fighting with his sister at the age of five and his father becoming very angry. He had one fight with a schoolmate, whom he frightened by his violence. The experience of his own violence terrified him. He said that he had never really fought since. At eleven, he discovered that he could not urinate if he thought that

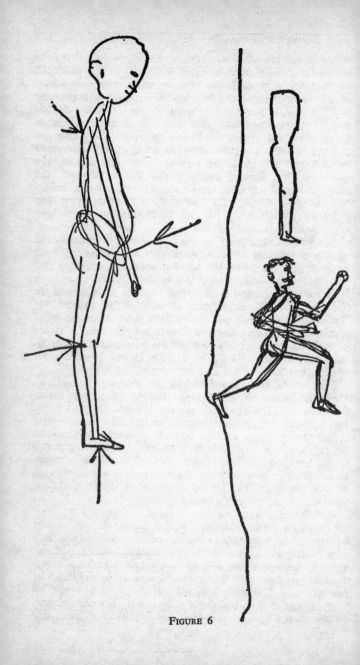

FIGURE 6

anyone was watching. He said that he still couldn't. From the ages of twelve to eighteen, he developed the practice of inserting things into his anus. He was not able to masturbate to orgasm until he was twenty-two years old. At that age, he underwent a circumcision to correct a condition of phimosis and painful erections. He also masturbated with a finger in his anus.

Jim said that he played a half-feminine role to appeal to bisexual men. Every couple of weeks, he went to bed with some man who, according to his expression, "punctured" him anally. Jim observed that he wanted this kind of relationship when he got the feeling that the world was closing in on him. His problems were either financial or related to girls and their demands, neither of which he could handle satisfactorily. Jim readily admitted his lack of manhood. He said that it was the reason for his homosexuality. His explanation of the latter, while very naïve, provides an interesting insight into homosexual motivation: "Going to bed with a man is a kind of incorporation of maleness. If you don't know what a man feels like, taking him into you is one way of finding out."

Edmund Bergler regards the bisexual as a homosexual whose heterosexual activity is a pretense. He writes: "Bisexuality ... is an out-and-out fraud, involuntarily maintained by some naïve homosexuals and voluntarily perpetrated by some who are not so naïve." According to Bergler, many homosexuals marry just to create an appearance of respectability and as a cover for their homosexual behavior. While this may be true in some cases, I believe that it is an oversimplification of the problem of bisexuality.

Every man is born to mate with a woman, and all his instincts urge him in this direction. Unfortunately, instinctual feeling and upbringing often conflict to a degree that makes the normal expression of the instinct difficult, if not impossible at times. Jim was not pretending about his sexual feelings for women. They were as genuine as his homosexual need to be "punctured" anally by a man. They collapsed in the face of stresses that produced the feeling that the "world was closing in." At these times, Jim could not obtain any release from his state of tension by an outgoing heterosexual expression. Enclosed in a cell of tension, Jim needed the homosexual penetration to open him so that he could make another attempt to assert his masculinity.

The bisexual has not surrendered his hope for a heterosexual life as has the confirmed homosexual. Most psychiatrists find that the analytic treatment of the bisexual produces better results than does the treatment of the confirmed homosexual. The bisexual should be viewed, therefore, as a person who cannot establish a dependable heterosexual pattern of behavior but who has not fully resigned himself to the "easy way out."

Robert was another patient, whom I saw briefly, whose heterosexual function collapsed whenever he was faced with the demands of a mature relationship. Robert had been married twice and had a child from each marriage. His first wife had left him because of his violent outbursts of rage, and his second marriage had failed for the same reason. I knew Robert and his second wife, and so I was able to follow the situation that led to the breakup of his marriage. Throughout his adult years, Robert had homosexual interests, but overt homosexual activity was not engaged in so long as certain conditions in the heterosexual relationship could be maintained.

The breakup of the second marriage came as a shock to his wife. She loved Robert dearly, and she was sure that he had considerable affection for her. She was a rich girl who had married a poor boy against the advice of family and friends. She did so because her sexual experience with Robert during the courtship was the best she had known. Robert was sophisticated and intelligent. He gave the impression of sincerity and conviction, although this was belied by concealments and false statements about his background. He seemed to be the kind of person his wife wanted.

The early months of the marriage were rather happy for both parties. Robert took command of his wife and of the home, decorating and furnishing the apartment. The only conflicts that arose to trouble them were financial ones. Although Robert earned some money, he contributed nothing to his wife's support. And he did not hesitate to spend her money for the home in a way to which she was unaccustomed. Sexual relations between them were fairly regular, if not fully satisfactory. This changed, however, as soon as his wife became pregnant. Robert said that he could feel no desire for a pregnant woman. He began to go out at night with a fast crowd that included a number of homosexuals.

After the birth of the child, the situation deteriorated rapidly. Following the collapse of a business venture, Robert seemed content to live on his wife's money. He made no effort to find a job. There was no sexual contact between husband and wife. Robert became more involved with his homosexual friends and stayed out quite late at times. A separation occurred following an argument in the course of which Robert became violent and his wife became afraid of physical harm.

I am certain that while Robert entered into this marriage with an eye to the convenience and comfort it could provide, he fully intended to maintain it as a meaningful relationship. Marriage, however, is not a game for children to play. And Robert was an immature person who would not accept responsibility if he could find a way to avoid it. As long as he was in the dominant position and free from responsibility and obligation, Robert could maintain some degree of heterosexual function. He could not maintain this function when faced with demands of a more adult attitude. His resentment of the power that his wife's money represented was intense. His hostility toward her for not sharing it with him was equally strong. These factors alone were enough to destroy the marriage. But it was his wife's pregnancy that undermined any attempt on his part to be a man. This fact changed his wife from a girl into a woman and raised the specter in his unconscious of his incestuous feelings for his mother. Robert fled into homosexuality.

Both Jim and Robert could function in a heterosexual relationship on condition that their immaturity was accepted by the partner. This acceptance removed the threat of castration or abandonment. A demand by the woman for a more responsible attitude was regarded as a challenge and was unconsciously responded to as a danger. Homosexuality was an escape.

To accuse the homosexual of marrying only for convenience, as Bergler does, is to overlook the desire in every person for a normal life with a family. If a homosexual enters into a marriage with his tongue in his cheek, it is because of fear of the outcome. The responsibilities and obligations that marriage and fatherhood entail will be, he suspects, too much for him to meet. The weakness and immaturity of his personality account for his relapse or escape into active homosexuality. The problem with the bisexual as with the homosexual is not the homosexual tendency but the immaturity and neurotic structure of the personality. Homosexuality in any form is a symptom of the inability to function as a mature and responsible adult. It is not a disease in itself but the symptom of a disease of the

total personality. It cannot be treated only as a sexual devia-
tion but completely in terms of the distortion of the whole
personality.

Homosexuality and heterosexuality can be regarded as
opposite ends of a scale of values that forms a continuous
spectrum. The two are not categories but limits. Persons
show homosexual tendencies to the degree that they are
neurotic. Since no one can fully escape the cultural forces
that cause neurosis, no one can claim to be perfect. There
are no 100 percent heterosexuals as there are not 100 percent homosexuals. If there are latent homosexual tendencies
in every individual, as Caprio asserts, there are latent
heterosexual tendencies in every homosexual person. Orgastic
potency is the specific value that distinguishes the heterosexual from the homosexual. The greater the potency, the more
the individual tends to the heterosexual pattern; the less the
potency, the more he manifests homosexual tendencies. Personality structures can be ranged on a scale of potency, with
homosexuality at one end, heterosexuality at the other, and
bisexual behavior and latent homosexual tendencies in between. This provides a good working concept, since it avoids
the division of people into one class or the other. People are
not heterosexuals or homosexuals; they are individuals with
varying degrees of orgastic potency associated with corresponding degrees of neurosis. This concept is illustrated in the
diagram below:

Scale of Sexual or Orgastic Potency

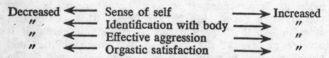

Homosexuality Bisexuality Latent homosexuality Heterosexuality
Personality characteristics

Decreased	←	Sense of self	→	Increased
"	←	Identification with body	→	"
"	←	Effective aggression	→	"
"	←	Orgastic satisfaction	→	"

I have attempted to show that homosexuality is related to
the loss of the feeling of self, the lack of an adequate
identification with the body, and a reduction in the effec-
tiveness of the total personality. The last item on the chart,
orgastic satisfaction, may require some explanation. The ability to achieve a satisfactory orgastic release is a function of
sexual potency. Despite any statements that homosexuals may

make to the contrary, it is limited to the heterosexual mode of functioning. The homosexual may derive some pleasure and satisfaction through identification and "acting out," but he forgoes the experience of the self. His satisfaction is experienced on an ego level, not on a physical level. Orgasm is a function of self-experience and self-realization in their deepest form.

There are important therapeutic implications in this analysis of homosexuality. If a patient can achieve a better identification with his body, a stronger sense of self, a better functioning personality, his sexual pattern will automatically shift toward the heterosexual end of the scale. To do this requires the working through of personality problems on the one hand and body tensions on the other. The corollary is also true: any increase in heterosexual feeling or behavior will result in an improvement in all personality functions. We must know more about heterosexual attitudes and behavior if this is to be our goal.

8

Heterosexuality

Heterosexuality is taken so much for granted that it is rarely subjected to the kind of analysis given to homosexuality. Yet it would be well to inquire in what ways it differs from homosexuality. This is the same problem we face in our attempt to understand health. It is so much easier to describe an illness than to define health. In the absence of such a definition, a person is regarded as healthy if he does not suffer from any discernible illness. Similarly, a person is considered to be heterosexual if he does not engage in any overt homosexual activity. Such distinctions are psychologically unrealistic. It is comparable to dividing people into thieves and honest men and viewing every man who is not a thief as an honest man. Many men are dishonest in ways that have nothing to do with thievery.

It would be simple to say that heterosexuality is the attraction and union of opposites, whereas homosexuality is the attraction and union of the same or the like. However, it has been shown that behind every homosexual act is the unconscious image of sexual union with the opposite sex. It is obvious that two homosexuals cannot play the same role. Can it be anticipated that under the façade of heterosexuality, one or both parties may act out homosexual attitudes and feelings?

The homosexual feeling derives much of its "charge" from the process of identification. The masculine partner in a lesbian relationship obtains most of her excitement and pleasure from the reactions of her partner. Her experience has been described as vicarious. A similar situation prevails in male homosexuality. The male who plays the feminine role has the vicarious satisfaction of experiencing the pseudomasculinity of his partner. Identification also occurs in many heterosexual relationships. The man whose excitement is dependent on the woman's arousal, whose pleasure stems from her satisfaction, is acting out a homosexual attitude. This attitude characterizes the man who knows more about female sexuality than he does about his own, who is less interested in his feelings than in the woman's.

Such an attitude was expressed and defended by a patient whom I saw for a short time. This man considered himself a "great lover," and he claimed that he was so regarded by the women he knew. His practice was to excite the woman's genitals by his oral activity until she reached a climax or was very close to one. Coitus was a secondary form of sexual activity to him. His expressed concern in whatever he did was the arousal and satisfaction of the woman, and his pleasure depended on her reactions. His own genital response was relatively unimportant, he said, since he obtained greater pleasure from the woman's reaction. It was difficult for me to picture this patient as a "great lover"; he was unromantic in appearance and unmanly in body attitude and movement. In fact, he impressed me as being an "old woman" as he sat opposite me, hunched within himself, smug and self-satisfied. Yet one woman told me that she felt a thrill go through her when this man looked at her. He devoured her with his eyes, she said.

This type of sexual activity is quite common. In fact, one of my female patients complained that "every man who is attracted to me indicates that he wants to 'eat me.' I was told by a friend that I was like the bottle in *Alice in Wonderland* which bears a label saying, 'Eat me.' One man told me that it was my swayback ass. One of these men, who loves to fight and will fight anyone at the drop of a hat, offered to wax my floor. He's very much like me. These are men who lower and degrade themselves. Why do such men choose me?"

The woman who made this observation had a strong masochistic element in her personality. She lacked a feeling of pride in herself as a person and as a woman. It was obvious that the men who were attracted to her had similar personality structures. My response to her question was, "Like attracts like."

How this kind of sexual activity can be distinguished from that of the male partner in a lesbian relationship, I do not know. The lesbian may even attempt to duplicate the male genitals by using an apparatus known as a dildo, which is strapped to her body and has an artificial penis. Similarly, it cannot be said that the male who has coitus with a woman is by that fact alone acting in a heterosexual manner. If the man uses his penis as the lesbian uses her dildo, that is, if it is used to satisfy his partner, the relationship may just as well be described as homosexual. It becomes even more homosexual if the man uses other parts of his anatomy to achieve this end. Identification with the feelings of the sexual partner is the mark of homosexuality, for it denies the antithetical nature of the sexes.

In addition to identification, another homosexual attitude that is often found in heterosexual activities is the concept of "service." The homosexual describes his activities as "servicing" his partner. But this is also true of a man whose primary concern in heterosexual activity is to bring the woman to a climax. The compulsion to have sexual relations with a woman simply because she is sexually excited betrays the need to "service" her. Under the banner of the art of love, some sexologists advocate a sex technique that is based upon this concept of "service." Albert Ellis, for example, writes, "The deeply empathic individual not only passively notes what his or her bedmate requires but actively looks for, seeks out this mate's requirements and then *caters to them*" (my italics). I have always believed that the sexual relation was the union of equals, each of whom was competent to take care of his or her own needs. The above quotation makes each sexual partner the servant of the other.

Helping a woman enjoy sex or helping her reach a climax is almost a socially accepted procedure in our culture. In part, this must be explained by the current fear of the frustrated female, the monster who can, and sometimes does, devour her children and destroy her husband. But the fear results only in further castration of the male, and this in turn leads to further frustration of the female. A man must be careful that in his desire for mutual pleasure and satisfaction, he does not surrender his own masculine identity or accept a subservient role in the relationship. The "good lover" is generally a poor male. Unfortunately, it seems to be part of the homosexual trend in our culture to equate masculine sexuality with the ability to satisfy a woman. However, the female is never truly satisfied with such a performance by the male, either in the course of coital relations or in any other way. The so-called sex techniques end with the man losing

more than he gains and with the woman losing what she truly
wants—a man.

Because of this inverted sense of masculinity in many men,
women frequently pretend to have orgasms. The justification
for this is that it would hurt a man's pride if he knew that he
hadn't satisfied her. One of my female patients complained
that her lover insisted that she have three or four orgasms
before he allowed himself to reach his climax. Her own
insecurity in the relationship made her feign feelings that she
didn't have. The result was that no one was really satisfied.
The sexual activity became a game in which each played a
part rather than a mutual experience of union. My patient
said that she was not happy with this arrangement, but since
her lover was so insistent, she went along with the game.

Satisfaction is not something one can give another person.
It depends upon the ability to surrender oneself fully to the
sexual experience, and it escapes the person whose sexual
activity is a performance. No man can satisfy a woman or
give her an orgasm. He can create the conditions that make
possible her self-fulfillment, but the rest is up to her. The
primary conditions are that he be fully himself, honest in his
relationship to the woman, and capable of enjoying sexual
contact with her. Let us not be deceived by the myth of the
multiple orgasm. It is, invariably, the expression of a woman
who is pretending. She may even be pretending to herself,
mistaking minor flutters of excitement for the deep feeling of
release that is the culmination of an enjoyable experience.

The need on the part of a man to satisfy the woman is
directly related to his fear of the woman and to his anxiety
about his own potency. Behind this behavior and need, one
can always find in the man a fear of premature ejaculations.
This doubt about his own potency renders him sensitive to
the woman's response. But again, it is part of a vicious circle.
The fear and anxiety about prematurity and the failure to
satisfy the woman increase the state of tension and augment
the prematurity. Finally, the man inhibits his own excitement
and sacrifices his sexual pleasure to maintain the image of
potency in the eyes of an unhappy woman.

Prematurity of ejaculation, or *ejaculatio praecox,* is one of
the most common sexual problems that afflict men in our
culture. In part, the fear of prematurity is irrational, for
there are no time limits to an act of sexual intercourse. The
ejaculation is premature if it happens before one has reached
the height of sexual excitation. To govern the timing of the

ejaculation by the response of the woman destroys the natural flow of feeling that alone guarantees mutual satisfaction. This point cannot be stressed too strongly. Inhibiting the buildup of the excitation for the sake of the woman limits the possibility of mutual satisfaction, whereas the opposite enhances that possibility.

One patient who had a fear of prematurity, coupled with the inevitable need to satisfy the woman, habitually took the feminine position in the sexual act. After analyzing his attitude and with some encouragement, he essayed the position on top. This is his report: "I was on top to try it, and I could feel that the friction was different, conducive to my coming. I got excited, and after two minutes I felt I could come. I stopped my movement so as not to come, and I lost my erection. So I came out and changed the position. In the position under the woman, I could last one-half hour."

At the same time that this patient expressed his feelings of being submissive to women, he voiced his rebellion: "The hell with women! All they want is a stud horse. I wish I never heard of sex."

A dildo can last longer than any man. What value is there in simple duration if the excitement is lost? Sex is not an endurance contest. Anyway, he understood that stopping his movement as his excitement veered toward the climax was a reaction of panic, since it resulted in the loss of his erection. There is nothing wrong with an act of intercourse that lasts only two minutes. Encouraged to try again, he came back the next week with a different story: "We started side by side, but soon I rolled over and got on top. I kept moving and got very excited. I came quickly, but I found that my excitement stimulated my partner and triggered her release. She came with me. I had a strong orgasm and almost lost myself in the release."

Identification with the woman's feeling and "servicing" her needs reflect not only a homosexual attitude in a man, but also a weakness in the total personality. Another patient described this relationship clearly in discussing his sexual attitude: "I am a big starter," he said, "and a big middleman but no finish. My concern has always been to please the woman. I have only rarely felt fulfilled. Reading Reich* has made me aware of this lack. After sexual relations—even

---

*Wilhelm Reich, *The Function of the Orgasm*. New York: Orgone Institute Press, Inc., 1942.

after several acts in a single night—I am still excited, unable to sleep. I feel no orgastic release. I feel this is typical of my whole life. I cannot bring situations to a resolution. I get stuck in them. I would like to resolve my own life. For so much of my life, I have escaped from my body. I was a mystical thinker."

This patient's inability to achieve an orgastic release was paralleled by his inability to achieve satisfaction in other areas of activity. The ability to gain satisfaction through one's endeavors is the characteristic of a mature personality that functions on the basis of the reality principle. It is lacking in individuals whose goal is to create an impression on others or to please others. This goal, as with my patient, indicates that the personality is "outer directed" rather than "inner directed." He correctly placed the cause of his difficulties in the lack of an adequate sense of self owing to his escape from his body.

What has been said about the man is equally true for the woman. Her identification with the man robs the sexual relationship of its heterosexual meaning and decreases the possibility of satisfaction or orgastic fulfillment in the experience. Where the identification with the male is a conscious preoccupation, there is a true lesbian situation. By far the more common situation, however, is an unconscious identification, apparent only in the behavior and attitude of the woman.

The unconscious identification with the male is manifested in the emulation of masculine activities, interests, attitudes, and comportment. The most popular example is the so-called career woman—not the working woman, but the one who has to establish her worth by competing with men. She is aggressive, tough, logical, and determined. Masculine values dominate her thinking. She talks like a man, walks like a man, smokes like a man, and drinks like a man. Masculine-style clothes fit her well. It is not surprising that these women are often quite successful in business or in their professions. They are free from the ego tension that burdens the male. They cannot fail since lack of success is no discredit.

The woman with a masculine identification often dominates the home situation. In her sexual relations to a man, she tends to take the initiative. And because her genital sensations are more clitoral than vaginal, she prefers the position on top. Analysis generally reveals the presence of unconscious feelings of penis envy in her personality. Freudian analysts assume that penis envy is typical of all women, but I have found that it is limited to the neurotic female. This masculine woman need not be a lesbian, although she has latent homosexual feelings. Her superficial orientation is heterosexual, and generally she is a married woman with children. In analysis or psychotherapy, one finds that she is dissatisfied, sexually unfulfilled, and complains about the inadequacy of her husband. While her complaint may have some validity, she overlooks the fact that her own attitude contributes to the trouble. She is heterosexual in appearance only, not in feeling. I have found it very helpful to point out to such a patient that her masculine identification transforms her sexual relationship into a homosexual one. It is not difficult for her to see that where both parties have identical values, the sexual relation becomes a union of the like. The charge of homosexuality is, in many cases, potent enough to jar the rationalizations of most sexually sophisticated individuals, the true homosexual excepted.

The masculine woman is sharply portrayed in Edward Albee's play *Who's Afraid of Virginia Woolf?* The play describes the attitudes and behavior of a married couple. George, the husband, is a college professor; Martha, his wife, is the daughter of the college president. The first scene opens with Martha's outspoken expression of contempt for her husband. She derides his manhood, and George defends himself and retaliates. Martha is ambitious and aggressive while George is content to be a scholar. The ostensible reason for her contempt is George's failure to become head of the history department. At the beginning, Martha proclaims her superiority by declaring that she can drink George "under any goddam table." It is significant that through most of the play, Martha is seen in a pair of slacks.

Martha plays the game of life by men's rules. As the plot unfolds, we learn that Martha has had affairs with many of the younger college instructors. Her penchant is for the he-man type, young, muscular, and athletic. A new instructor who appears to have these qualifications and his wife join Martha and George for some 2 A.M. drinks. As the liquor flows, tongues become looser and behavior less controlled. The pretenses, the weaknesses, and the hostilities of each character are clearly revealed. George announces that being married to the president's daughter is no sinecure and that the price he has had to pay for that privilege was the loss of his manhood. Martha expresses her admiration for her fa-

ther, who, like her, is ambitious and aggressive. It is obvious
that she has strongly identified with him.

Martha and George have a secret that, one gathers, holds
their marriage together. The secret seems to be that they
have a son, who is away at school and who is supposed to
return the next day, his twenty-first birthday. But both are
pledged not to speak of this son in the presence of third
parties. Martha violates the pledge by confiding his existence
to the other woman. This step, it appears, is the final straw in
George's humiliation. When he hears of this, he resolves upon
revenge.

Throughout the rest of the play, there are references to
this son in terms that are unusual and strange. George
corrects Martha by pointedly calling the son "him" not "it."
Yet in the next breath, he describes his son as "the little
bugger." Martha reacts by asserting that George is not sure
that their son is "his own kid." But George says that it's the
one thing in life he is sure of—his partnership in the creation
of his son. There is an argument about the color of the boy's
eyes—blue, says George; green, like mine, says Martha.

In the second act, there is further delineation of the
characters. George uses the term "heterosexual" as if to
imply the possibility of its opposite. Later, referring to their
son, George accuses Martha of "fiddling at him all the time"
in dishabille and with liquor on her breath. But George
admits that both have played this game when they were
alone. The masochistic element in George's personality is
emphasized by Martha as the reason for his marrying her.
Her insults are obviously designed to challenge George. They
do, and in the final act he meets her challenge successfully.

Martha's character is clearly revealed in her sexually aggressive behavior toward the young college instructor. To
seduce him, she intrudes her hand between his legs above the
knee in a very provocative gesture. It appears in the course
of the second act that she does seduce him but that the result
was far from satisfactory. It is difficult to see how it could be
otherwise in the tense and sordid situation that has developed, with everyone drinking to excess. This is the weakness of the play, for Martha is presented with so little appeal
as a woman that one wonders how any man could be interested in her sexually. Despite its sexual content and free use
of sexual language, the play is as devoid of sexual feeling as
are its characters.

The story begins at 2 A.M. and ends some hours later. The

game of humiliating one another is almost over. In the third act, the time has come for the final reckoning. Martha admits that George is the only man who has ever made her happy and that because he loved her, she hated him; because he understood her, she had contempt for him. But it is too late. George takes his revenge on Martha. He announces that he has received a telegram informing him that their son is dead. Martha protests, but it remains a fact, and in the face of this *fait accompli*, Martha collapses into a frightened little girl.

It quickly becomes apparent that the son is a fictitious invention. It is a game which Martha and George have played for twenty-one years and which George now terminates. The pretenses are over. No more games. George and Martha face the fact that they are a childless couple who have no one but each other. One cannot be content, however, with this obvious interpretation. Two intelligent and sophisticated adults such as George and Martha are too realistic to create such a shallow fiction unless it had a deeper meaning, one that would explain their relationship to each other.

I believe that the fictitious son refers to George's penis, to which Martha claims as much right as does its owner. The relationship between husband and wife is based on this shared object of veneration. Martha feels free to lay her hands on it at any time, since it represents "their son." Her aggressiveness compensates for George's sexual passiveness and explains why the marriage lasted as long as it did. This interpretation enables us to understand earlier references to the son as "it" and "the little bugger." Martha's obsession with the size of the male genital organ is well documented in the play.

Who's Afraid of Virginia Woolf? has been described as a homosexual view of women. But there are many women like Martha and many men like George who rationalize a distorted sexual relationship in the name of sexual sophistication. The play is not a homosexual view, but a view of homosexuality in married life. Every element of homosexuality that has been brought out in the preceding chapters is portrayed in the relationship of George and Martha: the identification, the hostility, the contempt, the preoccupation with the genitals, the sexual promiscuity, the lack of self-respect, the sexual dissatisfaction, and so on. Martha reveals these characteristics more than George, who fights to retain his integrity. In this sense, the play depicts a cultural tendency toward the masculinization of women and the dangers inherent in this tendency.

If the woman is not to be sexually aggressive in the same way that a man is, this does not mean that she is to be sexually passive. The sexual need of a man or a woman cannot be "serviced." Such an attitude on the part of a woman denies her personality and prevents the achievement of sexual satisfaction. If the concept of the equality of the sexes is to have any meaning, it must be applied in this most important relationship. The woman need not be as sexually excited as the man to begin the preliminaries leading to intercourse, but she must consciously want to engage in sexual activity for her own pleasure and satisfaction. It is not uncommon, even today, to find married women who view the sexual act as submission on their part to the sexual passions of the man. Some are submissive out of the mistaken idea that sexual pleasure is a male prerogative, while others are so to maintain the marital *status quo*. The result in either case is a loss of the feelings that bind the union, such that the marriage is threatened in its very foundations.

A woman can be sexually submissive only if she dissociates herself from her body. This is the mechanism that underlies the behavior of prostitutes and homosexuals. And by this action the woman denies herself the possibility of any satisfactory sexual response. It is far better for the woman to avoid any participation in the sexual act until some desire is experienced. This would require an assertion on her part of her right as a person to act in accordance with her own feelings. She is a person, and she has this right, but in the absence of an assertion of it, the right is not felt as natural. Psychiatric experience shows that once the woman begins to assert this right, it is not long before positive sexual feelings arise. Having reclaimed her body, the woman can experience its natural desires and feelings as her own. This may bring into focus latent feelings of sexual guilt that can then be resolved therapeutically.

Frequently, the attitude of sexual submission is demanded by the husband, even though he may then complain about the lack of sexual response on the part of his wife. One patient complained that her husband always wanted intercourse at times when it was inconvenient for her or when the children were around. At night, when the cares of the day had been left behind and privacy could be assured, he was too tired. It can be assumed that consciously or unconsciously, he chose those occasions when there could be no sexual feelings on her part and when her response could only be one of submission. In this particular case, the husband insisted upon his wife's submission in other areas of their relationship, none of which she could successfully resist as long as she was sexually submissive to him. Every attempt on her part to assert herself was countered with the complaint, "You are castrating me."

Such relationships, if heterosexual in appearance, are homosexual in attitude. The heterosexual relationship by its very nature is not one of dominance and submission. Heterosexuality implies the union of the different. If the difference in the sexes is to have any meaning, it must be respected. Simply stated, a heterosexual attitude is one in which the man respects the woman as a woman and the woman respects the man as a man. One cannot overemphasize the importance of respect in the sexual relationship. It allows the two parties to come together as equals, not as the same. It makes impossible the kind of sadomasochistic behavior that is so clearly portrayed in Albee's play. Because of her respect for the opposite sex, the heterosexual woman does not insult a man, nor would she do anything to make him feel inadequate or inferior. If she feels sorry for him because of any faults or weaknesses that he may show, she would keep her feelings to herself. To step in, as so many women seem anxious to do, with sympathy and help to "make a man out of him" is humiliating and degrading. Such help should only be offered when it is asked for. Under the pretext of helping a man to find himself, a woman can dominate a susceptible man and reduce him to the status of a dependent child.

It follows logically that the heterosexual man respects a woman as an equal, competent to run her own affairs and strong enough to protect her interests. The man who takes a father role toward "the helpless little creature" expresses thereby both his fear and his contempt for women. It is pathetic to see how many mature men marry young girls in the name of romance and devote their lives to the protection of what they regard as the "weaker sex." Obviously, as long as they can keep them weaker, their claim to manhood cannot be disputed. Then there is the man who expects the woman to take care of him, the man who turns his wife into a mother, and in the process loses his sexual feelings for her. This attitude had its origin in the man's lack of respect for his mother as a woman. He saw her as mistress of her home, cook, servant, drudge, wife, but not as a sexual person whose feelings of pleasure and physical excitement were counterparts of his.

Heterosexuality can be described as that attitude that is characterized by an identity with and a respect for one's body, one's personality, and one's sexual function. The corollary is respect for these aspects of the other individual. I have no hesitation in saying that this heterosexual attitude is the basis for orgastic potency and sexual satisfaction. Unfortunately, it is easier to describe a correct attitude than to achieve one.

How does it happen that a person loses identity with his body and, in the process, loses respect for his sexual nature? Years of clinical experience have established the fact that this happens in infancy and childhood. The newborn infant is an animal organism whose body is amorphously sexual. Aside from the focus of erotic pleasure in the mouth related to the overriding need for food, the infant's entire body responds pleasurably to contact with his mother's body. Limit this contact and the infant loses the feeling of pleasure in his body. Deny this contact and the infant's body becomes a source of pain. It is painful to long desperately for contact and closeness that are not forthcoming. It is painful to cry for a mother who does not respond. If the pain becomes too great, the child numbs himself to it by cutting off bodily feeling. He stiffens, inhibits his respiration, and makes no effort to reach out for pleasurable stimulation. Later in life, as an adult, he will avoid any excitation of his body because it can or does evoke the repressed feeling of pain that he experienced in infancy. Genital stimulation and excitation will be desperately sought as the only way to the physical sensation of being alive and feeling pleasure.

Important as is the need for total body contact with the mother, the child's need for oral erotic gratification is just as great. Nursing confirms the child in his sexual nature by the pleasure he experiences at his mother's breast. This is the first point at which a conscious conflict develops in the mother toward the sexual nature of the child. How long should she indulge this desire for pleasure on the part of the child, if she does indulge it at all? How important is physical pleasure in the life of a child—or in the life of an adult, for that matter? Isn't there the danger that if one abandons oneself to one's biological functions, one risks to lose all the higher values of civilization and culture? These questions are not consciously asked by mothers, but they exist in the unconscious of every civilized person. Are we beasts, or are we human beings? The animal functions by instinct only. Man has a mind that he can and should use to govern his actions. But let us use it as rationally as possible. Our minds did not evolve so that we would be unhappy, sexually frustrated, and defeated individuals. Our specifically human heritage did not arise to contradict and destroy our animal nature. The values of nature and culture need not become the source of conflict. The body pleasure of the child at the mother's breast or in contact with her body is the foundation upon which his personality and his intelligence will grow. One can live in a house with a poor foundation, one can function rationally without the support of a pleasurable body, but the danger of collapse is never absent. Emotional illness is too widespread today to accept blindly the old axioms.

Culture does not arise out of the sublimation of sexuality if the term "sublimation" is taken to mean a decrease in sexual feelings. On the contrary, in a healthy, normal person, cultural activities heighten sexual feelings. Similarly, the passions, excitements, and drama of sexuality provide the content for and inspiration of creative activity in art, music, and literature. Our moral heritage was based on an either-or attitude. Either one was committed to the higher values of life, culture, achievement, and morality or one was profligate, a pig, a sexual tramp. Either a girl was a virgin until she married or she was a whore. And the old dichotomy of good and evil, right and wrong, God and devil still continues to plague us.

However, man is not an animal *or* a human being. He is both. He must stand upon two feet if he is to stand for any length of time at all. He is not cultured *or* sexual. He is both cultured *and* sexual. His sexual behavior reflects his culture just as his culture reflects his sexual feelings and attitudes. My argument is that for the heterosexual person, sexuality is his way of life. He isn't fragmented into the asexual businessman from nine to five, the Lothario of the cocktail bars from five to seven, and the serious father when he returns home. He doesn't carry on an affair with his secretary in New York while preserving appearances at home. He doesn't discipline his children while asserting his own right to do as he pleases. He doesn't need alcohol to be free to express his sexual feelings. He isn't a pyramid climber, a status seeker, an organization man, or a conformist. He isn't a rebel or an outsider. He is a man who enjoys what he does because he enjoys everything he does. His pleasure is mostly in the satisfaction of doing, only partly in the reward or gain. He carries his good feelings with him; they are part of him, not derived from others. He loves those to whom he is close because he knows no other way of being close than through love.

In his sexual activities, the heterosexual man does not try to prove anything—again, simply because there is nothing to prove. He enjoys a woman because he enjoyed his mother. He loves a woman because he loved his mother. His expression of sexual feeling is free and unrestrained because the expression of affection and tenderness has always been the natural way for him. He gives himself to the sexual act without inhibition because whatever he does is wholehearted and spontaneous. Contrary to what some psychologists say, he isn't a "giving" person. He doesn't give himself to others—he simply is what he is. His positive qualities reside in a way of being, not in a way of doing. And since pleasure and satisfaction are the goals that motivate his actions, he experiences these in his sexual activities as he does in other activities. Naturally, he is orgastically potent, for this is only another way of saying that his sexual experiences are fully satisfactory—physically, emotionally, and psychologically.

The heterosexual man has been variously described. He has been called the "sexually adequate individual." Reich described him as the "genital character," the healthy character type, the one free of any neurotic complications. Unfortunately, he doesn't exist. People cannot be categorized as neurotic or healthy, heterosexual or homosexual, orgastically potent or orgastically impotent. No one in our culture can be considered a "pure" type. What I have described is an ideal type, a man joyous in his disposition, happy in his relationships, content with his existence.

Psychiatrists need criteria and standards if they are to guide their patients through the complex maze of neurotic rationalizations, but psychological standards are difficult to apply. I find it helpful to employ physical criteria to gauge emotional health. The case presentations have pointed out the correlation between psychological problems and their physical manifestations in the body attitude in the pattern of muscular tension, and in the limitation of motility.

The presence of chronic muscular tensions is a concrete,

palpable, and demonstrable sign of a disturbance in the organism. It cannot be argued that this disturbance exists on one level and not on another, that it is limited to the physical and does not include the psychological. A healthy body is alive and vibrant. Its features are harmonious, and its expression is pleasing. Skin tones and color are good; the eyes are bright; the muscles are relaxed, so that the body is soft and supple. A healthy body is characterized by its beauty and grace. If these criteria are open to subjective evaluation, they are at least visibly evident.

The heterosexual woman, or the sexually mature woman, however one wishes to call her, differs little from her masculine counterpart in the qualities I have described. She doesn't envy a man any more than a normal man would envy a woman. She is satisfied to be herself because her existence provides emotional satisfactions in the significant areas of her life. She almost always achieves vaginal orgasm during the act of love which "starts deep within her vagina and extends to all parts of her body."* It is not only in the sexual area that a mature woman finds her fulfillment. Her relations with her husband and children also provide deep satisfactions. The mature woman has a sense of reality and an awareness of personality which, as Marie Robinson points out, enables her to "select a husband who is good for her, almost near perfect." It can also be said that a mature man will almost invariably choose a good wife.

The quality of maturity that ensures the right attitudes and decisions in life is the full acceptance of reality. For each individual, the basic reality is the fact of physical existence in a body. A sexually mature woman identifies with her body. She knows that her pleasure derives from her body, and has experienced this pleasure in self-gratification. Robinson's view that masturbation is a "tasteless and pointless experiment" for the ideal woman represents a theoretically wrong position. It is true that a woman who is happily married has no need of masturbation except during the prolonged absence of her husband. But what shall one say of widows or divorcées? If a woman cannot experience pleasure in her own body through her own hands, then she has not fully accepted herself. It is my experience that such a woman is incapable of consistently achieving a vaginal orgasm. When a woman's

*M. Robinson, *The Power of Sexual Surrender*. Garden City, N.Y.: Doubleday, 1959.

sexual pleasure is fully dependent upon a man, she loses the independence that is characteristic of maturity.

The mature woman's acceptance of reality is manifested in a feeling of love for and pride in her body that is reflected both in her appearance and in her physical well-being. She takes care of herself so that she is not depleted or rundown. Drinking, late hours, and frequent parties are not consistent with the pride in one's body that constitutes the foundation of satisfactory sexuality. The sexually mature woman's identification with her body extends to childbearing and childraising. They are the natural functions of her body that only she can perform. Her positive attitude toward her responsibilities is not an example of "feminine altruism," as Robinson claims, and does not call for a eulogy. Because of her identification with her natural functions, the mature woman "wants to and does nurse her child at her breast." Thus, the sexual satisfaction she experienced with her husband is made directly available to the offspring of that union. Robinson's observation that the sexually mature woman ages gracefully is valid. Since she is free from neurotic conflicts and anxieties, her body retains its vitality and charm until old age. For the same reason, menopause brings no diminution in her capacity for sexual enjoyment.

This is not an idealized portrait. It describes a woman who has the capacity for sexual fulfillment. But this capacity cannot be realized apart from fulfillment of the total personality. Nevertheless, the relationship is also an inverse one. Personality is shaped and determined by sexual experiences, and to the degree that these provide greater satisfaction, the total personality will mature. The experience of full sexual orgasm transforms the ideal into an attainable goal.

9

Male and
Female Sexuality

It is a sad and frightened man who asks, like Professor
Higgins, "Why can't a woman be like a man?" Only a
rejected female would take this question seriously and try to be
like one. The values of masculinity and femininity have been
somewhat lost in the overall loss of identity that characterizes
the current situation in Western society. Sexual roles, which
were clearly defined in past generations, are now confused.
On one side, Simone de Beauvoir argues that woman has
become the "second sex" owing to her exclusion from the
world of masculine activity. On the other side, the poet
Robert Graves writes that "a real woman neither despises nor
worships men, but does everything she can to avoid acting
like one." The present confusion stems from the overthrow of
the so-called double standard upon which the old order was
founded. Yet this is no unmitigated tragedy, since the double
standard negated the woman as a person and ignored the
body as a source of truth.

The uncertainty about what constitutes the normal social
and sexual attitude is not limited to women. Men suffer from
a similar bewilderment about their role in the marital relationship. For example, if a man dominates his home, he is
considered dictatorial; if he is passive and submissive, he is
criticized as inadequate. It would seem that he must walk a
tightrope. However, when such problems appear in a family
situation, the trouble generally lies in disturbances of the
sexual relationship of husband and wife and in a lack of
clarity about the partners' sexual expectations. The man who
dominates his home does so because he consciously believes
that woman's role is to be submissive, sexually as well as

161

personally. He thinks that she expects him to "wear the pants," which he interprets as being the boss. The man who allows his wife to control their relationship acts in the mistaken belief that he is expected to serve the woman, that is, to satisfy her. Passive attitudes are often rationalized as expressions of altruism by both the man and the woman. Self-assertion is confused with selfishness, on the false assumption that one has an obligation to satisfy the sexual partner in return for the rights of the relationship. This neurotic attitude grows out of a lack of understanding of the biological factors that condition the relation of one sex to the other. To appreciate these factors, one must understand the different psychosexual development of the individual male and female.

I divide the psychosexual development of the individual into three periods: the pregenital, the latent, and the genital. This division corresponds to significant biological changes that take place in the organism during each period.

The pregenital period includes the time from birth to about six years of age. At about six years of age, the eruption of the permanent teeth occurs, an event that marks the end of what may be considered to be an infantile stage, broadly speaking. The choice of this age as the time to enroll a child in school must have some relation to this event and to the emotional changes that occur then. The pregenital period is devoted to the progressive integration of body movement and feeling into coordinated and goal-directed activity. Concomitantly, the pregenital libidinal impulses are integrated into a unitary pleasure striving that is focused upon the genital area. When this stage is completed, genital primacy has become established. This means that the genital area has superseded all other erogenous areas of the body as the source of erotic pleasure. Thus, by the end of this period, the child has given up his desire for oral gratification and no longer needs to suck on a breast, a pacifier, or his thumb. Toilet training has been completed, and the excremental functions no longer dominate the child's attention. Psychologically, the child has been weaned from his mother. He can stand on his own feet securely, and he has developed the motor coordination that enables him to function as an independent organism within the family group. Reality functions are anchored at both ends of the organism: above in the ego, below in genitality.

In the second half of the pregenital period, the child

becomes conscious of his genital area and of the pleasure he can obtain through masturbation. This is a period of considerable masturbatory activity, infantile sex play with other children, and sexual curiosity. The young child's interest in the sexual function promotes his acceptance of reality and reduces his dependence on his mother for erotic gratification. Masturbation during this stage does not have the adult significance of discharging excitation; rather, it produces a pleasurable excitation of a sensual nature in the total body. The masturbatory activity of the young girl is not directed at her clitoris, which is a minute organ, but at the whole genital area, including the clitoris. The boy touches his penis, but makes no attempt to stroke it to climax.

During this period, the parents' task is to fulfill the child's oral needs: food, security, affection, attention, and so on. These constitute the narcissistic supplies necessary to the growth and development of the ego and of the personality. Any severe deprivation at this stage fixates the child upon this pregenital, or oral, level. The personality will be marked by tendencies to cling and to be dependent. Sexual and personal relationships will be used to gain support for an inadequate ego. The need for body contact in sex will dwarf the desire for orgastic release. Such individuals become sensualists. It is unfortunate that the one natural way to fulfill these needs in the child, breast feeding, has become a lost art. In this one act, the child receives food, attention, security, and affection. Contact with the mother's body furthers the development of the child's body as well as its ego. The child discovers his body; that is, he develops a body image that grows out of the pleasurable experiences of contact with his mother's body. When this stage of development is over, the child has normally "found" his body in sense perception and motor coordination.

In the pregenital stage, there are no functional differences between male and female. The differences are there, but the child does not function according to them. There is little in the behavior of a boy or girl of four or five years to indicate his or her sex. Boys and girls are dressed differently in our culture and are given different toys to play with, but these differences are imposed from without. Young children function primarily as sexually undifferentiated individuals, although their awareness of sexuality would astonish the average adult. They are concerned with their emerging individuality, which will establish them in their own eyes as male or female if uninterfered with by adult feelings.

Most psychiatrists and psychoanalysts today believe that the personality of an individual is fully determined by the age of six. This means that the roots of all personality disturbances are to be sought in traumatic experiences that happened during the pregenital period. Indifference to the child's feelings is probably the most important violation of the child's needs. For example, parental disregard of the child's likes and dislikes about his diet is common and can be harmful. The insistence that a child eat what he does not want to eat is experienced by the child as a negation of his personality. Poking into his body orifices with Q-Tips, enema nozzles, or other instruments is a violation of his person. Ignoring his fears or not responding to his cries shows a lack of respect for the child as a feeling person. Each such experience weakens the child's faith that he is important, wanted, and loved.

The pregenital period terminates in a psychological phenomenon known as the oedipal situation. The girl becomes aware of her femininity and finds herself attracted sexually, not genitally, to her father. This means that she enjoys physical closeness to her father differently from the way in which she enjoys closeness to her mother. The boy experiences similar feelings about his mother. In fact, the establishment of genital primacy is associated with a peak of sexual feeling that is diffused throughout the body but includes a slight focus on the genitals. As a result, the boy may entertain ideas of supplanting his father as his mother's lover. Similarly, in the girl there is some competitive feeling toward her mother in regard to the father as a sexual object. I do not know whether this is a premature budding of genitality or whether it indicates that at some earlier phase of man's evolution, puberty was reached at this age. Analytic investigations have shown that a child of five or six has a full awareness of adult sexuality in his images and fantasies. His fantasies correspond, however, to his sexual feelings, which, barring adult interference, are diffused over his body and not strongly focused on the genital apparatus. Thus, a girl's desire to marry her father does not imply sexual relations with him but the feeling of wanting to be held and to be loved. The double efflorescence of sexual feeling, first in the pregenital period and later in adolescence, is similar to the double dentition. Its psychological significance has not been fully explored.

If normal development proceeds, the rather strong sexual fantasies and images of the child are repressed as he moves into the next stage, but the knowledge of sexuality is not lost. The child knows his sex, and he knows about sexual differences. However, the significance of these differences is pushed into the unconscious. When the child thus relinquishes his first foothold in genital functioning, he does so in the interest of the reality principle, which promises a greater gain later. Actually, he does not abandon his position; he only withdraws his interest.

This development proves that individuality and sexuality are closely linked. One does not occur without the other. The concept of genital primacy is functionally identical with the growth of individuality. Thus, if the pregenital phase is one of undifferentiation, it ends when differentiation takes place.

From the age of six to puberty, the child passes through a stage that is known in psychoanalytic language as the latency period. This period is characterized by a subsidence of the sexual interest and feeling that had reached a peak in the preceding years. The child is aware of sexual differences, but the main interest now lies in the child's recognition of the role of boy or girl. The emphasis shifts to the total personality and to the important task of acquiring knowledge and learning the skills that are necessary for efficient functioning in our complicated world. One can argue, as Reich did, that this is an unnatural development owing to the antisexual moral code of our culture. Such a view assumes that the restrictive influences in a highly developed culture are antagonistic to life. They may operate in this fashion, but not necessarily. In a culture that requires extended educational training for life in society, the reduction of sexual interest and feeling facilitates the transfer of attention to this task.

The degree of latency varies with the individual. In cases where the oedipal problem is not resolved and repression fails to occur, the latency phenomenon is disturbed. I had one patient who told me that during this period, he masturbated as often as twenty-two times a day, each time to some climax. This is not normal, and this patient in adult life developed an acute type of paranoid schizophrenia. His illness was in no way due to excessive masturbation. Rather, the disturbances in his personality that later caused his mental breakdown created such anxieties in his early years that he was forced to masturbate excessively in order to control them. The sexual situation in his home was one of open conflict. He was emotionally seduced by his mother, who at the same time violated his feelings by force-feeding him and giving him an excessive number of enemas. He was rejected by and afraid of his father. In such an emotional climate, healthy growth and development can hardly be expected.

Many children engage in some sexual activity during the latency period, such as masturbation or sexual play with other children. Generally, it indicates the persistence of some unresolved sexual problem from the preceding stage. Sexual activity that occurs in this period is an attempt on the part of the child to release the tension that the problem produces. And since children mature at different rates, no absolute criteria exist about the normal. To the extent that such sexual activity interferes with the ability of the child to devote himself to the normal activities of this period, it is a sign of a disturbance in his personality.

The latency period is the time when the individual develops his conscious identification with his body. Physical activity strongly dominates most of this period in both boys and girls, only slowly giving way to intellectual and cultural pursuits. The body image is almost completed in this period. The feelings and sensations that underlie the body image provide the somatic basis for the sharpening and delineation of the personality. Strength and confidence in his personality are the child's unconscious objectives in this stage, and they are intimately related to his feeling about his body.

The third stage is designated as the genital stage. It can be further subdivided into adolescence, late teens, and sexual maturity. For purposes of brevity, these distinctions will be overlooked.

In the boy, development continues along the same line it had previously followed. Feeling in the genitals gains an urgency that is experienced as an outward force in the erection of the penis. In the course of these early erections, the foreskin stretches and the head protrudes. Masturbation activates the mechanism of ejaculation, which comes as a stunning revelation to the neophyte. Energetically, the penis may be considered to be an extension of the body. This idea is based on the feeling of the pelvic thrust in the man. The excitation for this thrust is perceived as flowing down through the body and pelvis and into the penis. It may also be perceived as two distinct sensations. One is a feeling along the back of the body that has an aggressive quality and is associated with sensations in the buttocks and pelvic floor. Another is a sensation of melting and streaming in the front of the body that has a tender quality. Both streams of feeling unite to create an outgoing impulsion in the penis.

In the girl, marked changes occur at puberty as compared with the boy, whose development proceeds in a straight line. The girl's pelvis enlarges disproportionately and tilts backward. As a result, the vagina, which in the young girl lies in a forward position like the penis, is now located between the thighs. The downward tilt of the pelvis causes an inward rotation of the thighs, bringing them together at the midline. Of even greater significance is the change in the direction of the flow of excitation. Instead of flowing outward as it does in the boy, it *turns inward* along the walls of the vagina. This change in direction serves the function of mature sexuality and reproduction.

The term "vagina" comes from the same root as the word "invaginate," which means to "turn inward." It may be surprising, therefore, to learn that the vagina does not develop embryologically as an invagination from the surface. It is actually formed by the fusion of the embryonic Müllerian ducts, remnants of which also persist in the male. Although the vagina is formed in early embryonic life, it does not become operative until feelings (or energy) invade the vagina after puberty. When this takes place, the more intense genital feelings become located deep within the vagina. These feelings are aroused only by the full penetration of the penis. The presence of these strong vaginal feelings allows a distinction to be made between a superficial and a deep response. This distinction is absent in the feelings of the pre-pubertal female. This development also explains the so-called transfer of excitation from the clitoris to the vagina. Actually, no transfer occurs. The clitoris retains its sensitivity in the mature woman; however, its importance is reduced in view of the stronger, deeper, and more intense feelings that pervade the vagina.

The normal development of the girl, as described above, depends upon the undisturbed maturation of her individuality and personality in the earlier stages. Neurotic elements in the family situation can prevent or impede this normal turning inward of the sexual feelings. If the feminine role is regarded as inferior by her parents, the young girl will attempt to compensate for her feeling of being unacceptable by identifying with boys or with the masculine. She will become aggressively assertive rather than receptive, hard rather than soft, pushing rather than yielding. This will have the effect of diverting the flow of her feelings or energy into an outward rather than inward channel. Instead of bypassing the clitoris to invade the vagina, the genital excitation will become fixated at the surface and on the clitoris. Through this organ, she can feel her identity with the male, but her vagina will remain unalive and unresponsive. The differences between male and female will be distorted: the distinction will be between the superior male (large penis) and the inferior male (small penis = clitoris) rather than between male and female as equals.

One of the difficulties that students of sex have in comprehending this development of female sexuality stems from a mechanical view of sex. The argument is that since there are no sense corpuscles (nerve endings) in the walls of the vagina, the latter is without feeling. On the other hand, the clitoris has many sense endings, like the penis, and it is, therefore, the organ of greatest sensitivity in the female. But sensitivity to touch is a sensual phenomenon; it becomes sexual only when excitation charges the total body on a deeper level. This is also true in the male. His sexual arousal is an emotional phenomenon that involves the whole body and is not limited to the erection of the penis. The vagina is not only an organ; it is also the entrance to the woman's body. Only through her vagina can a woman respond fully to a man. Sexuality is primarily a function of movement and only secondarily a function of erotic contact. The deepest feelings in a man and woman are mobilized by sexual movements, voluntary and involuntary. In no other physical relationship between two people is there both the intimate contact and the strong movement that are characteristic of normal intercourse. Mouth-genital contact, hand-genital contact, or other forms of sexual activity provide neither the degree of physical contact nor the freedom of movement that can be experienced through the penile-vaginal relationship when it functions normally. For these reasons, it can be stated that only the relation of vagina to penis provides the setting and conditions for full orgastic discharge in the male and the female.

How are the differences between male and female sexuality related to the development sketched above? First, the fact that excitation in a man focuses upon a point and is directed outward accounts for his tendency to be more quickly aroused genitally than a woman. This tendency can be compared with electrical or electrostatic energy, which focuses and discharges more quickly from a point than from a round or flat surface. Second, the fact that the man has the organ of penetration assigns to him the initiative to institute the sexual act. Third, the fact that his body is more muscularly developed explains why he is generally the aggressor in sexual relations.

The word "aggression" is used here in the psychiatric meaning of "to step forward, to approach, to assert oneself." "Aggressive" is used in psychiatry as the opposite of "passive" and does not carry the dictionary meaning of "hostile." Aggression in an individual is regarded as a positive quality and denotes an ability to "move toward" objects in the world. Movement is a function of the musculature. Since the human male is endowed with greater muscular development than the female, it can be assumed that the function of movement is more important in his nature than in hers. It is interesting to speculate upon the outward flow of energy in the man and his greater muscular development. Throughout all mythologies, the male or the masculine principle has been considered to represent the moving spirit. On the other hand, the female or the feminine principle has been regarded as the receptacle that transforms that spirit. The feminine functions of reception, containment, and transformation are as necessary in the sexual act per se as in the production of offspring.

I do not mean to suggest that a woman's role is passive or submissive. So many women, consciously or unconsciously, reject their sexual nature because they believe that it imposes a submissive attitude upon them. No woman wants to feel that she is an object, sexual or otherwise. Everyday observation shows that women are as active as men in proposing sexual relationships. Women have their own way of indicating desire or willingness for the sexual relationship: a look, a touch, a gesture—rarely the spoken word. In the sexual encounter between a man and a woman, it is impossible to know who initiated the contact. Once the contact is made, however, the man generally becomes the pursuer and the woman the pursued, but she has her own ways of keeping the chase exciting and challenging to the man. Since a woman is as much an individual as a man, she is only slightly less aggressive than he is in life situations. Her attitude can be described as aggressively receptive. If this expression seems confusing and sounds like an oxymoron (a combination of incongruous or contradictory words, as in "thunderous silence"), it denotes that the feminine function of reception is not a passive process. She is as eager to receive the male as he is to enter her. Her aggression is more subtle, but not less effective.

On the other hand, most men resent the woman who is overly aggressive sexually and who tries to take the initiative in the sexual relationship. They feel that they are being called upon to perform, and they unconsciously resist. The effect of this unconscious resistance is to reduce the man's desire and occasionally to render him impotent. Too often, men with passive tendencies in their personality marry women who are overly aggressive. While this may seem to be a good combination in theory, it rarely works out in practice. The man unconsciously resents the woman's assumption of the dominant role. She in turn resents his passiveness. She reacts with increasing demands that he prove himself which only further alienates him and decreases his interest. The frustrations that develop in such marriages lead to severe conflicts, often ending in divorce or alcoholism. It would be easy to say that the man must not adopt a passive or dependent attitude. But such advice is meaningless in view of the usual severity of these emotional problems, which may call for the competent help of a marriage counselor or psychiatrist.

In most sexual situations, the desire of a man for a woman will condition her response. Normally, a woman is more sexually aroused if a man is aggressive and moves toward her. It is sometimes said that a woman wants to be taken. I believe that this statement exaggerates her attitude. She wants to be needed, she wants to be wanted. She responds to the sexual excitement and desire in the man. It can work the other way around, too (that is, a man can be aroused by the sexual desire of a woman), but that is not the usual way. It may be that the turning inward of her energy and the lack of a sharp focal point for her sexual excitation make her somewhat dependent upon the male or his image for full arousal. If this is true, it would explain why primitive peoples regarded the phallus as the symbol of life and fertility. Its erection is the visible evidence of the flow of the creative impulse.

Among mammalian animals, the male assumes the dominant, covering position in the sexual act. This is also true in most human sexual relations. The dominant position (on top) means that the man sets the pace and rhythm for the sexual activity. He determines the quality of the pelvic movements in the voluntary phase, the speed and the strength of the thrust, and the moment of withdrawal. A woman has to adapt her movements to a man's rhythm as long as he is on top. She may indicate to him by word or touch that she would prefer a slower or faster rhythm, but it is up to him to make the change. She cannot move counter to his rhythm without upsetting the harmony of their actions. If she responds to his movements, then his climax, with its strong, involuntary pelvic movements, will frequently trigger her climax. If in our culture simultaneous orgasm is rare, this is owing to neurotic disturbances that interfere with normal sexual feelings and function.

On the psychological level, the above differences are reflected in the woman's attitude toward a man. She feels dependent on him in a way that is not true of a man in relation to a woman. This feeling of dependence has its roots in the sexual function. It is exemplified in one difference not mentioned above: his failure in the sexual act results in her failure. The reverse is obviously not true. Loss of erection dooms the sexual act for both parties; the loss of a woman's sexual feelings has no such effect. Because of this dependence, a woman will react, sooner or later, consciously or unconsciously, with hostility to any weakness in a man with whom she is emotionally involved. A woman can be and will be sympathetic, understanding, and helpful to a man in his need. She will support him in every effort he makes to overcome his difficulties or limitations. But if this doesn't work and the weakness continues, she will leave him or destroy him. I think that men are unconsciously aware of this tendency in a woman. Their concern about satisfying a woman sexually reflects their fear of her hostility should they fail. But a woman is not deceived by such tactics. Her intuitive sense for the natural penetrates all pretense. No man can hide his weakness from a woman. If he attempts to do so, she will probe his personality with uncanny instinct and smash his defenses with the power of a battering ram. This is the psychology of the female. It may stem from some obscure biological drive to improve the race by mating with the best, but whatever the origin of this need, it characterizes the behavior of a woman. For all the identity and equality between them, man and woman are on opposite sides of the equation: their natural antithesis can easily degenerate into conflict and strife.

It is rare to find hostility on the part of a man toward a woman for any failure in her sexual function. Men may complain that a woman is sexually unresponsive or frigid, but this feeling seldom turns into hostility. Normally, a man tends to take upon his shoulders the responsibility for the success of the sexual relationship. He feels that it is up to him to arouse the woman and even to satisfy her. While I have suggested earlier that this attitude resembles the homosexual approach, it must be recognized that it has some basis in the dynamics of the normal sexual relationship. For the man is aware that a woman would have little to complain of if he were manly enough. If a woman at times needs to have her femininity affirmed by a man, it can be done only by a "full-bodied" man.

This situation is illustrated in the following incident. A female patient related her difficulties with her husband in the course of a therapeutic session. She said, "He wanted to make love to me last night. He sidled up to me and then, hesitatingly, tried to caress me. The worm! I was so disgusted, I shoved him out of the bed."

I could feel her contempt for him, and it angered me. I replied spontaneously, "If I were your husband, I'd have beaten you up."

To my surprise, she said, "I wish he had."

In all the years of my clinical experience, I have never known a woman to resent a strong, aggressive assertion of intention or feeling by a man. On the contrary, she welcomes such an attitude and resents his fear and weakness. Physical force is not called for; the man who hits a woman is a coward unless it is done in self-defense, but the man who allows a woman to beat him or to ridicule him is a fool.

There is another area in which the psychological differences between the sexes are revealed, that is, in their respective attitudes toward infidelity. A woman can tolerate sexual infidelity more easily than she can accept the transfer of her husband's affection to another woman. The opposite seems to be true of a man. A husband is more hurt by the sexual infidelity of his wife than he is by her affection for another man. These are broad generalizations, of course, but they point to an important psychological difference. The sexual infidelity of a wife threatens the husband's manhood. It is experienced as an insult to his pride in his virility, that is, in his ability to hold and to satisfy a woman sexually. A cuckolded husband is an object of ridicule; the wife who is left for another woman is an object of pity. On the other hand, as long as a husband supports his wife in her accustomed position, she is respected by the community regardless of his dalliances.

Few women question their ability to satisfy a man sexually. A woman's pride is based upon a broader foundation: the appeal of her personality as expressed in the role of wife and mother. Her pride is not identified with her sexual function alone, but with her total body. Her body represents the two functions of sexuality and reproduction. These two functions of her body determine her dual nature—one based on her relationship to the man, the other stemming from her relationship to her children. By virtue of this dual relationship, it can be said that woman is man's bridge to the future via children.

Duality exists in the nature of the man, too. It inheres in his relationship to his body and to his genital organ. A man identifies with his penis as an extension of himself. Since it is not subject to his will or to his ego, he often speaks of it as having an independent existence. It may be referred to by a different name—Peter, John, or, as the French say, *mon petit frère*. His identification with his body is more direct, but it is in terms of the ability of his body to function in the world of men. His pride on this level is related to his muscular development and coordination. His body belongs to the world; it is geared for action vis-à-vis other men or nature. His genital organ, however, belongs to the woman. Because of his dual relationship to the world and to the woman, man is woman's bridge to the outside world. He brings its romance and excitement home to her. While a woman's necessary preoccupation with the birth and care of children limits her range of movement, she can bring other values to a man, values as important and as necessary as those he offers her. To his intellect, she brings a wisdom derived from her intimate connection with the vital processes of life and death. And she is the inspiration as well as the recipient of the fruits of his activities.

10

Sensuality
versus
Sexuality

The terms "sensuality" and "sexuality" are sometimes used interchangeably, as if they refer to the same thing. Sexuality is considered by many people to be a sensual experience, and sensuality is often mistaken for sexuality. The dictionary gives two meanings to the term "sensuality" that are somewhat contradictory. One links sensuality with the animal instincts or desires. The other identifies sensuality with voluptuousness and associates it with free indulgence in carnal pleasure. The idea of voluptuousness, however, cannot be equated with a normal indulgence in carnal pleasure; it carries the implication of overindulgence rather than free indulgence. I have chosen the terms "sensuality" and "sexuality" to designate two different approaches to the sexual experience.

The sensualist is primarily interested in those aspects of the sexual act that involve stimulation and sensory excitement. He strives to prolong his state of excitement as long as possible. The sexual person aims for the pleasure that is realized from the discharge of the excitation. In sexual relations, the sensualist concentrates upon activities that are described as forepleasure. The objective of the sexual person is the satisfaction that derives from endpleasure, or orgasm. This is not to say that the sexual person denies himself sensual pleasure entirely. My purpose here is to draw a distinction between the attitude of one who seeks constant excitation and that of one who aims for fulfillment and satisfaction.

The sexual experience consists of two phases. In the first, the emphasis is on the buildup of excitation through sensory stimulation. The second phase is directed toward the release of the excitation through movement. Normally, these two phases are so continuous that no sharp line of demarcation can be drawn between them. The sexual act, from the first erotic contact through forepleasure, penetration, movement, and release, constitutes a unified experience for the individual—but pathological disturbances in the personality can fixate an individual upon one or the other of these phases of the sexual experience to the relative exclusion of the other. For some persons, stimulation is more important than release, while for others the need for release is so imperative that the pleasure of erotic stimulation is bypassed. To understand these disturbances, it is necessary to analyze the sexual process in terms of the excitatory phenomena in each of these phases.

These two phases of the sexual act correspond to a dual aspect in the nature of the pleasure function itself. One of the reasons for the confusion that surrounds the nature of the orgasm is the lack of understanding of the dynamics and mechanisms of pleasure. Important as pleasure is in the lives of people, it is not discussed in any of the standard textbooks on physiology. In my years as a medical student, I rarely heard the term mentioned. The concept of pleasure seems to have no place in the scientific view that regards the body as a machine. Only in analytic writing and psychology is an attempt made to understand the nature of pleasure.

Freud propounded the idea that pleasure results from the release of tension. He related the amount of pleasure to the intensity of the tension that was discharged and to the time interval in which that discharge took place. The shorter the time, the greater the pleasure. Examples are easy to find. There is pleasure in the satisfaction of hunger. Hunger may be regarded as a state of tension that is discharged in the process of its satisfaction or satisfied in the process of discharge. The pleasure derived from the satisfactory evacuation of a bowel movement stems from the discharge of a state of tension. Even the pleasure of achieving a difficult task can be related to the discharge of the tension that arose from the confrontation and challenge of the task. The same principle applies to sexual pleasure. Sexual excitation is perceived as a state of tension.

The prospect of a good meal when one is in a state of hunger tension produces a feeling of pleasure. The exhilaration in the face of a dangerous or challenging situation is experienced pleasurably. Pleasure is perceived in the buildup of excitation as well as in its discharge. I shall use the term "anticipatory pleasure" to describe this response. It represents a mobilization of energy and constitutes a feeling that seeks release. The discharge of this energy or tension through a satisfactory sexual experience produces the significant feeling of pleasure that is called orgasm.

Thus, there is, however, a kind of pleasure that does not fit Freud's definition, which has led to some modification of his theories. Freud's statement that pleasure results from the discharge of tension has been interpreted to mean that life strives for Nirvana, a state of no tension and no struggle. This conclusion, which seems to follow logically from the imperious nature of the pleasure principle, led Freud to formulate his concept of a death instinct. Many facts, however, contradict this conclusion. Psychologists and analysts have pointed out that man often seeks situations of stress and tension. Actually, one can experience a certain amount of pleasure in the state of tension itself under certain conditions.

The tension of a challenge is pleasurable if one can anticipate the satisfactory resolution of the tension situation. The anticipatory pleasure in a state of tension is contingent upon the prospect of its release. Take this prospect away and every state of tension or of excitation would become unpleasurable and frustrating. In fact, frustration can be defined as a state of excitation or tension from which there is *no* prospect of release. Given the prospect of release, one can tolerate tension until the possibility of its discharge occurs. This is known technically as the reality principle, which is a modification and extension of the pleasure principle. According to the pleasure principle, an organism seeks to avoid pain and to feel pleasure. The reality principle states that the organism will postpone the realization of pleasure or tolerate a situation of pain to gain a greater pleasure or avoid a greater pain in the future. The search for pleasure is an expression of the life force in an organism. Contrary to Freud's view, the pleasure principle denies the validity of a Nirvana concept. In his search for pleasure, man will often consciously create situations of tension in anticipation of the pleasurable release.

Pleasure has a dual nature. There is first the pleasure of the excitation, provided that one can anticipate its discharge; and then there is the pleasure of the release of the tension or the discharge of the excitation. The first pleasure, anticipatory pleasure, is associated with the buildup of excitation. The second pleasure is perceived specifically as satisfaction and is related to the discharge of the excitation. It is the nature of living organisms that the buildup of a state of excitation carries within itself the unconscious prospect of its release or fulfillment.

Seen in this light, pleasure is not the experience of a static state but of a dynamic one. The organism does not seek to discharge tension as an end in itself, nor does it seek to build tension as an end in itself. If a state of excitation were not discharged, the organism could not get excited again. If it seeks anything, teleologically speaking, an organism seeks the flow of feeling, the buildup and the decline of excitation, the movement from one condition to another within the limits of its available energy. Pleasure cannot be divorced from movement, either physical or psychological. Movement is basic to the function of the living organism. An organism is alive because it moves spontaneously, and it moves because it is alive. Feelings can be defined in terms of movement and excitation. For example, frustration is the inability to move out of a state of excitation or to decrease the excitation. On the other hand, depression is the inability to move into a state of excitation or to increase the excitation.

In an organism, movement results from an increase or decrease in its state of excitation. An increase of excitation moves an organism toward the exciting object, while a decrease in excitation moves it away from that object. This is the nature of life and of the sexual function. The result is a quickened movement that produces a greater sense of aliveness and is experienced as pleasurable by the organism. Movement, excitation, and pleasure contribute to a heightened preception of the self, because they are different aspects of the process of living.

Excitation and movement are energetic phenomena. The sexual drive is also an energetic phenomenon; it depends upon the existence of excess energy in the organism, that is, upon the availability of energy over and beyond that needed to maintain biological survival. The production of excess energy is a natural function of living organisms. Any factor that depletes the energy of the organism reduces its sex drive. Illness, fatigue, neurotic tensions, and lack of sleep are among the factors that act in this direction. The factors which act in the opposite direction are those which promote the natural health and vitality of the organism. I know of no artificial stimulants that provide energy for the sexual drive. Alcohol may increase the desire but it decreases the function.

Normally, this excess energy is diffused throughout the organism, or it may be said to exist as a state of latent excitation, ordinarily experienced as a feeling of well-being or aliveness. In its diffused form, it is available for any situation. When the energy reaches a certain level of intensity in an adult person, it will flow toward its natural avenue of discharge, the genital apparatus. This accounts for spontaneous erections in the male, spontaneous desire in the female, nocturnal emissions, and the like. In daily life, there are sufficient stimuli to focus the excess energy upon the genitals. Once this focus occurs, that is, when the energy charges the genital organs, one becomes conscious of the sensation of sexual arousal and desire. Arousal is not a process of putting life or feeling into a person; the feeling or life must be there first. Arousal is a process of focusing excitation upon the genitals through either psychic or physical stimulation or both.

After focus occurs, any further contact with the sexual object will operate to increase the focus and raise the level of sexual excitation. Genital arousal is, therefore, a pleasurable experience, despite the accompanying feeling of tension, as long as the prospect of discharge is present. Most couples engage in a variety of sexual activities that serve to raise the level of sexual excitation. This is known as forepleasure.

Forepleasure serves two purposes in the sexual function. First, through the erotic contact of the different parts of the two bodies, all the available excess energy normally diffused throughout each body is mobilized for the genital activity that is to follow. The stimulation of the mouth, the face, the neck, the breasts, the back, the legs, and so on, evokes feelings that flow toward the genital region. Second, the excitatory level is raised, so that a greater urgency is felt for sexual union and sexual discharge. This buildup of excitation through forepleasure mechanisms is experienced pleasurably as a positive life force in the body as long as one can anticipate the release of the tension through the sexual discharge.

The second phase of sexual activity comprises those actions that lead to sexual discharge. These constitute endpleasure mechanisms, the goal of which is not to heighten the tension

but to release it. The pleasure of the discharge differs from
the pleasure of excitation. This difference can be described as
the feeling of fulfillment and satisfaction as opposed to that
of excitation and anticipation.

The endpleasure of discharge is only as intense as the
excitation that preceded it. However, I do not wish to give
the impression that the sexual process can be or is easily
divided into distinct periods. The process of excitation continues through the act of coitus itself until the involuntary
movements of discharge occur. The discharge takes place in
seconds as compared with the relatively long period of buildup. The division of sexual activity into two periods with
respect to the buildup and the discharge of excitation is only
for the purpose of describing and understanding the problems
one encounters in disturbances of the sexual function.

"Sensuality" is one of the manifestations of a disturbed
sexual function. Normally, sensuality is part of the sexual
process. The stimulation of all the senses plays an important
part in the preliminary phase of sexual excitation. Forepleasure is predominantly a sensual experience, but sensuality can
become opposed to sexuality if the search for excitation
becomes an end in itself. The sensualist differs from the
sexual person in that he is less interested in the endpleasure
of discharge than in the exploitation of the means of creating
tension and excitation.

Sexual orgies as an extreme instance, are not sexual experiences in the true sense of that word but exercises in
sensuality. The important function of sexual discharge is
relegated to a minor position, and the endpleasure experience
is empty, flat, and meaningless. It would be accurate to say
that little or no orgastic experience can be had under these
conditions. Intimacy, with its need for privacy, is completely
ignored. The mad search is on for excitement, and anything
goes; but satisfaction escapes the sensualist. His excitement
inevitably fades away. It has to be rekindled with new
devices, further maneuvers, and additional stimulants to
awaken a jaded sensibility into feeling. Orgies end only in
exhaustion or drunken stupor, for the real end of sexuality
has been denied in favor of a perverted vision of sexual
excitement.

The sensualist hopes that he can bring the excitement to a
high enough pitch to take him out of himself. He looks for
an ecstasy that forever escapes him. Each failure is interpreted as due to the lack of sufficient stimulation. Each new

attempt is doomed to a greater failure. Sensuality, limited as it is to the senses, is a function of the surface only. By its very nature, it disregards the inner feelings of the body that alone hold the true key to sexuality. Meaningful sexuality involves the guts, the heart, and the mind of a person. But these are precisely the areas that the sensualist has blocked off from feeling.

Sexual orgies are relatively rare in our culture—at least they are not ordinary occurrences in the lives of average people. But sensuality is present both as a temptation and as a disturbing force in the sexual behavior of many people. The prolongation of forepleasure activities for the sake of the excitement they provide is not without its danger to endpleasure satisfaction. Normally, forepleasure activities should terminate as soon as the genital organs are ready for coitus. Once the vagina is well lubricated and the penis fully erect and charged, any delay in commencing coitus risks a decrease in the excitatory state rather than an augmentation of it. Much as one may have to give up a pleasure that is so enticing and alluring, one risks missing the boat at the other end of the voyage.

Sensuality is an element, too, in the promiscuous search for new sexual contacts and experiences. Surely the novelty doesn't lie in the different sexual responses of new partners, for the sexual response of the same partner is different on each occasion. The novelty of a new partner is primarily a sensual phenomenon, one that usually fails to provide the sought-for intense excitement. And much of the talk or writing about different sexual positions or approaches can be criticized on the same grounds.

What factors in the personality of an individual incline him to a sensual attitude rather than to a sexual one? On the basis of my clinical experience, I would name two factors. One is the lack of aliveness or feeling in the body; the other is a fear of the sexual orgasm. The search for excitation is typical of persons who are unalive, emotionally repressed, and physically unresponsive. Lacking an inner feeling of excitement, they find life boring and empty. Sex, like any other strong stimulant, gives them a temporary feeling of excitement or aliveness. They use sex as an alcoholic uses drink, compulsively and without regard for the sensibilities of others. Since the stimulation is only temporary, the pursuit of excitation is pushed to greater lengths. Forepleasure is extended to a point where it becomes a perversion, as Freud pointed out. If this is not enough, the sensualist seeks excitement by creating external situations of tension. He engages in sexual activity in exposed places or in the presence of third persons. The sexual act is performed before mirrors so that the visual excitement can increase the feeling. Special techniques to excite the partner are employed to gain a vicarious thrill.

The popular notion that the sensualist is bored because of a surfeit of sexual pleasure is completely erroneous. Quite the contrary is true. The more sexual pleasure a person has, the more discriminating is his attitude. No one I have ever met has complained of too much sexual pleasure. Appearances to the contrary, the sensualist is a person who is unable to enjoy the full pleasure of the sexual experience.

I am not a sexual moralist, and my intention is not to condemn these individuals. The sensualist needs such practices to gain sufficient excitement to make any sexual function possible. He needs sexuality, as we all do, to overcome the isolation and loneliness of his individual existence. However, his means defeat his end. The immoderate use of sensuality, like that of alcohol, leads only to disappointment and to a hangover. The sensualist wakes up the next day with no feeling of cleanliness, no feeling of fulfillment, no feeling of renewal or rebirth. His activity has been of no help in overcoming his characterological condition of deadness and boredom.

The second reason for the sensual attitude is fear of orgastic discharge, with its strong involuntary and convulsive movements. Reich called this fear "orgasm anxiety." It may seem strange that an individual should be afraid of pleasure, but if we bear in mind that pleasure, especially sexual pleasure, is associated with feelings of sin and guilt, this apparent strangeness is easily explained. Clinical studies of patients repeatedly show that pleasure anxiety is characteristic of neurotic persons. While sexual guilt has diminished considerably since Victorian times, it has by no means been eliminated. Beneath the surface of our present-day sexual sophistication, one can find deep layers of sexual guilt in most individuals. For reasons that will be discussed more fully in the next chapter, this guilt attaches more to orgastic sexuality than to sensual sexuality. It is my experience that sexual sophistication has lowered the barriers to sensuality without significantly affecting or relieving orgasm anxiety.

Patients sometimes experience orgasm anxiety directly, as shown by the following illustrations. One young woman remarked recently, "I have a climax, and it's just too much—so I don't move, I hold myself still. Even when the climax is beginning to come, I say, 'No, no, no!'" The "no" expresses the patient's fear of being overwhelmed by the orgastic feeling. Not moving, holding still, and becoming rigid in the face of the mounting sexual excitement are the means used to restrict the feeling and to combat the anxiety.

Here is another report (by a divorcée):

> "I started masturbating with my legs bent. At first, I had an almost overwhelming desire to straighten my legs out and make them rigid. I kept them bent, however, and soon felt a warm surge of excitement through the genital area. I could still feel some tension in the backs of my legs. It was hard to tell how much was suggestion from our discussions, but I do believe I got the feeling that I was afraid too much energy would come up from my legs and that orgasm, though slower, would be too powerful for me to handle if I didn't straighten my legs out."

Most patients unconsciously control the buildup of excitation so that it doesn't overwhelm them. I was told of one case where it did become overwhelming with a frightening result. This patient described a scene with her husband who was a rigidly inhibited individual: "With John, on two occasions I let myself go. I had a feeling of abandon, and John had a strange reaction. We had made love, but I wanted more, so I started to love him all over. John started to tingle over all his body and then felt numb and paralyzed. I became alarmed and called a doctor. By the time the doctor came John felt better and the doctor passed it off."

The orgasm is a reaction of the total being, the total body. Genital sexuality aims at this response. Sensuality is limited to the surface of the body and to the superficial aspects of the personality. I have said that the sensualist is afraid of a deep personal involvement, of a full commitment to sex and to love. In orgasm, love and sex unite in the strongest physical expression of these feelings. Is orgasm anxiety, then, a fear of love? At first glance, this is the logical deduction. Analysis of the character structure of the sensualist provides another explanation.

Love and sexuality are at the core of every living organism. They give its life meaning and provide the strongest

FIGURE 7

pleasure motivations for its behavior. Unfortunately, the upbringing of children in civilized communities is accompanied by authoritative attitudes that instill fear into the child and lead to the development of negative and hostile feelings. When these negative feelings are repressed, in the course of a necessary adjustment to family living, they form a layer of hate in the personality that encloses and seals off the deeper feelings of love and sexuality. The surface layer of the personality, which forms the content of consciousness, is polite, positive, and adjusted. This layering of the personality, in simplified form, can be shown diagramatically. It will help us greatly to understand the problem of sensuality. (See Figure 7.)

If the depth and intensity of the repressed hate are strong enough, the individual cannot reach the center of his being, where love and sex are located. He is limited to the surface and to a sensual approach to life. Any attempt to break through to the core of his being threatens to mobilize these powerful and repressed negative feelings, with their associated elements of fear and anxiety. Psychologically, orgasm anxiety stems from the anxiety associated with these repressed hostile feelings. Every psychotherapeutic effort, regardless of the form of therapy, aims to release these negative feelings in the controlled setting of the therapeutic situation. Physically, orgasm anxiety is the inability of rigid, tense, and contracted bodies to tolerate strong sexual excitation. Any kind of physical therapy that softens and resolves chronic muscle tension will help to increase sexual pleasure.

When the negative feelings invade the surface layer of the
personality, true sexual impotence develops: erective impotence in the male and frigidity in the female. It is relatively
simple in the case of a man to distinguish between erective
impotence and orgastic impotence. The first condition indicates a negative attitude toward the female in the surface
layer of the personality. In the second condition, the negative
feelings are repressed, so that while a sexual function is
possible, sexual satisfaction is missing. The situation in a
woman is complicated by the fact that her ability to perform
the sexual act is not dependent upon outwardly visible evidence of her desire. Her submission to the sexual partner
may or may not have any relation to her sexual feeling. Yet,
physical evidence of her sexual desire does exist. The lubrica-
tion of the vagina is comparable to the erection of the penis in
that both phenomena result from the congestion of the genital organs with blood. If a man who erects is not impotent, I
believe that it is not valid to describe a woman who lubri-
cates as frigid.

Probably no fiction has been more exploited in our culture
than the idea that a woman who does not desire sexual
relations is frigid. The chief exploiter of this fiction is the
man who tries unsuccessfully to seduce a woman. She may or
may not be frigid, but her response to one particular male or
several is no criterion of the presence or absence of sexual
feelings. Similarly, it is not true that the woman who does
have sexual relations is therefore not frigid. The confusion
stems from the equation of sexual feeling with sexual activity. I have treated a number of women who were promiscuous in their sexual activity precisely because they lacked
sexual feeling. Their promiscuity could be understood as a
search for sexual feeling. It terminated when the woman was
capable of experiencing spontaneous sexual excitement.
Promiscuity is the most common form of sensuality.

Among most sexologists today, there is a tendency to
describe a woman as frigid who does not achieve a sexual
orgasm. While it is valid to say that a woman who is frigid
will not achieve a sexual orgasm and that one who does
cannot be frigid, clarity of thinking requires that we distinguish between frigidity and orgastic impotence in a woman
and, similarly, between erective impotence and orgastic impotence in the man. Frigidity refers to the inability of a
woman to become aroused or excited and not to her inability
to discharge that excitement or have a vaginal orgasm. For

while these two are obviously related, they are not, strictly
speaking, the same thing. Women whom I considered warm
and tender persons lacked the ability to achieve satisfactory
orgasm, yet their sexual feelings were strong enough so that
one could not call them frigid. Orgasm requires a degree of
integrity in the personality and a kind of aggressive strength
that may be lacking in women who are otherwise soft, warm,
and yielding.

Words should be taken in their literal sense if they are to
serve as meaningful ways of communicating. Literally speaking, "frigidity" means "coldness," and a woman who is frigid
is sexually cold. But one cannot be cold sexually and warm
emotionally, and the woman who is sexually cold is also
emotionally cold. I have seen any number of these emotionally cold women, toward whom a sexual approach would be
extremely ill-advised. They are hard, rigid, and aggressive
personalities from whose appearance alone one could sense
the absence of soft, tender feelings. In other words, the
hardness or rigidity is so structured in the body that it is
readily apparent in behavior and movement. This physical
rigidity is the somatic equivalent of psychological attitudes of
negativity and hostility that extend to and embrace the whole
outer aspect of the personality. Even in these individuals, the
inner core of their being is alive with love and sexuality, but
it cannot come through to the surface. Since the sexual
feeling reaches consciousness only when the excitation charges the erotic areas on the surface of the body, such a
strongly "armored" individual, to use Reich's expression, is
incapable of sexual arousal. This is a true picture of the
frigid woman as distinguished from that of the woman who
does not achieve vaginal orgasm. The frigid woman may
engage in sexual activity; if she does, she is emotionally
unresponsive, vaginally dry, and mechanical in her body
movement.

On the superficial level, the sensualist is a warm person,
pleasure-loving and outgoing. The male is not erectively impotent, and the female is not frigid. The problem of the
sensualist stems from a fixation upon the oral stage of development. This fixation can be due to either oral deprivation
or overindulgence. Oral deprivation in childhood fixates development because it creates a feeling of unfulfillment of the
basic needs for body contact and oral-erotic gratification.
The lack of satisfaction in this phase of life is responsible for
the oral tendencies that are so evident in our culture: the

addiction to smoking and alcohol, passive attitudes in entertainment, the need for erotic stimulation, and the overindulgence in food. Exactly the same tendencies develop through the overindulgence of a child in his oral needs, since this is always done to prevent a child from growing up and becoming a sexually mature individual. Overindulgence is not an excess of love. The overindulgent mother yields to a child's demands because of her anxiety. She is overprotective and restricting. Her attitude has been described as "smothering." Its effect is to keep a child in a dependent relationship to her, which undermines the natural process of maturation.

The oral personality that develops through deprivation or through suffocation is an immature individual. He lacks the aggressive drive to do things for himself, and he lacks the aggressive concept necessary to achieve satisfaction. The absence of this aggressive component in his personality forces him into the sensual way of life. Sensuality is essentially the passive mode of experiencing pleasure. The sensualist is often pictured as reclining in a bower while someone hands him a bunch of luscious grapes. The only effort demanded of him is that he reach out and take one, but even this is sometimes omitted from the picture. This is the picture of an infant; and in his sexual activities, the sensualist plays the role of an infant. Oral activities—fellatio and cunnilingus—dominate his concept of the sexual function. The prevalence of these two forms of activity is a manifestation of sexual immaturity that parades as sexual sophistication.

Sexuality demands maturity of body and mind. The sexual individual as opposed to the sensual individual, the genital as opposed to the oral, is a person who stands on his own feet and acts aggressively to obtain the satisfaction of his needs. His life is oriented to achievement and fulfillment because he is unafraid to mobilize his aggression in the service of his desire. However, the responses of the sexual individual, whose focus is upon genital discharge, can also be distorted by pathological anxieties. If sensuality is a defense against the fear of sexuality, an exaggerated emphasis upon genitality may hide a fear of sensual feeling. This is the only interpretation that explains the behavior of men who avoid forepleasure and insist upon immediate genital contact and release. Many women complain about the lack of tenderness and sensitivity in husbands who act in this fashion. Superficially, it would appear that this attitude is normal. But women describe such sexual activity as mechanical and impersonal. The ejaculation is followed by an immediate withdrawal of interest and feeling from the woman. This is hardly what one would expect of a healthy person.

The fear of sensuality is the fear of emotional warmth and physical closeness. The sexual behavior of this person is compulsive and egoistic. His sexual activity is designed to prove his manhood in the face of an underlying fear of the female. Thus, he does it, and having done it, he escapes.

Exaggeration of the sexual attitude is characteristic of the rigid individual who is compulsive in all aspects of life. His achievements, like his sexual activities, provide an ego satisfaction, but never an emotional or physical satisfaction. His rigidity takes the pleasure out of satisfaction just as it takes the meaning out of sex. The rigid individual works, achieves, plays, and makes love because these are the "things to do," not because he is interested in the pleasures they can yield. In other words, he acts compulsively.

Rigidity is a defense against collapse—collapse into infantile behavior. To put it simply, the rigid person says, in effect, "I will show you that I am a man, not a baby." What he is trying to prove is that he is not a "crybaby." It is not difficult to guess at the background factors that produce this personality structure. In cutting off his desire to cry, the rigid character suppresses all feeling in general. By eliminating sensual pleasure, the rigid, compulsive individual destroys his opportunity for self-fulfillment.

The concept of orgastic potency is the most important development in the analytic understanding of sex and personality to be introduced since Freud. It was originally formulated by Wilhelm Reich in 1927. According to Reich, the orgastically potent individual does not suffer from a neurosis. The reasoning behind this conclusion is that the orgasm, if it is full and complete, discharges all the excess energy of the organism; thus there is no energy left to maintain the neurotic conflict or the neurotic repression.

It can be shown clinically that every emotionally healthy individual is orgastically potent; that is, he consistently derives full gratification from his sexual experiences. In this respect, Reich's theory is rather widely accepted today, for it would be inconceivable to label a person emotionally healthy if he lacked this capacity. The corollary proposition, however, has met with considerable argument. Is the person who is neurotically afflicted incapable of orgastic experience? Reich and his followers have steadfastly answered this question in the affirmative. The early Freudian analysts and many others have pointed to the fact that some of their neurotic patients claim to experience orgastic satisfaction in the sexual act. What is one to believe?

Reich was led to his conclusion by two discoveries that he made in the course of his analytic work. First, he found that only to the degree that a patient's sexual function improved as a result of therapy was he able to hold on to and integrate the fruits and experiences of his analysis. Second, he found a positive correlation between neurotic disturbances and the lack of sexual fulfillment. This meant that there could be no neurosis in the presence of a satisfactory sexual life. The confusion and disputes that arose over this concept stemmed from different ideas about what constitutes a "satisfactory sexual life." One school of thought then held and still holds that every climax is an orgasm. However, Reich restricted the meaning of the term "orgasm" to total release and fulfillment. Between these two schools of thought, there may be a world of difference.

In part, this difference may be explained by the fact that the orgastic experience varies among different individuals and in the same individual under different circumstances. This should be self-evident, since no two people can have identical reactions and since no one person reacts the same way all the time. An orgasm can thus vary in intensity. At one time, it can be a sublime experience of the ecstatic; at another, it can be experienced as a solid feeling of satisfaction as the body lets go. All orgastic experiences have one element in common that, I believe, provides the clue to the understanding of this phenomenon. That element is the physical feeling of satisfaction. A sexual release, if it is to merit the term "orgasm," must be physically satisfying. "Climax" implies no such element. A premature ejaculation in a man is considered a climax, which, in fact, it is, but it is not felt as satisfying. It is often just the opposite. A woman may reach a clitoral climax, the so-called clitoral orgasm, with some feeling of release but no feeling of satisfaction.

We are dealing here with subjective experiences that are not open to objective evaluation. Who is to say whether an experience is satisfactory or unsatisfactory except the individual who undergoes that experience? In this area, the statements of individuals are very unreliable. There is too much self-deception; in addition, most people are unwilling to reveal their failures and shortcomings. Most patients assert at

the beginning of therapy that their sexual responses and
experiences are satisfactory, only to retract these statements
later on the basis of new insights. Too many men regard
sexual experiences as satisfactory when they feel that they
have satisfied the women. Others substitute ego satisfaction
for physical gratification and regard seduction as a satisfactory experience in itself, quite apart from their own physical
reactions. And many women are satisfied to lie close to and
be held by a man they care for, even if there was no climax
at all.

If personal disclosures are not to be trusted, can one rely
upon the physical reactions of the individual? There is a large
group of sexologists who believe that any involuntary or
convulsive reaction in an act of sex constitutes an orgasm.
The orgasm is a convulsion, but it is a special kind of
convulsive reaction. Twitches, jerks, spasmodic contractions
of the body should be regarded as defenses against orgastic
movements rather than synonymous with them. They do not
produce the physical sensation of satisfaction, although they
are not necessarily unpleasurable. Sighs, cries, moans, and
groans tell little except that something is happening. Aside
from the utterances of surprise that often occur as climax
approaches and the orgasm overtakes one, a satisfactory
sexual experience can be a quiet, relaxed but intense affair.
Moans and groans betray suffering rather than pleasure and
should be so interpreted.

This leaves only the idea of satisfaction as the basic criterion of sexual orgasm. The person who has experienced an
orgasm is satisfied. He is not irritable, depressed, argumenta-
tive, restless, or moody. I'll never forget one patient, himself
an analyst, who asked me about his wife. In the sexual act,
she moaned and sighed and gave every indication that she
was having an orgasm. To his point-blank question, she
answered that she did. But, he asked me, if this was true,
how could she be so angry upon waking in the morning? Why
was she so irritable with the children? So short of patience?
Why didn't she feel contented, satisfied? I am sure that other
husbands have been puzzled by this contradiction in their
wives. I surmised that my patient's wife had not had an
orgasm. It was either pretense, not beyond a woman, or
ignorance. His wife consulted with me some time later, and I
found that my suspicions were correct. She, however, had
come to complain about her husband.

The ability to obtain satisfaction is the hallmark of the

mature, integrated, and effective personality. Aside from the truly frigid woman, almost everyone can find some pleasure in sex. The sensual approach is oriented toward pleasure rather than satisfaction. Satisfaction implies a goal-directed effort and the total commitment to that goal. It can be obtained from almost any activity, but only if one commits one's entire energy and feeling to that activity, whether it be playing a game of tennis, writing a book, or remodeling a home. And this is true even if the outcome is not always favorable. Win or lose, having committed yourself totally, you can only feel satisfied with your effort—and yourself. Anything less than a total commitment cannot provide the physical feeling of satisfaction that is directly related to the mobilization and expenditure of all one's available energy and feeling in the activity.

These principles apply to sexual activity. In the absence of a total commitment to the sexual act and to the person who is one's partner, a satisfactory experience cannot be expected. Clearly, any diversion of attention such as listening to music or thinking of business while having sexual relations is such an obvious lack of commitment that it merits no discussion. But sexual fantasies during the sex act also indicate an inability to make a full commitment to the sexual partner. Often the holding back is unconscious. One can gauge the commitment only by the result. Subjectively, the degree of commitment can be perceived by the extent to which the body is suffused and charged with sexual feeling. I shall say more about this in the following chapter. Only if the sexual feeling and movement embrace the total body and total being will the experience of climax provide the satisfaction of orgasm.

The orgastic experience can vary in the same person. Even the fullness of commitment can differ in intensity or depth of feeling. One doesn't give oneself over to every activity with the same intensity of feeling. In its greatest depths, the sexual response touches and actively involves the heart. This is not a metaphor. At rare moments, one can feel the heart respond. This is in addition to the normal tachycardia, or rapid heartbeat, that occurs as the respiration deepens and the climax approaches. When the heart responds in the sexual climax, the deepest and fullest feeling of opening up and release has been achieved. And since the response literally comes from the heart, it can be said that sexuality has been experienced in the very center of one's being. This is the deepest meaning of love.

In Chapters 2 and 3, I described the relationship of sex to love. In analyzing that relationship, I pointed to the connection between the heart and the genitals via the blood. Sex was viewed as an expression of love. And so it is, but only to the degree that the individual experiences pleasure and satisfaction in sex. If this is true, the fullest, deepest, and most satisfying expression of love in sex is the response of orgasm.

I have used the term "satisfaction" to describe the quality of pleasure of the orgastic experience. Satisfactory it truly is, but this term is inadequate to convey the full extent of this pleasure. The orgasm is not only pleasurable, it is joyful. It is joyful because it is free, unrestrained, unlimited, and spontaneous. It has the same quality as the joyfulness of children's responses: it comes directly from the heart. In orgasm, the adult expresses the joy of the child within. For this reason, the orgasm is the greatest experience of joy available to adults.

If the activities of the sensualist are characterized by the search for excitement and pleasure, the truly sexual person is known by his joyfulness.

11

The Sexual Orgasm

The preceding chapter dealt with the psychological concomitants of orgasm. I emphasized that the orgastic experience is perceived as a sensation of physical satisfaction based upon the total commitment of the self to the sexual action. The physical reaction that is the basis for this feeling of satisfaction is the participation of the total body in the involuntary pleasurable movements of sexual discharge. This emphasis upon the total body distinguishes heterosexuality from homosexuality and the kind of climax that is limited to the genitals from the climax that Wilhelm Reich described as orgasm.

While this distinction is valid and important, it is, nevertheless, incomplete. Since every sexual climax has some elements of the orgastic experience, it would be more correct to speak of partial and full orgasms. A partial orgasm is by its nature limited and unfulfilling and is not experienced as physically satisfying. It is, however, a form of sexual release, and temporarily, at least, it abates the sexual tension of the organism. For women who have never experienced any form of climax in the sexual act, the partial orgasm is often a rewarding and revealing experience.

It is easy to make verbal distinctions; it is difficult to apply them to specific cases. No one but the individual involved can state definitely whether or not he or she has experienced an orgasm in the sexual act. The perception of orgasm requires the subjective experience of satisfaction. But it frequently happens that the individual involved is not himself clear

193

about the quality of his subjective experience. The problem is sometimes compounded by the presence of ego satisfactions that may be unrelated to the physical sensations involved. Thus a woman may derive a certain satisfaction from the fact that a special man has succumbed to her charms, or, what is even more common, a man may get a feeling of satisfaction from a successful seduction. Even if one makes due allowance for these possible distortions, another source of confusion exists. Subjective states or feelings are not commensurable. The term "satisfaction" can embrace many degrees of feeling. The orgasm, even if full and satisfying, is not the same for different people; it will vary with their personalities. The orgasm also varies in the same individual according to the intensity of the initial feeling, the special time, place, and circumstances for any particular sexual relation. Nevertheless, one has to rely upon the feeling of satisfaction as the only criterion of orgastic response.

To facilitate our discussion of the orgastic experience, a brief description of the feelings and movements that are part of the normal sexual act follows. The preliminary erotic contacts subsumed under the heading of forepleasure prepare the way for the coital act. They serve to mobilize the diffused body sensations and make them available for the climactic experience. They focus the excitation upon the genitals and prepare them for the consummation of the sexual act. However, if forepleasure is unduly prolonged the vagina tends to lose its excitation and becomes dry, while the penis becomes overexcited and primed for discharge. If the urge to penetrate is absent in the male, it may indicate a fear of the vagina. In the absence of a sexual disturbance, the excitement of forepleasure naturally leads to the desire for the closest possible physical contact between the two individuals. This can be achieved only by the normal act of penile penetration of the vagina. In the course of penetration, the sensory pleasure of contact increases sharply until penetration is full and complete. Soon after this is accomplished, there is a leveling off of the excitatory state—love has achieved its first objective; the two are as close together as possible.

If one inquires into the feelings of the man at this time, one learns that he feels at home. There is a feeling of belonging that is experienced as a sense of relaxation. In *Thalassa: A Theory of Genitality*, Sandor Ferenczi postulates that the act of sex is, for the man, a symbolic return to the womb, his original home. The womb, according to Ferenczi, represents the sea, in which life first started and from which it emerged long ago. The return to the womb is literally true for the sperm cells. The feelings of the woman are quite different. She has no identification with the man in his symbolic return to the womb. Several women whom I questioned said that they felt complete, filled. Others said that they felt that they now had the man inside them, that he was now part of them. This also gave them a relaxed, contented feeling. If in the act of penetration, the man symbolically returns to the womb, the woman symbolically is the womb that receives him.

This feeling of relaxation, as after a journey ended, is only an interlude. It is followed by an increasing urgency, to bring the experience to a climax. The situation calls forth the specific sexual movements that will give rise to new sensations and stronger impulses. To the experience of sensory pleasure is added the new experience of kinesthetic pleasure derived from the sexual movements.

During the first phase of coitus, the sexual movements are under ego control and are completely voluntary. At the beginning, they are slow, gentle, and relaxed. Generally, the movements of the man dominate during this period, but this may change if the woman assumes the more active role. The position and rhythm that the partners adopt should be whatever suits their individual needs and mood at the time. I shall proceed on the assumption that the man is on top of the woman and takes the more active role. In this case, the woman tends to be passive until a rhythmic pattern is established by the man with which she can harmonize her movements. Before this happens, however, the man may interrupt his movements either for a short period of rest or for an adjustment of position. Interruption at this time does not interfere with the course of the excitation, which tends to remain at a fairly steady level. But interruptions of the sexual act can diminish the final pleasure if they interfere with the establishment of a rhythmic pattern of movement.

The voluntary movements serve to unify the body so that the rhythm of breathing and pelvic thrust are synchronized. If there are no inhibitions, the forward thrust of the pelvis coincides with the exhalation of the breath. In the course of the voluntary movements, the man attempts to "ground" his body by making the forward movement of the pelvis with his legs while digging his feet into the bed. The shift of emphasis to the lower half of the body prepares the way for the involuntary pelvic movements. During the voluntary phase, the consciousness of both parties is directed toward the perception of pleasure in the genital areas and to the quality of the pelvic movement.

Before a definite rhythm can be established and maintained, the movement of the pelvis must become full and free. Pushing the pelvis rather than swinging the pelvis will prevent the involuntary movements from occurring. The kinesthetic pleasure of sexuality depends on the quality of the pelvic movement. Civilized human beings are ordinarily restricted in their body movements. Compared with primitive people, their hips are more bound and their pelvic musculature is more tense. This restraint of pelvic motility must be overcome if the act of coitus is to be fully satisfactory. The pelvis should move with the smoothness of a well-oiled hinge but not independently, like the free swing of a dangling leg. In the man, the impulse of the movement comes from the legs and is fully ego controlled. While the man is "grounded" through his legs, the woman in the supine position is "grounded" on the man through the contact between her legs and his body. This allows her movements to become synchronized with his.

The phase of voluntary movement ends when a definite rhythm has become established that harmonizes the movements of both partners. This phase occupies the longest time period of the sexual act. Its function is to involve as much as possible of the body in the sexual movements. It prepares the way for the transfer of control over movement from the head to the pelvis. It smoothes the transition from ego function to id function. This phase should end when these objectives have been reached. It terminates earlier in a premature ejaculation because of the inability to sustain the mounting tension.

At this point, the tempo of the sexual movements increases. It is accompanied by the desire on the part of the man and woman for deeper penetration and greater friction. It begins as a voluntary action by the male initiated when he feels that he is ready for the ascent to the climax. As the tempo increases, the pelvic movements suddenly take on an involuntary quality and induce a deeper response from the body. There is an accompanying strong increase in genital sensation as the friction between penis and vagina is intensified. Melting sensations are felt in the pelvis as an immediate preliminary to the discharge.

Orgasm commences with the contraction of the bulbocavernosi in the man and in the woman. These muscles surround the base of the penis in the man and the introitus (opening) of the vagina in the woman. The orgasm is experienced as the opening of a dam, with the release downward of a flood of feeling while the body convulses as a unit in response to each involuntary forward swing of the pelvis. Feelings of melting and streaming downward now pervade the whole body. If the acme is intense enough, the sensation of heat increases and is perceived as a glow in the pelvis and as an overall body sensation of lumination. When ejaculation begins in the man, his excitement mounts and remains at a high peak for a few moments. During this phase the orgasm may be experienced as "flying," "spinning," or some similar sensation. The orgastic experience of the woman parallels that of the man in every respect except for the sensations of pulsatory ejaculation. Ejaculation is produced by the contractions of the smooth, involuntary musculature of the prostate and seminal vesicles. It consists of pulsatory squirts of the semen. The woman experiences the ejaculation as an added stimulus to her pleasure.

The orgasm in the male ordinarily consists of two involuntary responses: the response of the total body in its convulsive reaction and the ejaculatory response. It is a matter of record that one can have an orgastic discharge without the ejaculation of semen (Kinsey). It is also known that one can ejaculate without the involuntary body reaction described above (Reich). Each in itself would be only part of a total orgasm. If neither of the involuntary reactions takes place and the semen flows out instead of being discharged in pulsatory squirts, it must be regarded as an inability on the part of the man to achieve orgastic release.

In the woman, the counterpart of ejaculation is the contraction of the smooth musculature surrounding the vagina. This action is perceived by the man as a "pumping" of the penis. Thus there are two involuntary responses in the woman that combine to give her the experience of a total orgasm: the convulsive reaction of the whole body, similar to the man's and the rhythmic contraction of the muscles surrounding the vagina and in the pelvic floor. If the woman reaches her climax at the same time as the man, both responses are intensified.

After the climax, the excitation subsides rapidly, while the feelings of glow and satisfaction continue for an indefinite time. The involuntary movements may persist for several moments; then relaxation, frequently leading to the desire for sleep, takes over.

At the acme, there tends to occur a loss of ego consciousness. This is a temporary eclipse of the ego and is not to be confused with a feeling of abandonment. One doesn't become unconscious in the process of orgasm. It would be more correct to say that the individual tends to lose consciousness of the self. The self disappears in the fusion with the love object: love has achieved its final goal. There is not only a feeling of complete unity and merger with the partner, but also a feeling of being part of the total pulsating universe. This latter feeling supports Reich's idea that in orgasm, man finds his identification with cosmic processes.

If the first stage of coitus can be regarded as a symbolic return to the womb by the man, the second stage can be considered to represent the emergence from the womb. In its very intensity, the orgasm makes one think of the birth process. Man is reborn through orgasm. If this is speaking figuratively, let us not forget that orgasm is often experienced as a rebirth. One feels renewed and refreshed through orgasm. The whole act of sex can be viewed for the man as a symbolic return to the womb and rebirth. Now, what of the woman's role? Since her first stage is a filling up, her second stage is an emptying. Whereas the man is reborn in orgasm, the woman has given birth to him, symbolically, of course. This may explain why some women actually experience the process of birth as an orgasm. Women have related that they found the capacity to have orgasms only after having given birth to a child.

The confusion that exists in sexology about the nature of the orgasm has its roots in the failure of most students of the sexual function to appreciate the importance of movement in the orgastic experience. Attention is focused upon the sensory element in sexuality almost to the neglect of its motor component. It is generally assumed that the function of the sexual movements is to increase the friction between the genital organs. It is not generally appreciated that the sensory elements of contact and friction serve to provide the excitation for the movement. The sensation of orgasm is a function of the movement; that is, if the movement is stopped, the orgastic sensation immediately disappears. Contact and friction alone, such as when the penis is masturbated manually or orally to climax, can produce ejaculation but never orgasm.

On the other hand, the orgastic feeling can be derived from movement alone. For example, a woman can reach an orgasm under conditions in which contact with the penis is reduced to a minimum. If the man has reached his climax and the penis has shrunk to its flaccid state and even slipped out of the vagina, the woman can bring herself to orgasm by continuing her movements until the involuntary reaction occurs. Among animals such as the dog, it can be observed that one animal masturbating upon another is capable of achieving a release through movement even though there is no contact of the genital organ with the body of the other animal. What is the special quality of the sexual movements that gives them this property?

The answer to this question is that only the involuntary sexual movements involve the total body in the feeling of the action. Voluntary movements, no matter how strong, are by their very nature subject to the control of the ego. This controlling force, the ego, exists as an entity apart from the movements. The analogy that comes to mind is that of a rider on a horse. The rider is carried along by the movement of the horse, but he does not share the kinesthetic sensations that the horse experiences. Involuntary movements are expressions of the body on the primitive level of functioning in which the ego is reduced to the role of participant rather than director. This is the domain of the id, which includes the ego as part of itself. On this level of functioning the rider is part of the horse. In the orgasm, the ego is eclipsed and absorbed in the id.

The specific property of the involuntary sexual movements is that they involve the whole body in the final release. Orgasm is a pleasurable convulsion of the whole body. The full orgasm, as Reich defined it, is the result of "the involuntary contraction of the organism and the complete discharge of the excitation." Not all involuntary movements involve the total body. Many convulsive movements may occur during climax that do not discharge the excitation. I referred earlier to twitches, vibrations, and spasmodic contractions that are defenses against orgastic release. These movements do not lead to satisfaction, because they are the result of two forces: one seeking to let go, the other trying to hold back. This situation is the same as that which would develop if at the moment one let go of a bowstring, one also attempted to hold it back. The bow would quiver, but the arrow would fall impotently to the ground.

The analogy of the bow is strictly appropriate to the sexual act. The bow and arrow have been used as a symbol of love since ancient times. The arrow represents the male genital organ; the bow corresponds to the body of the individual. Each of the pelvic movements can be considered equivalent to the flexing and relaxing of the bow preliminary to the flight of the arrow (sexual release). The flexing and relaxing are analogous to the ego-controlled voluntary movements of the first phase of the sexual act. Each retraction of the pelvis charges the organism (places more tension on the bow). The higher one allows the excitement to mount before release, the greater will be the pleasure of orgasm (the greater the tension of the bow, the greater the flight of the arrow).

In terms of its movement, the body is structured like a bow. In this analogy, the shaft of the bow corresponds to the backbone, together with its ligaments and accessory muscles. The bowstring is functionally identical with the large lumbodorsal muscles of the back, which act to hyperextend the backbone. The force that extends the body is the strength and intensity of the feeling. To see the human body in action as a bow, one has only to watch a baseball pitcher throw a ball. The power of his motion stems from the hyperextension and release of the back, to which is added a whiplike action of the arm. In this action, the power of the back is transmitted through the arm to the hand and finally to the ball. The gallop of the dog illustrates the principle of the bow in reverse. The dog's back is flexed as the four legs come together, and then extended to provide the force that, flowing into the hind legs, moves the animal forward. When the body functions according to the principle of the bow, it acts as an integrated unit. If the body lacks unity and integration, its ability to function according to this principle is lost. The sexual problems of a neurotic personality can be illustrated in terms of the principle of the bow. The chronic rigidity of the compulsive individual (with his stiff backbone) would act to sharply decrease the flexibility of the bow and to reduce the power of the release. The weakness of the oral character would have a similar effect because of the limpness of the bow shaft. Any break in the integrity of the body structure is equivalent to the fracture of the bow shaft. It is not hard to visualize the resulting impotence of the action of the bow.

For the human body to function as a bow, the two ends of the body that correspond to the ends of the bow shaft must be sufficiently anchored to support the tension. The upper end of the body (bow) is anchored in the functions of the ego. The lower end of the body is anchored through the contact of the legs with the ground. An individual so anchored is entrenched in reality. He has his feet on the ground, his head on his shoulders, and feeling in his body. If these anchorages don't hold against the increasing tension, a premature release occurs. The strength of the ego determines, therefore, the height of tension and excitation that can be reached.

Sexologists are confused about the role of the ego in sexuality. Edrita Fried, for example, believes that the individual with an underdeveloped ego can "let go" easier and, therefore, can more easily achieve orgasm. But what value is there in "letting go" if no significant tension or excitation has been created? This is commonly overlooked. Another possible source of confusion is about the role of the legs in the sexual act. How can a man ground his feet when he is lying on top of a woman in bed? The answer is rather simple. One can either dig one's toes into the mattress to gain an anchorage or use a footboard or wall as a means of support for the drive. If the legs lie without dynamic tension, the pelvic movement takes on the quality of "pushing," which localizes sensation in the genitals to the exclusion of the body.

The principle of the bow in the human organism is the physical mechanism through which the reality principle operates. Body movements that are motivated according to the reality principle are purposeful, controlled, coordinated, and effective. These movements involve the total body as a unit. In contrast, the movements of an infant, who functions according to the pleasure principle, are random, haphazard, and uncoordinated. An infant can tolerate no tension; his body reacts immediately to every stress placed upon it. His movements are not goal directed or consciously controlled. This is not to say that the random movements of an infant have no meaning. The meaning has to be sought in terms of what is happening within the infant; it cannot be determined by reference to external goals. This analysis of movement can be used to show the difference between the concept of motility and that of mobility.

Motility describes the spontaneous motions of the living body; it includes such involuntary actions as breathing, crying, laughing, and so on. These spontaneous responses are conditioned by the fluidity of the living body, which allows the waves of feeling or excitation to flow through the body. An infant is extremely motile; every feeling is immediately expressed in appropriate body movements. On the other hand, he lacks the stability and rigidity that would allow him to stand on his own legs and move effectively toward the satisfaction of his needs or desires. Motility is closely related to the expression of feeling; it is the biological basis for the pleasure principle. Mobility describes movements which are consciously motivated and goal directed. Generally, it refers to the displacement of a body in space. Thus, a very young infant, while highly motile, is relatively immobile. But an adult may be mobile, yet deficient in motility if the spontaneous expression of feeling is blocked.

The voluntary phase of sexuality as a goal-directed genital activity is a function of the mature organism. It requires mobility, stability, and tonicity. This is the principle of the bow, which I have described above. It explains the dynamics that underlie the voluntary movements of the sexual act. The involuntary movements that lead to orgasm do not follow this principle, since they are not ego controlled. They are an expression of the motility of the body, since they aim, like the movements of the infant, at the immediate discharge of tension.

Again, the analogy of the bow is helpful. The voluntary movements, as I said earlier, correspond to the repeated flexing of the bow to increase the tension. The involuntary movements result from the "letting go." The convulsion of the body is the reaction of "letting go." Persons who are afraid to "let go" don't have orgasms.

The involuntary movements follow directly from the voluntary movements, as smoothly as night follows day. They develop spontaneously from the voluntary ones after a certain intensity of feeling has been reached. This happens when the feeling of excitation in the body becomes so strong that it overwhelms the ego. The excitation takes possession of the body and mind of the individual and reverses his normal orientation. Whereas the voluntary movements are ego directed, the involuntary movements are under the control of the pelvic sensations. It is as if a center of excitation and feeling develops in the pelvis that is strong enough to overthrow the hegemony of the conscious ego. Before orgasm, the flow of excitation and energy was from the head to the genitals. Once orgasm begins, this direction of flow is reversed. The excitation then flows backward from the pelvic area to the body. Reich described this reversal of flow as one of the criteria of the full orgasm. The normal pattern of movement can be expressed in the phrase "dog wags tail." In orgasm, this pattern changes into "tail wags dog." The loss of ego consciousness in the orgasm is the result of the take-over of the command of the body by a deeper life process. In orgasm, the id asserts its ultimate authority. It can be compared to an earthquake that shatters man's confidence in his ego and makes him realize how dependent he is upon the stability of the earth. It is interesting to note that Hemingway described the experience of orgasm as the perception that "the earth moved." In the orgasm, the self, not the ego, is realized on its deepest level.

The organism is by its very nature an isolated individual. No matter how much it may feel part of its surroundings, it exists within the closed system of its limiting membrane, the skin. Its motility and mobility are dependent upon a free and renewable supply of energy contained within an enclosed body. It has been previously pointed out that every animal organism needs to give up its individuality, to overcome its sense of aloneness and apartness, to become part of the greater whole. It accomplishes this through sexuality, by means of which it joins with another organism and loses its sense of isolation and incompleteness. But for this to happen fully the very quality of its movements, which is inherent in its individuality, has to change. It has to move in a different way, in a mode of movement that is part of a larger movement, a kind of movement that goes back to its manner of origin and creation.

One can also overcome the sense of aloneness and incompleteness by certain passive procedures. Meditation, religious isolation, self-communion, and mysticism are some of the practices employed. These passive maneuvers involve an abandonment of the ego, a surrender of self-consciousness. They have a place in the framework of an active life, but they cannot become a substitute for life. Passivity is not the natural mode of existence. By union with another organism, an excitation is set up that is capable of *moving the organism* at the level of its biological foundation. In the passive techniques this does not happen; the experience is one of inner calm and peace. The distinction is between active and passive, between partial and total. Any response that actively involves the total organism is perceived as a "moving experience." In this feeling of *being moved*, we sense ourselves as part of the universal. Precisely because religious communion can move us (in the emotional sense), we experience it as a valid expression of our link with the universe or God. Sexual orgasm is a deeper, more biological experience of man's unity with nature and the universe.

The following statement is one woman's experience of this phenomenon; her description is concise and informative: "Once I had an experience during intercourse which was so different from anything else that I don't think I will ever be satisfied until I experience it again. During this experience, without any effort or trying on my part, my body was moved from within, so to speak, and everything was right. There was rhythmic movement and a feeling of ecstasy at being part of something much greater than myself and finally of reward, of real satisfaction and peace."

Glow and lumination are other aspects of this phenomenon that bear some resemblance to cosmic events. The full orgasm is generally accompanied by a feeling of glow that is a "higher," perhaps hotter, stage of the phenomenon of sexual heat. If the intensity and extent of the orgasm reach a high peak, the glow may extend over the whole body and be experienced as a feeling of lumination. The external manifestation of this feeling of lumination is seen as a radiance that is the natural expression of a person in love. Glow and lumination are properties of heavenly bodies. The person in love feels that he is in heaven. In love, the individual transcends the experience of his finite existence; in orgasm, he transcends the feeling of his physical existence.

The orgastic experience has other meanings. It is experienced as a rebirth and as a renewal. There is some explanation for this experience in the feelings of melting and flow that precede and are also part of the orgastic reaction. Structure, Reich once said, is frozen motion. Certainly, it is the antithesis of movement and is therefore, in one sense, the antagonist of life. Life begins with very little structure, in the form of a fertilized ovum. It ends when the energy of the organism is incapable of sustaining and moving the final structure that the organism has developed in the course of its life. When rigidities are dissolved in orgasm, one is to that extent being reborn, as the perception of that experience indicates. Orgasm is also experienced as a creative event. Sometimes it results in the creation of a new life, the conception of a new individual. But at all times it results in the creation of a new and fresh vision of life.

I have said that in orgasm, one reverts to the kind of movement that lay at the origin of one's being. It is a sensation that is experienced as overwhelming, as if one is being *moved* by life's deepest force. In normal daily activities, the movements of the individual are ego controlled and ego directed. Activities are purposeful. The average person walks to get to a destination. When one observes people walking in a city, one is often strongly impressed by the mechanical quality of the movement. Both in ourselves and in others, we frequently sense a lack of pleasure in walking. We are aware only of an urgency to get somewhere. Of course, as soon as one goal is reached, another is envisioned. On the cultural level, this continued striving is ennobled with the term "progress." The pleasure of moving, the feeling of joy in the coordination and gracefulness of bodily motion, is missing from our normal daily movements. We are so ego conscious that we have lost consciousness of the self, represented by the body in motion.

Less civilized peoples manifest in their movements a different quality of the relationship between the ego and the bodily self. When one watches a West Indian woman walk, for example, one is aware of the ease and freedom of her movements. Her hips sway loosely, her legs move effortlessly, while the upper half of the body rides gracefully upon this carriage. The native woman feels no compulsion to arrive anywhere on time. Most people in our culture move compulsively. What strikes us most about the walk of the West Indian woman is its sexual quality. It is sexual not because it is sexually provocative, but because it looks alive, vital, animal-like. It is sexual because the woman is conscious of her body, conscious of her movements, and identifies with the sexual nature of her being.

Sexuality is the strongest link to our animal nature. The animal knows no goals other than the satisfaction of its needs. It labors under no compulsion to progress. It finds its pleasure in the activity of the moment. The natural state of the animal, as Dostoevsky so charmingly pointed out in the *Brothers Karamazov,* is one of joyfulness. In some respects, we are more than animals. We have gained the knowledge of good and evil, and we order our lives according to values. We have a consciousness of ourselves and others, of space and time, which relates us to the gods. But in another sense, we are only a different kind of animal—superior if you look at our cultural achievements, inferior if you see our bestiali-

ties and our cruelties. In love, we are human; in sexuality, we
are animal. Let us not forget that the former grows out of
the latter. Sexual activity has no goal other than pleasure.
One "goes" nowhere with sexual movements. In sexuality as
in children's play—one gives oneself over to the excitement
of moving and feeling. In this state, we are closest to being
pure animal, but we are also closest to experiencing pure
joy.

The ability to let the body move the person is the capacity
to have the orgastic experience. But one cannot let this
happen unless one is secure in one's body and identified with
it. Bodily security as contrasted with ego security depends
upon the integrity and coordination of the body movements.
It is based upon the strength of one's contact with the
ground. Just as a tree has its security in its roots, so a man
has his security in his legs. To feel "grounded" means to be
rooted in the earth and in the animal functions. It is synonymous with the ability to stand on one's feet and to feel them.
Identification with the body requires that one accept its
animal nature, that is, not to be above it. Any feeling of
disgust or revulsion about bodily functions destroys this sense
of identification. Above all, one has to accept the sexual
nature of being.

If I seem to emphasize the physical, the animal, and the
sexual sides of our nature, it is only because these aspects of
our being have been denigrated in our culture. The human
being who is not also an animal is inhuman, but the human
being who is only animal is infrahuman. The strength of the
body cannot be divorced from the strength of the mind. The
security of the body is as much dependent on the functions of
the ego as it is on the functions of the legs. Emotional health
represents the ability to be in two places at once; that is, one
has to have the strength to tolerate the tension of a polar
situation. When I stand before an audience giving a lecture, I
am aware of the audience and aware of myself. I am in
touch with the audience and in touch with myself. Yet one
knows that one cannot be in two places at one time. It is
possible, however, to oscillate the attention so rapidly that
there is no apparent break in the dual perceptions. The
attention revolves like a rotating beacon, now directed inward, then outward, and inward and outward again. If this is
done smoothly, there is no disruption in the feeling of contact
between the inner self and the outer world.

Similarly, one is in contact with the body and the ground

at one moment and with the thinking and sensing self at another. Here, too, the oscillation of attention must be quick enough to avoid a lapse in the continuity of perception and awareness. It is in this sense that one can speak of a healthy person as being a sexual person. It means that the healthy person is a thinking individual and a moving animal organism at the same time. It means that his movements also partake of this dual relationship. They are sexual, animal-like, and grounded below; they are poised, controlled, and goal directed above. If these experiences are part of one's daily life, then the transition from ego control and voluntary movement to the strong involuntary movements of orgasm is easy and not frightening. Otherwise, the orgasm looms as a danger equal to the threat of being whirled into space at the end of a rocket. Sexuality is not a leisure or part-time activity. It is a way of being.

12

Orgastic Impotence
in the Male

Sexual disturbances can be divided, roughly, into two categories: (1) those involving the diminution or loss of sexual desire and (2) those manifested by the inability to achieve orgasm. Included in the first category are the problems of erective impotence in the man and frigidity in the woman. The second category comprises such disturbances as premature ejaculation and delayed ejaculation without any feeling of climax in the man and, on the part of the woman, the inability to reach a climax or to reach one only through clitoral stimulation. The justification for this division is that the problems included in the first category represent disturbances of arousal and sensory response; while orgastic impotence, or the inability to achieve a satisfactory climax, is basically a disturbance in the motoric aspects of the sexual function, owing to a deficiency either in motility or in mobility. But the two aspects of the sexual function, sensory and motor, are parts of the unitary response. Any decrease on the sensory level diminishes the final response; any limitation in motility reduces the sensory experience. My emphasis upon the problem of orgastic impotence is based on clinical findings which show that the anxieties and fears associated with full surrender in the sexual act are primarily responsible for disturbances in arousal and desire. This chapter will be devoted, therefore, to an analysis of these fears and anxieties and their relation to orgastic impotence in the male.

Two criteria determine whether a climax amounts to an orgasm or not. Subjectively, the experience of climax must include the physical sensation of satisfaction. Objectively, the physical response at climax must involve the total body in a

unified and integrated reaction. Even with these criteria, the
question of orgasm may be difficult to decide in any particular case. "Satisfaction" is not an absolute term like the grade
75 on an examination. At one end of the scale, there is a
clear-cut feeling of disappointment and dissatisfaction. At the
other end, the experience of climax is one of fulfillment and
ecstasy. These extremes of feeling are clearly perceived.
Somewhere in between, satisfaction fades imperceptibly into
disappointment and the nature of the response is indetermi-
nate. Similarly, the point at which the total body becomes
involved in the sexual response may be difficult to determine
in some cases. The problems involved in orgastic impotence
are most evident in extreme cases.

Disturbances of orgastic potency are intimately related to
the fear of the sexual movements. The idea of moving in the
sexual act is identified with many of the taboos and anxieties
that are associated with sexuality. Some time ago, I treated a
young woman who, among other difficulties, complained of a
lack of sexual satisfaction. She had never experienced an
orgasm, although she had been rather promiscuous in her
sexual activities. To help her, I gave her a copy of an article
that I had written for the *Encyclopedia of Sexual Behavior*
entitled "Movement and Feeling in Sex." Her response to this
article revealed many of the distortions that surround the
concept and the function of sex in our culture. She wrote
down her thoughts as they occurred to her while reading this
material, in the form of a dialogue with herself:

> Began to glance at your article—didn't like the title
> "Movement and Feeling in Sex." Movement! That both-
> ers me. Feeling is fine—but movement. Movement is
> embarrassing. It's an open commitment of intent for
> pleasure.
> So why not openly admit intent?
> Because you're not supposed to want it.
> Why?
> Because it's bad.
> Why is it?
> If it happens to you, it's okay, but you're not sup-
> posed to seek it.
> Why not move?
> If I move, mother will see me moving. If I lie still, I
> can make it happen and they won't know. I won't get
> caught.

I read a story once: animals when they are scared—some of them lie very still and then it's all right. So I'll lie very still and I won't get hurt.

But how can you feel anything? Don't you like to move? Sometimes you do and you enjoy it with a man.

Yes, I've tried that, but just when maybe something is about to happen, it slips away. The feeling is there, then it's gone.

You move when you are really attracted sexually to a man.

Yes. I get on top, and I move, but then, I'm the man. The man is supposed to move, the woman to lie still.

Aren't you embarrassed to be on top of a man and to move like this?

No. I believe it's pleasing to him to have it happen. He is pleased that I am also being pleased.

Why don't you move?

Movement is a lot of crap! I could move and have a heart attack trying to impress the bastard I'm with. Doesn't mean anything. Covers up the emptiness. Pretending. Movement hides the complete lack of any authenticity in the act. Fools men. The more you move, the more they believe you are enjoying it. The faster sometimes, the better. That's work for which I should have been paid and admitted what I was instead of covering up as an act of love.

What really bothers you about "Movement in Sex"?

The open admission, the confession of desire.

Is that what movement means to you?

Yes, also it means a giving of pleasure to a man.

Why is that wrong?

Not wrong, confused. Usually when *I* move, it is phony. Done to impress or excite or stimulate partner. Rarely done for self. Must be highly "self" to be free enough to try for me.

Why?

Bad sex doesn't deserve good feelings.

It can't be that hard for other people—books—movies, all so easy.

You're no different. Sex—good sex—is not easy.

I don't enjoy it—only sometimes.

Mostly when it's over, they leave me anyway—good or bad. So what to do.

Read and stop getting yourself so damned involved.

So, to move in a positive way for one's own pleasure is a difficult thing to do. How true! It requires a self that is free enough and strong enough to demand satisfaction, not only in sex but in all other aspects of life. In view of this requirement, it is easy to see why every neurotic disability will impede or prevent orgastic fulfillment.

The big question is whether this requirement applies to the male as well as to the female. By virtue of his position on top, he dominates the sexual relationship. Consciously, at least, the man has no inhibitions about movement. And having a penis that can ejaculate, he is almost always assured of some kind of climax. Yet, clinical experience shows that in terms of full satisfaction, the male suffers from orgastic impotence as much as the female does.

The most widespread disturbance of sexual function in the male is premature ejaculation. How common it is no one truly knows, since no time definition of prematurity has been formulated. Alfred Kinsey notes: "For perhaps three-quarters of all males, orgasm is reached within two minutes after the initiation of sexual relations, and for a not inconsiderable number of males, the climax may be reached within less than a minute or even within ten or twenty seconds after coital entrance."* I would venture to say that about one-third of the men I have seen in my practice suffered from this condition. Its effects extend beyond the lack of satisfaction in the man. If the prematurity is severe, it deprives the woman of an opportunity to achieve a vaginal orgasm even if she is capable of it. The overall result is a lack of fulfillment in sex for both partners, with a strain upon the marriage that frequently leads to its collapse.

There are many degrees of prematurity of ejaculation. In the severe case, the ejaculation occurs before the man penetrates the woman. In the milder form of this disturbance, ejaculation happens as soon as the man starts his rhythmic movements. In all cases, premature ejaculation is experienced as a disappointment. Normally, the act of coitus will take from about three to twenty minutes from penetration to climax. The elapsed time varies according to the degree of excitation of both parties prior to the commencement of the sexual act. Prematurity, therefore, cannot be measured against a timetable. By definition, it indicates that the man has

*Alfred Kinsey *et al., Sexual Behavior in the Human Male.* Philadelphia: W. B. Saunders Company, 1948, p. 580.

reached his climax before he himself was ready. Obviously, premature ejaculation occurs before the woman has reached her climax, but this is no criterion of prematurity, since her reaction may be delayed or may never occur.

The lack of an adequate concept of orgasm can easily lead to a confusion about the question of prematurity. On the basis of reports that most primates, notably the chimpanzees, are extremely rapid in their sexual response, Kinsey and his collaborators came to the absurd conclusion that the quick response of the premature individual is the superior type of reaction: "It would be difficult to find another situation in which an individual who was quick and intense in his response was labeled anything but superior, and that in most instances is exactly what the rapidly ejaculating male probably is."* It is not difficult to find a situation analogous to premature ejaculation. Take a soldier in the front lines who fires his rifle at every sign of movement or noise. His reaction is quick and intense, but who would regard it as superior? If anything, it is the reaction of a very anxious soldier, much as premature ejaculation is the sexual response of an anxious male in a tense situation. The common admonition, "Don't shoot till you see the whites of their eyes," is as applicable to the sexual act as it is to the action of the soldier in war. But the more serious error in Kinsey's statement lies in its misunderstanding of the problem. If prematurity were a sign of superiority, one would hardly expect to find men who complain of this disturbance. The fact is that many men come to therapy with the specific complaint of lack of satisfaction due to prematurity.

What has to be explained is why many men who suffer from prematurity of ejaculation are unaware of it. The main reason for this lack of understanding is that they have no standard of comparison. Several women who consulted me remarked that their husbands ejaculated immediately or soon after entering, but they thought that this was perfectly natural. Since the women themselves had never had an orgasm, they too, knew no better. In the absence of knowledge, a man could easily assume that his habitual mode of response was the normal one. Often the cloak of normality can be a defense against facing oneself. When this cloak is shed under analysis, no pretense is made that prematurity is anything but a severe lack of sexual satisfaction.

Ibid., p. 580.

On the other hand, there is a form of prematurity that is partly conditioned by the knowledge of its likely occurrence. The man who has had a premature ejaculation on previous occasions with his partner will worry about its happening on his next attempt. His concern and fear will augment the tension of the situation to the point where excitation cannot be contained, and prematurity will result. Such a man is caught in a vicious circle of prematurity: worry, tension, prematurity, worry, and tension again. This vicious circle is often very difficult to disrupt once it has taken hold of a person.

Often a man may experience a premature ejaculation in his first sexual encounter with a new partner. As his anxiety about the relationship decreases and as he feels more at ease and more secure in the woman's response, his premature reaction may disappear and his sexual response take on a more normal pattern. Observations such as these indicate the close connection between prematurity and anxiety. In fact, the greater the anxiety, the more premature the ejaculation. The most obvious cause for anxiety is the fear of rejection by the woman. This fear is consciously experienced in those situations in which the male senses the hostility of the woman or her reluctance to engage in sexual activity. If he persists in his attempt to have intercourse with her in the face of her negative attitude, he is liable to develop anxiety and have a premature ejaculation. Such situations are more common among young unmarried males for whom the sexual act has the connotation of a conquest. Since the conquest is achieved as soon as the penetration is accomplished, the orgasm is an anticlimax and is, at best, only partial.

Prematurity may also occur in the presence of a positive attitude on the part of the woman to the sexual relationship. Instead of the fear of rejection, the man may experience the fear of failure. He may become anxious that he will lose his erection or that he will be premature. Given enough anxiety, if the former doesn't happen, the latter will. The common denominator in all these cases is anxiety.

Since the problem of prematurity is the problem of sexual anxiety, the man who is consciously aware of his anxiety can often remove it by confronting the situation. Thus, if he senses that the woman is not fully receptive to his sexual advances, he can either refrain from any activity until he meets a more favorable response or discuss the situation with his partner. An honest discussion of sexual difficulties is one of the best ways to overcome them. It is also the best advice a physician can offer to married couples who have difficulties. And it is an approach that is generally welcomed by both parties. If the man fears that he may be premature, he should mention this fear to his partner. I am sure that in the great majority of cases, he will find to his surprise that the woman will be very cooperative. The inability to discuss sexual problems openly indicates that the relationship lacks the communion and acceptance that are essential to healthy sexuality. Such an approach, however, may be difficult if the individuals are not free from neurotic conflicts about sexuality and regard them as a personal stigma.

In most cases, the anxiety that conditions premature ejaculation stems from unconscious sexual conflicts. The only indication of the anxiety may be the fact of prematurity. Yet it is evidence enough, for by its very nature, prematurity denotes a state of anxiousness. Despite our sexual sophistication, sexual pleasure is still the forbidden fruit. And despite the woman's acquiescence in the sexual act, the premature male has not resolved his guilt about sexuality. It persists in his unconscious in the form of fear of the woman, fear of offending her by his sexual aggressiveness, and fear of not satisfying her by his sexual performance. Few men will admit to themselves that they are afraid of women or that they feel any hostility toward them. On the conscious level, neither the fear nor the hostility is experienced in relation to the specific sexual partner. Unconsciously, the fear and hostility have reference to the female in general, whose prototype is the mother. Underlying the phenomenon of prematurity is the problem of the unresolved oedipal attachment to the mother.

The specific mechanism of prematurity is an overexcitation of the penis. In prematurity, the penis becomes as excited in the initial stage of the sexual act as it normally does just before orgasm. In the latter case, however, this excitation is the result of the sexual movement; while in the premature reaction, it precedes these movements. The logical deduction is that the premature male is afraid of the sexual movements; that is, he is afraid of making aggressive sexual movements in the sexual act. Premature ejaculation may be interpreted as an unconscious wish to terminate the coital relationship as soon as possible. In the premature reaction, there is fear not only of the sexual movement, but also of the vagina. The latter fear is more clearly evident in cases in which ejaculation occurs immediately after penetration or even just prior to penetration.

The hypothesis that prematurity represents a fear of the sexual movements finds support in the physical condition of the male with this problem. His body structure is characterized by its rigidity. And, broadly speaking, the degree of prematurity is commensurate with the degree of rigidity. This rigidity is manifested in a lack of flexibility in the back or backbone, with the result that the rigid individual has difficulty in executing movements of extension such as I outlined in the preceding chapter in discussing the concept of the bow. In these persons, the muscles of the back, especially those in the lumbosacral region, are tense and contracted. The effect of this rigidity is to reduce both the motility and the mobility of the body and to impose a restriction upon the amplitude and freedom of the pelvic movements. In addition, one also finds in these individuals that the iliopsoas muscle, which flexes the pelvis on the thigh, the *levator ani* muscle, which constitutes the pelvic floor, and other related muscle groups are spastic. The result of these muscle tensions is that the body cannot hold the sexual charge or excitation, which flows immediately into the genital organ and overexcites it.

The pelvis, together with the belly and the buttocks, serves as a reservoir for the sexual feeling. When these structures are fully relaxed, they can accommodate and hold a large amount of sexual excitation until the sexual movements become rhythmic and involuntary. If this reservoir function is missing or greatly reduced because of tension, the excitation is released into the penis as soon as the man moves his penis in the vagina. To counter this tendency to overexcitation of the penis, the premature male tries to move as little as possible. Such a maneuver may delay the ejaculation in point of time, but it has no effect upon his functional prematurity. And since the fear of movement increases the tension, this maneuver only completes the vicious circle, trapping the man in his anxiety.

Premature ejaculation reflects a state of tension resulting from the man's fear of his aggressive impulses toward the woman. The normal pelvic thrust of the man is an aggressive action. In the unconscious of the premature male, this aggressive movement is associated with hostile and sadistic impulses towards the female. For him, the sexual thrust has the significance of piercing or raping the woman. Men for whom the sexual act has this meaning consciously do not suffer from prematurity but often need a sadistic fantasy to achieve a climax—without orgastic satisfaction. The repression of the sadistic feelings and impulses is responsible for the pelvic rigidity and the resulting prematurity. Coupled with the hostility toward the woman is the fear of retaliation or retribution by the woman. In the final analysis, this always turns out to be a fear of castration.

The problem of prematurity can be resolved through the analytic working out of the underlying castration anxiety, together with the release of the repressed hostility toward the female. This procedure is facilitated if at the same time the muscle tensions of the back and pelvic areas are released through appropriate exercises.

The unconscious hostility toward the female, which lies at the base of the symptom of prematurity, stems from early frustrations in erotic gratification. In the chapter "Love and Sex," I pointed out that the feeling of love arises in the child through the satisfaction of his erotic needs by the mother. The child obtains this satisfaction through his closeness to the mother's body in being held, in being nursed, and so on. If these needs are not fulfilled, the child develops feelings of deprivation and of anger toward the mother. These feelings are suppressed and eventually repressed, but they condition the adult male's response to every woman. The desire to pierce the woman or to rape her combines both the sadistic impulse to hurt the love object, as a representative of the mother, and the desire to get as close to her as possible. If these feelings are repressed, both objectives are lost: the man can neither hurt the woman nor get really close to her. Premature ejaculation betrays this repression.

Characterologically, the male who suffers from prematurity may be described as a "good" man, just as he was a "good" boy to his mother. "Good" in this context means that he makes an effort to please the woman. He is hardworking, ambitious, and generally rather successful financially. His orgastic impotence threatens him greatly, since it undermines the image he has of himself as a responsive and responsible person. There is a very lovely song, from the show *Carousel*, that expresses this idea clearly: "A girl who is in love with a virtuous man is doomed to weep and wail. ... There's nothing so bad for a woman as a man who thinks he's good." The idea is that a "good" man is no fun. I do not claim that such statements are invariably true. They contain the germ of a truth that, if properly understood, can help to clarify the dynamics of this sexual disturbance.

Several interpretations are possible to explain the relationship of this character attitude to prematurity. The so-called virtuous male or "good" man is attempting to cover up his hostility toward women with this attitude. Psychologically speaking, his virtue may be regarded as a defense against negative feelings. Another interpretation would explain his attitude as an attempt to gain the woman's love and approval by being virtuous. When virtue serves this purpose, it is suspect, for it masks the lack of self-respect and manliness. One may also discern in this attitude a feeling of veneration for the woman, who is idealized and idolized in her role as wife and mother. In most cases of prematurity, this tendency to idealize the woman exists. Again, this tendency is a defense against repressed feelings of hostility and contempt stemming from the man's early childhood experiences with his mother.

If the virtue and the goodness are defenses against negative feelings, we can anticipate that the repressed feelings will come through in disguised form. The so-called good husband is often critical and disparaging of his wife. The hostility that cannot be directly expressed is insinuated in subtle remarks and invidious comments. His very prematurity may be viewed as a denial to the woman of her pleasure in him. And alongside the veneration, the premature male is contemptuous and denigrating. Any man who places a woman on a pedestal does so in order more clearly to reveal her "feet of clay." In the very process of doing this, however, he is doomed to fail. His prematurity makes him feel inadequate and inferior, and the insecurity that it creates forces him to greater lengths to compensate for his impotence and hide his true feelings. In the end, he will blame the woman, accuse her of castrating him, and seek in an extramarital affair some proof of his potency. It should not be surprising to learn that there are latent homosexual attitudes in the premature male. Many of the elements that make for homosexuality are present in his personality, though repressed. These are the fear of the woman, hostility toward her, and contempt of her sexuality.

This analysis of the dynamics of the premature ejaculation points to the advice that should be given in this problem. Since the condition stems from fear of the sexual movements the premature male should be discouraged from all attempts to inhibit or restrain his movement. This advice runs counter to his tendency to move as little as possible in order to avoid becoming excited. However, such a maneuver only increases his fear. He should move easily and freely, without regard for the climax. If he concentrates upon the movement, it will diminish the overexcitation of the penis. Attention should be paid to the breathing. If respiration is full and synchronized with sexual movements, excitation will remain longer in the body. Full, deep, and relaxed respiration is the best safeguard against prematurity, since it focuses the feelings upon the body. The belly should be loose and allowed to extend freely. The common practice of holding the belly in tightly and under tension decreases the capacity of the pelvis to hold the sexual charge. Finally, pulling the pelvis back and arching the back before each forward movement prevents the excitation from flowing into the penis too quickly. Prematurity can be avoided if the entire body is actively engaged in the sexual act.

Intercourse should not be engaged in under conditions of tension and strain. The relationship between the sexual partners should be one of ease and confidence. Otherwise, the sexual act loses its quality as an expression of love and becomes a compulsive "acting out" of ego drives. The circumstances in which the sexual act takes place should allow for freedom of movement and sound. Movement creates sound, and the fear of moving may have some roots in the fear of being heard. This fear may stem from the days of adolescent masturbation. While it cannot be hoped that these few recommendations will help every man who suffers from prematurity, an understanding of the physical and psychological factors that create this difficulty may aid those individuals who can examine their feelings and sense their inner attitude.

Another form of orgastic impotence in the man is known technically as *ejaculatio retardans*. In this condition, ejaculation is restrained or does not occur until the excitation has subsided. The result, of course, is a very weak climax with no feeling of orgastic satisfaction. Contrasted with this disturbance, in which there is often no feeling of climax at all, the premature response is an exciting experience.

I have said that normal intercourse takes from about three to twenty minutes. These limits are not fixed but merely describe the range of the majority of normal sexual acts. The time period for the act of coitus depends on many factors:

the age of the man, the degree of excitation, the frequency of
sexual relations, and so on. Younger men tend to reach
climax sooner than older ones. When ejaculation is retarded,
the sexual act may take from one-half hour to two or more
hours for its completion. However, the time required is no
true criterion of *ejaculatio retardans*. In this condition, ejaculation occurs as a result of exhaustion rather than as the
product of an overwhelming excitation.

As a rule, the man who suffers from *ejaculatio retardans*
doesn't regard his type of response as a disability. On the
assumption that the longer he holds his erection, the more
pleasure he gives the woman, the man with delayed ejaculation often regards himself as a superior lover. The sacrifice of
his sexual pleasure for the woman doesn't disturb him, since
this sacrifice is often consciously made. He attempts to compensate for his loss by deriving his satisfaction from his
partner's reactions. I shall illustrate the personality problems
involved in this kind of sexual behavior with a case history.

Paul was a forty-year-old male who was referred for
psychiatric treatment following an abortive attempt at suicide
by carbon monoxide inhalation from the exhaust of a car.
There was no evidence of psychosis. Paul suffered some slight
loss of memory following shock therapy at the state hospital
in which he was first treated. He was depressed but without
agitation. He had a history of headaches, beginning in adolescence, which were thought to be migraine. However, the
headaches were generalized, without any visual disturbances
or auras. They lasted anywhere from several hours to several
days. He would frequently be awakened from his sleep early
because of a headache. They tended to be more severe on
weekends, when he was with his family, and at work, where
difficulties that required decisions often arose. Paul had been
repeatedly hospitalized since early adulthood because of these
headaches, and in the hospital his headaches usually subsided.
He had been treated by numerous psychiatrists and other
physicians and had frequently become quite toxic from the
medications which he took and which he seemed to crave.
Placebos would often relieve him dramatically. He had never
gone through a full year of work without hospitalization, and
he was often hospitalized several times during the year.

When I saw Paul in consultation, we discussed his suicide
attempt. He said that he wanted to end a meaningless life of
failure and to do something for his wife. She would have the
benefit of a considerable amount of insurance money if he

died. I pointed out to him that his motives were questionable.
The money his wife would receive was blood money. Any
pleasure she could obtain through it was paid for by his life.
Did he think that his wife could enjoy the money? I asked
Paul whether his attempted suicide was intended to make his
wife feel guilty, but he made no answer.

Paul was a tall, somewhat stoop-shouldered man. He was
quite thin in the waist. His buttocks were pinched together
and very tense. His belly was flat and contracted. He had a
very rigid backbone, a round, tight shoulder girdle, and he
was bent over as if he were carrying heavy burdens on his
back. Paul's manner was friendly and gentle, and at times he
could be extremely humorous. He wore a rather cynical
smile. He loved to talk; before he became depressed, he had
had a reputation as a raconteur. He felt defeated in life, and
he was fascinated by the success of others.

Paul's psychosexual development was marked by an unusual fear of masturbation. He could not recall any acts of
onanism in early childhood or adolescence. The problem was
so severe that he could not discuss it in his therapy. He said
that it was abhorrent to him. As a young man, he had had a
sexual liaison with an older woman. His mother was the
dominant figure in the home during his childhood. His father
was a dull, hardworking man who clung to old business
methods despite repeated failure. His mother compared her
husband unfavorably with her older brother, who was a
business success. At twenty years of age, Paul developed a
mild case of tuberculosis. Since his return from the sanatori-
um, he had been regarded as an invalid by his family, first
because of the TB and later because of his chronic headaches.

Paul married a woman much younger than himself whom
he described as attractive and vivacious. In the early years of
the marriage, he struggled to free her from her family's
influence. The union produced three children. Discussing his
sexual life, Paul said that intercourse generally lasted an hour
or more and sometimes as long as two hours. He took great
pride in the fact that his erection could be maintained for so
long and that his wife often experienced several orgasms in
the course of a single act. His own climax, when it occurred,
was empty of pleasure or meaning, but he negated its significance in view of the pleasure and satisfaction he gave his
wife. However, he gradually lost interest in sexual relations
with his wife, and over the years the sexual contacts dimin-

ished considerably. At the same time, Paul became increasingly more depressed.

In the course of therapy, Paul's pattern of sexual behavior and feeling became evident. As his depression lifted, Paul would begin to have a spontaneous return of sexual feeling, accompanied by morning erections and "wet dreams." This would lead to sexual relations with his wife. Following several sexual experiences, Paul developed a feeling of despair and went into a state of depression that lasted for several months, during which time he had no sexual desire. During the period of depression, his headaches became more frequent and more intense. They occupied all his attention and interest. All his efforts were directed toward obtaining relief through medication. He could not understand why sedatives were withheld from him. Even his fantasies were concerned with the relief of his headaches through medication. Throughout this time, Paul maintained that sex was no problem for him, that he had no sexual desire, and that all he wanted was relief from the headaches.

The relationship of the depression, the headaches, and the loss of sexual feeling was clearly revealed by the observation that whenever Paul woke with an erection, he didn't suffer from a headache that day. This observation was repeated often in the course of therapy. It could be postulated that the headaches resulted from Paul's inability to focus his sexual excitation upon the genital organ. Instead, the excitation became localized in his head, producing an unbearable tension. The muscles of his neck and scalp became inordinately tense. In view of his exaggerated erective potency and lack of satisfaction, it could be assumed that the headaches resulted when Paul suppressed his sexual feelings. The suppression was, of course, unconscious. Paul felt only the tension of the effort.

It was possible to reduce both the frequency of the headaches and their severity by therapy that included physical exercise and muscle massage to decrease his tension. Through his identification with the therapist, he was able to become more aggressive in his business. He was able, for example, to discharge employees who had taken advantage of him for years. On occasion, he had even become more aggressive with his wife and less tolerant of her financial demands. However, each assertion of his manhood and individuality was followed by a collapse and retreat into passivity and dependence upon the therapist and upon his wife. Although seemingly close to it on several occasions, he never expressed any realization of his resentment toward his wife or his family.

Paul complained about his wife's financial demands upon him, but he always acceded to them. He expressed the wish that his wife would be the sexual aggressor, but he was unable to assume a sexually passive role with her when she ridiculed his tendencies to passivity and dependence. Consciously, Paul wanted to be taken care of like a child: his demand for medication, his desire to be sexually passive, and his invalidism testify to this element in his personality. On another level, Paul was unconsciously obsessed with the need to prove that he was a man. He took the top position in the sexual act, he maintained his erection for unusually long periods, and he was convinced that he gave his wife pleasure and satisfaction in sex. Then when he lost his sexual feelings and became depressed, he retreated into fantasies which were either almost openly homosexual or in which the therapist or another person was having a sexual affair with his wife. Thus, Paul oscillated between the attempt to function as a responsible adult and the wish to regress to the position of an infant. Neither effort was successful. Regression meant a loss not only of manhood but of self. The "mother" would swallow him up, he believed. On the other hand, Paul was convinced that he could not possibly satisfy the voracious appetite of the female. This is the meaning of the fantasies in which he pictured another man satisfying his wife.

Paul's relationship to his wife paralleled and reflected his earlier relationship to his mother, whom he idealized and idolized. At no time was it possible to dethrone the image of the good, sacrificing, and devoted mother. He never made any negative remarks about his mother, but at the same time, he never said anything positive about her either. If it is assumed that his hostility against his mother, as against his wife, was deeply repressed, then his failures and his self-destructive behavior could be viewed as an attempt to get back at her through spite. This assumption finds support in Paul's rejection of food, which is a universal symbol of the mother. Paul ate so little at times that he became emaciated.

What is the explanation of the retarded ejaculation? How is it possible for a person to maintain an erection for two hours during intercourse without either losing it or reaching a climax? The phenomenon seems so strange that it requires an effort of the imagination to comprehend it. It is not difficult to realize that the sexual act was for Paul a means of "servicing" his wife. In fact, Paul was able to maintain the erection only by concentrating his attention upon her needs, her feelings, and her responses rather than upon his own. Obviously, he couldn't serve her if he were premature or if he lost his erection. Paul rationalized that this ability was something to be proud of.

If the penis is used to serve another, it loses its character as a genital organ and becomes, functionally, a breast or nipple. In this sense, Paul was feeding his wife's hunger for sexual pleasure, and the erection would persist as long as the need continued. Two dreams supported the idea that his penis functioned as a teat. In one dream he pictured his dog sucking his penis. Paul had a dog to whom he felt closer than to his wife. Whenever his wife complained about the dog's sleeping in their bed, Paul would leave her to sleep in another room with the dog. He experienced his wife's rejection of the dog as a rejection of himself, and he obviously identified with the animal. In the dream, Paul projected upon the dog his own repressed wish to be nursed. But in view of his sexual behavior with his wife, she can be identified with the dog in the dream. Accordingly, the dream can be interpreted as an unconscious expression of contempt for his wife. In the second dream, Paul pictured his penis as being triangular and wrapped in aluminum foil. His associations with this dream were memories of his high-school days and of geometry, a subject in which he excelled. For his excellence in school, Paul was admired and approved by his mother. His penis shaped as a geometric object and wrapped as food was the offering he now gave his wife.

In other cases where the male attitude is one of serving the woman, erection is not so easily maintained. In addition to the idea of service, the continued erection in Paul's case suggested the idea of challenge. It was as if Paul were saying to his wife, "You cannot defeat me, you cannot destroy me." This was another example of Paul's ambivalence—submission in service, but rebellion in endurance. I believe that without the concept of challenge, the problem of *ejaculatio retardans* cannot be understood. In the end, the challenge must fail, as it invariably did in Paul's case, for the lack of satisfaction leads to futility and despair and ends in the pit of depression.

The physiological pattern that became so striking in this

case, that is, the alternation of headaches with sexual feelings, made me speculate about the mechanics of such a phenomenon. Psychodynamically, it was apparent that when Paul felt defeated in his challenge to the woman, he responded as a "sorehead," regressing in his behavior to helplessness (invalidism) and using his symptoms as a weapon to enforce his will. His physical structure gave me the impression that all his energy appeared to be drawn up out of the lower half of his body and held immobilized in his chest, neck, and head. His legs were thin, with tense muscles, and he had poor skin color. His pelvis was narrow and tight. Pelvic motility was greatly reduced. The forward movement of his pelvis was achieved by contracting the abdominal muscles to draw it forward and by squeezing the buttocks to push it forward. Such a movement lacked any resemblance to an aggressive thrust. This tension in the lower half of his body limited his respiration to the thorax. When Paul was able to establish a pattern of more natural abdominal breathing and when, through exercises, he began to feel some vitality and movement in his legs, his sexual feelings returned.

The picture Paul presented was one of masochistic spite—unconscious "holding back." His inability to let his feelings down into the lower half of his body spontaneously paralleled his inability to "let go" in sex. The rigidity of his body was duplicated in the rigidity of his penis. When the pattern of "holding back" yielded, there was an immediate feeling of release. A special technique was employed to accomplish this. If Paul was thumped lightly on his back so as to "shake up" the rigidity, his reaction was immediate and positive. His eyes lit up, his expression cleared, and he felt a sense of relief and release. This is a typical masochistic reaction. Paul had to be made to "let go," since he was unable to do this for himself. The same mechanism explains the "need to be beaten" of the true masochist, for whom beating is a necessary preliminary to sexual pleasure. Paul's condition was due to a severe block in genital aggressiveness and to strong castration anxieties. His masochistic submissiveness was a defense against his fear of castration; that is, by serving the woman, Paul avoided the perception of his underlying castration anxiety. On another level, Paul's rigidity was an attempt to compensate for his masochistic submissiveness.

We have now examined two problems of orgastic potency—the premature ejaculation and the retarded ejaculation. In the former, the climax comes too soon; in the latter, it hardly

comes at all. There is another disturbance which is less severe
than these two but which is perhaps even more common,
although it is not usually recognized as a disturbance. For this
phenomenon, I use the term "local climax," to distinguish it
from the orgastic response, which involves the total body. A
brief description of what happens will indicate the nature of
the problem. An ejaculation that is neither premature nor
retarded occurs just before the involuntary movements take
over. The full feeling of satisfaction escapes the man because
his whole body does not take part in the sexual response. He
is not moved. However, the feeling at climax is one of
pleasure, and for this reason, such a reaction is not usually
viewed as a disturbance. From the point of view of orgastic
potency, it must be regarded as a partial orgasm.

It is this local orgasm that caused so much confusion about
Reich's orgasm theory. Few sexologists or psychologists
would argue that premature ejaculation or retarded ejaculation is normal. For in neither of these responses is there any
feeling of satisfaction. The local climax, however, is different.
Without a knowledge of what the full orgastic experience
should be, it is easily taken for the complete response. And,
unfortunately, knowledge of the full orgasm is rare.

In the partial orgasm, body sensation is limited to the
genital area or extends slightly to the pelvis and legs. The
man may experience some streaming sensations in his pelvis
and in his legs, but these do not extend into the upper half
of his body. Specifically, consciousness is not clouded, and
there is no feeling of dissolution of the personality or of
the body boundaries. Any experience of melting sensations is
limited to the genital area. There is no feeling of glow or
lumination as a result of the climactic response. On the
other hand, in this partial orgasm, there always is a feeling
of release and of relaxation following the climax. This may
even induce a feeling of drowsiness, and the man may fall
asleep after such a climax.

The difference between the local climax and the full orgasm is the absence or presence of the involuntary pelvic
movements and body convulsion that I described in the
preceding chapter. In this connection, it is important to
distinguish between these involuntary movements and other
involuntary reactions that are often mistaken for the orgastic
response. Kinsey lists six kinds of orgastic response in the
male subjects he studied. If we analyze these six different

reactions, we shall see that not one of them approaches the full orgastic response. They are as follows:

1. The reaction is limited to the genitals, with little or no body reaction. In the penis there are a few mild throbs, and the semen flows out without the normal ejaculatory, pulsatile squirts. The climax is one without any significant feeling. Kinsey states that about one-fifth or more of all males experience this most inadequate response.

2. A second reaction, which is said to be most common, involves some "tension or twitching of one or both legs, of the mouth, of the arms or of other particular parts of the body." In this response, the whole body becomes rigid. There are a few spasms but no aftereffects. This reaction is said to occur in about 45 percent of all males. It should be noted that the rigidity of the body is a defense against "giving in to" the orgastic convulsion and not an orgastic reaction. This is the kind of response that I have called the local climax.

3. The third type of response appears to be a more violent reaction than the preceding one but is of the same nature. The descriptive terms used by Kinsey, based upon statements of his subjects, are: "legs often become rigid with muscles knotted and toes pointed, muscles of abdomen contracted and hard, shoulders and neck stiff and often bent forward, breath held or gasping, eyes staring or tightly closed, hands grasping, mouth distorted . . . whole body or parts of it spasmodically twitching, sometimes synchronously with throbs or violent jerking of penis."* In addition, there may be groans, sobbing, or violent cries. The aftereffects are not marked. This type of response was reported by about one-sixth of Kinsey's subjects.

Again, it is my contention that rigidities, tensions, and spasm are contrary to the nature of the orgastic reaction. How pleasurable can a climax be if it is accompanied by the manifestations described above? One would expect such reactions from a person undergoing torture rather than the delights of an ecstatic experience. No, this is not orgasm but fear—fear of an orgasm that threatens to overwhelm the ego.

4. A small percentage of males, about 5 percent, reported reactions of laughter, talking, sadistic or masochistic feelings, and rapid motions "culminating in frenzied movements."

**Ibid.*, p. 161.

Such reactions are hysterical in nature and need no further comment.

5. A smaller group of males also reported the above reactions, but "culminating in extreme trembling, collapse, loss of color, and sometimes fainting of subject." This sounds like a panic reaction, which I suspect it is.

6. The survey also notes that a number of males complained of pain and fear at the approach of orgasm. It seems that the penis became very sensitive just before orgasm, and Kinsey says that "some males suffer excruciating pain and may scream if movement is continued or the penis even touched." Some of these males may fight away from the partner at the approach of climax, although they report "definite pleasure" in the whole experience.

Kinsey's contribution in making these findings available for study is valuable. But how he can confuse them with orgasm is beyond my comprehension. The theoretical basis for his position is the argument that the biologist is concerned only with physiological responses and not with subjective experiences. But even the biologist must be aware that physiology involves more than the measurement or description of isolated organ reactions. For example, physiologically, the organ response in flight or fight is similar: increased adrenaline output, elevated blood pressure, faster pulse, increased respiration; yet one would expect the biologist to know the difference between flight and fight. Kinsey believes that it is a confusion in the literature to equate orgasm with orgastic pleasure. If one takes the pleasure out of orgasm, had one not better speak of climax, which can be considered a physiological reaction, rather than orgasm? On this issue, Kinsey specifically states that "all cases of ejaculation have been taken as evidence of orgasm." This is a misuse of the term "orgasm."

So much for Kinsey and the attempt to study sexual behavior as a mechanical response. The problem of the local climax, or partial orgasm, is characterized by the development of rigidity at the approach of orgasm. Instead of the rhythmic movements becoming stronger, faster, and involuntary, the body becomes stiff, movement ceases or slows down, and the breath tends to be held. This type of response is a clear indication of some fear of the orgastic reaction. What is the nature of this fear?

Orgasm, as many psychologists and psychoanalysts know,

is a process of surrender. Surrender to the woman, surrender to the unconscious, surrender to the animal nature of man. It is precisely the fear of surrendering that inhibits the average male from experiencing the full orgasm in the sexual act. Without surrender, full union with the partner is impossible. But surrender in the sense in which it is used here is not a conscious act. It involves the ability to give oneself fully to one's sexual partner without unconscious reservations. It is possible to surrender only if one is in love with one's sexual partner. By the same token, however, the full surrender to the woman in the sexual act is an expression of love on a level deeper than words can reach.

The inability to surrender to the woman stems from unconscious fears of and hostility toward women. We take this state of affairs so much for granted that we speak of the "war between the sexes." We need not be psychiatrists to be aware of the hostility that pervades most marital and sexual relationships. I find it hard to answer the patient who demands that I show him a happy marriage. Such marriages exist, and I know of some, but they are so rare that I would feel foolish to argue on the basis of their number that marriage is a happy state. My psychiatric patients are not the exceptions; they are exceptional only in that they have come for help and have revealed their difficulties.

It has been truly said that no man can love a woman unless he loves all women. I have taken this to mean womankind. Each woman is an individual, and yet for the man each woman is also a reflection of his mother. All his unresolved conflicts with his mother are unconsciously transferred to his wife or partner. On the conscious level, he can very well distinguish between the two. It is on the unconscious level that they fuse into an indiscriminate image. But it is precisely on the unconscious level that orgasm occurs. And it is the fear of the transition to unconscious behavior, involuntary movement, that stops the man at the threshold of orgastic response. He knocks at the door, it is opened, but he becomes afraid to pass through. His body becomes rigid, his legs stiffen, his jaw becomes hard, his abdomen contracts, his breath is held or comes in gasps, and his chest becomes tense. If the sexual feeling is strong enough, he may respond partially with what I have called the local climax, but the barrier of fear has not been breached.

In the process of neurotic adjustment in childhood, the ego learns to accept intention in place of deed. It creates an image of the "good mother" to counter the negative experiences assigned to the "bad mother." These experiences are necessarily repressed in the interest of survival and adjustment. But they are repressed, not gone, even if they are forgotten. The ego commands behavior as a captain commands his ship. And all is well and safe as long as this command is exercised. But the ego dare not abandon the helm, for strange forces lurk in the dark night of the unconscious. If one has continually maintained control over one's negative feelings and over the image of the "bad mother," this control cannot be relinquished in the sexual act.

On the ego level, sex is accepted as the natural expression of love between two people. The ego is right in this acceptance, as it is right in the knowledge of mother love. But the personality is divided. The ego opposes the unconscious to preserve peace and stability, but it is a truce in an unresolved war. Never must the border guards sleep or lose consciousness. The moment they do, the neurotic individual is seized with a panic, as if an enemy were invading his territory. This is the panic that the neurotic person experiences in the face of orgasm. It appears unreasonable, as unreasonable as the fear of a child in the dark. Yet no amount of logical argument can make the child lose its fear. All one can do is explore the dark with the child and show him that there are no monsters lurking in it. The knowledge of the nature of orgasm is a light that illuminates the darkness.

13

Orgastic Impotence
in the Female

Orgastic impotence in the man is often masked by the experience of ejaculation, which in itself constitutes a form of climax. In the woman, however, the problem of orgastic impotence is more sharply defined. There are many women who have never reached any kind of climax in the sexual act. Some are quite ignorant of the fact that a woman is capable of having an orgasm and that her experience of this phenomenon parallels that of the man. Other women achieve an occasional orgasm when the relationship between the sexual partners is harmonious and affectionate. Still others have known the orgastic experience during one period of their sexual lives or in one particular relationship. The woman who is orgastically potent in the sense that she is sexually satisfied in almost all her sexual experiences is rare. But on the basis of Kinsey's report, Reich's observations and my clinical experience, I would say that the man who is fully satisfied in his sexual experiences is probably equally rare.

One result of the sexual revolution that has been in progress since World War I is the increasing recognition by women of their right to sexual fulfillment. The corollary is that they have also become aware of their lack of fulfillment or sexual satisfaction. This is especially true of the younger generation of women, who are more sophisticated in these matters than are their parents. The inability to achieve a proper orgasm is regarded by these women as a sign of sexual immaturity. They equate orgastic potency with womanhood.

One of my patients expressed this idea very clearly. She remarked one day, "I still don't have any orgasm. Instead, I feel sad and it makes me cry. I feel that if I would have a vaginal orgasm in intercourse, I would feel like a woman."

The significance of orgasm for the concept of womanhood is a relatively recent development. In Victorian days, the symbols of womanhood were marriage and the family. These symbols were undermined by psychoanalytic investigations that revealed the defenses and rationalizations covering the inner feelings of frustration and emptiness. To the degree that knowledge about the nature and function of the orgasm has penetrated the modern consciousness, women have become aware that personal fulfillment cannot be divorced from sexual fulfillment.

The problem of orgastic potency in a woman is complicated by the fact that some women are capable of experiencing a sexual climax through clitoral stimulation. This kind of response is called a clitoral orgasm as distinguished from a vaginal orgasm. What is the difference between these two reactions? Is a clitoral orgasm satisfying? Why are some women capable of having only a clitoral orgasm? These questions should be answered if we are to understand the problem of orgastic impotence in the female.

A clitoral orgasm is produced by the stimulation of the clitoris either manually or orally, before, during, or after an act of coitus. Some women respond to this stimulation and reach a climax that they cannot achieve through vaginal stimulation or penile-vaginal friction. Most men, however, feel that the need to bring a woman to climax through clitoral stimulation is a burden. If it is done before intercourse but after the man is excited and ready to penetrate, it imposes a restraint upon his natural desire for closeness and intimacy. Not only does he lose some of his excitation through this delay, but the subsequent act of coitus is deprived of its mutual quality. Clitoral stimulation during the act of intercourse may help the woman to reach a climax, but it distracts the man from the perception of his genital sensations and greatly interferes with the pelvic movements upon which his own feeling of satisfaction depends. The need to bring a woman to climax through clitoral stimulation after the act of intercourse has been completed and the man has reached his climax is burdensome, since it prevents him from enjoying the relaxation and peace that are the rewards of sexuality. Most men to whom I have spoken who engaged in this practice resented it.

I do not mean to condemn the practice of clitoral stimulation if a woman finds that this is the way that she can obtain a sexual release. Above all, she should not feel guilty about using this procedure. However, I advise my patients against this practice since it focuses feelings on the clitoris and prevents the vaginal response. It is not a fully satisfactory experience and cannot be considered the equivalent of a vaginal orgasm. On this point, however, I think that women should speak for themselves, since they alone know what it feels like. The following remarks were made by several patients who were asked to describe the difference:

1. "The clitoral orgasm is felt on the surface of the vagina like a trickle of sweet pleasure. There is no satisfying release. The vaginal orgasm is like the opening of a dam which floods my body with pleasure and leaves me with a feeling of deep release and satisfaction. There is no comparison. The next day after a clitoral orgasm, I am hot, disturbed. After the other, I wake up in one piece, relaxed."

2. "The vaginal orgasm I experience, limited as it may be, fills me with a sense of completeness, of satisfaction. I have a feeling of being full—filled up. The clitoral orgasm is more high level in excitement but leaves me with no aftereffect of completion. I feel I could have one clitoral orgasm right after another."

3. "I start masturbating with the clitoris, but while this excites me—it gives me a frenzied feeling which doesn't go to any conclusion; it is too much on the surface—it makes me want to go deeper. Then I masturbate vaginally and it feels good. The orgasm is deep and satisfying. I feel warm, melting, and relaxed, satisfied that it is all finished."

These observations by women support the idea that there is a significant difference between a vaginal and a clitoral orgasm: the vaginal orgasm is experienced in the depths of the body, the clitoral reaction is limited to the surface. From what they say, it appears that only the vaginal orgasm produces the feelings of fulfillment, complete release, and satisfaction. In my years of clinical experience as a psychiatrist, I never heard a woman assert anything to the contrary.

In view of the distinctions made by the women themselves, it is difficult to understand why many sexologists argue that a clitoral orgasm is the equivalent of a vaginal orgasm. The argument is based on the theory that since the clitoris is a more sensitive organ than the vagina, all orgasms are essentially owing to some form of clitoral stimulation. Thus in Kinsey's discussion of the sexual response in woman, there is the following statement: "In view of the evidence that the walls of the vagina are ordinarily insensitive, it is obvious that the satisfaction obtained through vaginal penetration must depend on some mechanism that lies outside the vaginal walls themselves."* There is an obvious truth in this statement; there is also a less obvious misunderstanding. The truth is that the mechanism of orgasm is independent of any stimulation of the vaginal walls. Orgasm is a motor phenomenon the mechanism of which is a specific kind of body movement described earlier. The error in the statement lies in its implication that since the vaginal walls are insensitive, the female orgasm must result from stimulation of some other area. Kinsey suggests four areas as the source of the excitation leading to orgasm: (1) tactile stimulation of the body surface when one partner lies on another; (2) tactile stimulation of the clitoris, the labia minora, and the vestibule of the vagina; (3) stimulation of the levatores; and (4) stimulation of the pelvic floor and perineal body.

The emphasis upon stimulation, tactile or other, as the mechanism of sexual arousal and release distorts the true nature of sexuality. It introduces a mechanical element into an act that has meaning only as an expression of feeling. In the name of physiology, it overlooks and ignores the emotional significance of the sexual function. It is a limitation of science to describe a caress as tactile stimulation. The difference between the two is the difference between the mechanical act of sex and the expression of love for the sexual partner. Kinsey's statement implies a dissociation between action and feeling. A caress is distinguished from other forms of tactile stimulation both by its quality and by the special feeling that motivates the action. This special feeling (love, affection, tenderness) gives the caress its special quality. But even with this distinction in mind, it is inaccurate to base the phenomenon of orgasm upon body contact alone.

Tactile stimulation in itself is not the causative factor in erotic arousal. This is clearly evident if one considers the fact that the detumescent penis after intercourse is relatively insensitive to any form of stimulation. Yet in this state, its anatomy includes the same nerve endings and sense organs that are present in the condition of tumescence. But how

*Alfred Kinsey *et al., Sexual Behavior in the Human Female.* Philadelphia: W. B. Saunders Company, 1953, p. 581.

different is the feeling. The excitation or energetic charge in the organism manifested in the feeling of desire determines the fact and degree of arousal and not the act of stimulation itself. If the act of stimulation appears to produce a state of arousal, it does so because a latent desire for love is present in the individual. The act of touching or kissing serves to bring this feeling to consciousness. Erotic contact calls up the images and fantasies of love. Since it is not possible to dissociate the action from its image, one can confuse the gesture with the feeling, the mechanical act with the emotional expression.

The vaginal orgasm differs from the clitoral orgasm in that it is a total body response of love. It is, therefore, relatively independent of any single part of the body, either the clitoris or the vagina, but it is dependent on the total bodily feeling of contact, intimacy, and fusion with another person. Otherwise, one could not explain the fact that men and women can have sexual dreams with the experience of orgastic satisfaction without any actual stimulation or contact with the opposite sex. Although stimulation can be dispensed with, movement cannot. For a person to have an orgastic experience in sleep, he must dream that he is executing the sexual movements. But even this is not enough. I believe that the sleeper who dreams of sexual release and experiences orgasm is executing the sexual movements while sleeping. This is not a difficult idea to accept, since it is known that people move quite a bit during sleep without being aware of it. The basis of the orgastic feeling is the kinesthetic experience of the involuntary sexual movements.

If it is possible to have a vaginal orgasm without penile-vaginal contact, as in a dream, is it not possible to have a vaginal orgasm through clitoral stimulation if the woman makes the appropriate sexual movements? The answer to this question must be yes: it is possible but not probable. If a woman is not fixated on the clitoris, its stimulation will induce the desire for deeper contact. She will want the feeling of penetration by the man. If she inhibits this desire because of unconscious fears about vaginal penetration, she will reduce the level of excitation and fail to achieve a full orgasm. It is also possible for a woman to achieve a satisfactory orgastic release through masturbation. If this is so, what is the special value of the normal coital contact? Does it serve merely the function of reproduction? Normal intercourse is preferred to masturbation because it is a deeper,

richer, and more fulfilling experience. Penile-vaginal contact
allows the excitation in one body to be directly transmitted to
the other. This sharing of feeling increases the intensity of
the excitation. If some individuals have recourse to a mode
of lesser satisfaction when the means for greater satisfaction
are available, it is because of neurotic anxieties and fears
associated with the more satisfactory mode.

Most psychoanalysts contend that when the clitoral response is the sole mode of obtaining a sexual release, it is a
manifestation of an immature personality. F. S. Kroger and
S. C. Freed note, "Hence in the child the clitoris gives sexual
satisfaction, while in the normal adult woman the vagina is
supposed to be the principle sexual organ. . . . In frigid
women the transference of sexual satisfaction and excitement
from the clitoris to the vagina, which usually occurs with
emotional maturity, does not take place."* Freud had made
similar statements earlier: "The clitoris in the girl, moreover,
is in every way equivalent during childhood to the penis. . . .
In the transition to womanhood very much depends on the
early and complete relegation of sensitivity from the clitoris
to the vaginal orifice."† And, ". . . in the phallic phase of the
girl, the clitoris is the dominant erotogenic zone. But it is not
destined to remain so; with the change to femininity, the
clitoris must give up to the vagina its sensitivity, and with it,
its importance, either wholly or in part."‡ The evidence to
support these statements was the repeated analytic observation that patients who reported being able to experience only
clitoral excitation and release had immature personalities.
But these analysts were in error on one point. The clitoris
does not transfer any of its sensitivity to the vagina. It retains
its sensitivity throughout the life of the normal adult woman.
If it loses its assumed importance, it is because the vagina
takes on a function in relation to sexuality that is superior to
that of the clitoris.

In Chapter 9, I pointed out that sexual maturity in the
woman involves the development of a new function, the
function of vaginal receptivity. The addition of a new function doesn't eliminate an older one. An adult can crawl
almost as well as a child; he prefers to walk because it is a

*F. S. Kroger and S. C. Freed, "Psychosomatic Aspects of Frigid-
ity," *J. Amer. Med. Assn.*, 143: p. 528, 1950.
†Sigmund Freud, *A General Introduction to Psychoanalysis.* New
York: Perma Giants, 1935, p. 278.
‡Sigmund Freud, *New Introductory Lectures on Psychoanalysis.*
New York: W. W. Norton & Company, Inc., 1933, p. 161.

more effective and satisfying modality. Similarly, the clitoris does not lose its sensitivity in the adult woman, as the following statement shows: "I feel that my clitoris is very sensitive, so sensitive that I don't want to touch it. I get a better feeling through the vagina." I have known other women whom I regarded as sexually mature who felt the same way, namely, that the sensitivity of the clitoris interfered with sexual pleasure. Since these women became sexually excited when their tender and affectionate feelings for a man were aroused, they had no need of clitoral stimulation to focus their erotic desires on the vagina. Kissing, body contact, and caresses served this purpose adequately.

A mature woman can reach a climax through other means than penile-vaginal contact. However, this climax is not what she wants. Her preference is for the normal form of sexual relationship. In view of this preference, it is beside the point to say that one is as good as another, that "an orgasm is an orgasm." This is like saying that a meal is a meal or that it is absurd to prefer steak to hash. It is interesting that the arguments in favor of the clitoral orgasm are advanced by males. No woman whom I have questioned has expressed a similar view. Scientific support for the equality of the clitoral orgasm with the vaginal orgasm was sought in the experiments of W. H. Masters and V. E. Johnson. Under laboratory conditions, they observed the physiological responses of women to stimulation of different erogenous areas. Their conclusion: "The human female's physiologic responses to effective sexual stimulation develop with consistency regardless of the source of the psychic or physical sexual stimulation."* The error in such studies is that it equates the physiological response with the emotional response. To appreciate this error, one should know that the physiological response to hash is identical to that of steak. Yet the experience of eating the two is not the same. If we ignore the factors that determine feeling and emotional response, we lose sight of the human and spiritual qualities that make life meaningful. The great importance of the sexual function for human happiness requires that it be studied in terms of its emotional significance and not as a mechanical or physiological act of release or discharge.

Another argument against the validity of conclusions

*W. H. Masters and V. E. Johnson, "The Sexual Response Cycle of the Human Female; III, The Clitoris: Anatomical and Clinical Considerations," *West. J. Surg.*, 70, p. 254, 1962.

drawn from the observation of sexual activity under laboratory conditions is advanced by S. Pagan. After hearing about
the experiments of Masters and Johnson, she wrote to them:
"I just know that if someone would watch me copulate with
a partner, the best I could do would be a little outer clitoral
climax, as fast as possible to get the silly situation over with.
I do not call that an orgasm." Wilhelm Reich had made a
similar observation during experiments to measure the psy-
chogalvanic response of erotogenic areas to stimulation. In
the absence of privacy, the typical pleasure response did not
appear. I find it incredible that anyone could equate the
subjective experience of copulation under observation with
that which one has when the sexual act is an intimate
communion of two individuals in private.

Unlike the urethra or the alimentary canal, the vagina is
not just an organ with an orifice. Physiologically, it is that;
but psychologically and emotionally, it is an opening into a
woman's body. A man who penetrates the vagina also penetrates the body of the woman. His sperm cells may go much
farther. If no barriers exist, they will ascend the cervical
canal, traverse the uterus, and, at times, fertilize the egg in
the oviduct. In a deeper sense, a woman's sexual organ is her
whole body. When a woman responds sexually with her
whole body her reaction is the vaginal orgasm.

The clitoris is the homologue of the male penis. Anatomi-
cally and physiologically, it is similar to the penis. It is,
however, a rudimentary structure, which explains its very
small size and lack of functional significance. It neither penetrates nor discharges anything. Yet we are asked to believe
that this structure is the sexual equal of the vagina. In what
way is the stimulation of the clitoris to bring a woman to
climax different from the manual stimulation of the penis to
achieve orgasm? The physiological response in both cases is
the same. Are we not justified in assuming, therefore, that the
woman who can achieve a climax only through clitoral stimulation can find sexual release only through identification
with the male? In other words, the inability to achieve
vaginal orgasm denotes the incapacity of the female to accept herself as a woman sexually. One should not be surprised when such a female complains that she doesn't feel
like a woman.

It seems necessary to point out that as an organ, the
vagina is a receptacle to receive the male. But it is not a
static receptacle. It receives and embraces the male, who is

represented by his penis. But receiving and embracing are only preliminary to the complete union that occurs when the two meet in a mutual orgasm. That this fails to happen in most instances of sexual love indicates the degree of sexual disturbance and maladjustment that exists in our culture. The disturbances and maladjustments are not confined to the sexual function. They pervade the personality of the individual, female as well as male. There is a correlation between disturbances in personality and disturbances in sexuality in the female as well as in the male, as is shown in the following case.

May is a woman who consulted me because of her inability to achieve a vaginal orgasm. In answer to my question about her sexual response, she said:

"I get very excited in the sexual act, but when it comes close to a climax, it shuts off. I get a wonderful warm glow all over. I can feel it building up. Then when I feel he is ready to come or that he is holding back, I give up. I say to myself, 'All right, forget it. We'll try again next time.' I feel if I could free myself, I'd have a vaginal orgasm.

"The feeling starts in the clitoris, but it spreads all over. I feel it around the vagina but not inside. It's an overall warm, flushy, glowing feeling.

"For years I used to get some release through manipulation of the clitoris after the sexual act. But I feel that it's not enough. And I don't want my husband to do it now. Before, it was much more erotic. We necked and played, and it was a slow process. When I was young, I needed a lot of foreplay. I would get very excited, and he would, too. Then he would reach a climax, and I would have one before or after he did. With my former husband, we had a fantastic amount of sex, but it was never enough. He seemed to need it all the time.

"Now it's different. My present husband is not so sensual. The whole act now takes no more than one-half hour. With my former husband, we would lie together for hours playing with sex.

"My first husband was a liar; the whole relationship was a farce. My present husband is sensitive, honest, and true. I was completely dependent on my first husband. When he left, I fell apart. I didn't realize how dishonest my former marriage was. It was all superficial. Now I want a deeper feeling and a deeper response."

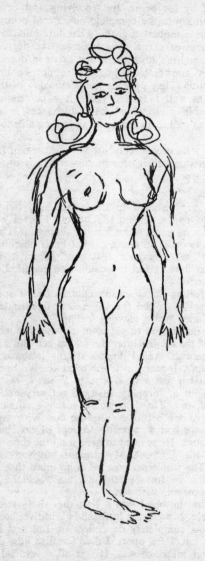

FIGURE 8

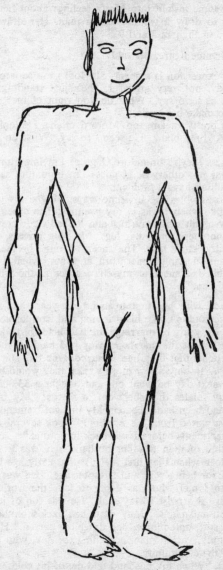

FIGURE 9

To obtain some insight into May's feelings about her body, I asked her to draw a woman and a man. Her drawings are reproduced in Figures 8 and 9.

Of the female figure, she said:

> "Her expression is a sneer. She looks too square, kind of dowdy, not very graceful. She's just standing there waiting, as if to say, 'What do you want of me?' I was trying to make her smile.
>
> "He's pretty vacant, too. More than she. He looks like a boy. Awfully blank. He seems to say, 'What do we do next?'
>
> "I guess they're immature. I guess I'm immature sexually, but not otherwise. I guess I'm immature sexually or I wouldn't have a problem.
>
> "She resembles me in some ways. Maybe it's what I looked like when I was in my twenties. The other figure is pretty much what my husband looked like: crew cut, broad shoulders, muscular legs. Me—big breasts, round hips, fluffy, curly hair. The sneer—it must be me. I do feel I am sneering underneath at times, when I don't feel fulfilled. I sneer at myself, I sneer at the world, I sneer at men."

May lived with her first husband six years and left him because she couldn't take his drinking and irresponsibility any longer. In six years of marriage, he had held thirty jobs. Just before the end of the marriage, May had paid off more than $2,500 in debts that they had incurred. One day she told her husband that in only a few more weeks, they would be out of debt. The next day he went out and bought a $3,000 car on credit. May relates that she went to pieces: "My face blew up like I had been badly beaten. My lips got tremendous. My eyes almost closed from the swelling. It took several weeks of doctor's treatments before I was back to normal."

What kind of man was her husband? He was twenty and May eighteen when they first met. At that early age he had a reputation for being wild and irresponsible. "He was the first young man I met who was going to take the world by the tail and give it a twist," May said. "He was full of ideas and had a thousand plans." May described Jack's mother as "a very cold, stiff, unfeminine, and unfeeling person." His father was an empty, vacant man, according to May, who posed as a pillar of the community.

She said, "When my husband told me of his cold, unfeeling

family life, my heart went out to him. I wanted to love him and make up to him for all those unhappy years. I wanted to fill his life with love, warmth, children, and a happy home."

This reaction to a lost man seems so noble and fine that one would hesitate to characterize it as immature. Yet immature it is, for it is the kind of feeling one might expect in a young girl, not in a young woman seriously considering matrimony. It reflects a lack of self—self-worth, self-esteem and self-preservation. Her husband completed half a year at college when they were married. Everyone thought she was mad, but May's emotion was too strong for reason: "I just glowed, came to life, when he was near me." May felt that he was a superior being. "Older people found him most charming," she remarked.

Following the marriage, the young couple moved into May's parents' home. May went to work, but her husband couldn't find a job. She gave him her salary to put into a savings account. When he finally got a job, they stayed on with her parents so that they could save for a honeymoon and their first home. Then May discovered that all the money was gone. Her husband had gambled it all away, with the excuse that he wanted to give her a really fine honeymoon.

This description enabled me to see that May had married a man with a psychopathic personality. Good-looking, suave, irresponsible, and unprincipled, such a psychopath always finds a woman who will devote herself to him. Once the relationship is established, the psychopath becomes a little boy who expects to be taken care of. And for six years, May indulged him as a child. In the course of my practice, I have run across a number of such marriages, all of which ended unhappily. When this one broke up, May was left without support for herself or her children. She returned to her family.

What kind of woman is attracted to this kind of psychopathic male? May's description of herself was accurate: big breasts, round hips, square, dowdy, and not very graceful. There was a markedly passive element in her personality. "What do you want of me?" expressed an attitude of submission. Her lack of a sense of self reflected the masochistic character of her personality. In her life with her first husband, May made almost no personal demands; her individual needs were continually being subordinated to the irrational demands of her husband.

May related that she was "a very good, quiet child" who was kept very clean by her mother. "She shined my shoes twice a day, curled my hair, and did everything she could to make me pretty and clean." The passivity in her nature was manifested very early, and her tendencies in this direction were encouraged by her mother, who treated her as a doll rather than as a person. In one special area, her mother's interference furthered the child's passivity and deepened her submissiveness. May relates that as a child, she had a great deal of trouble with constipation, and her mother gave her enemas all the time.

The practice of giving regular enemas, I have found, is extremely harmful to the psychosexual development of the child. The insertion of the enema nozzle into the child's anus has such an obvious sexual symbolism that I wonder why its significance has been so consistently overlooked by psychologists and sexologists. Joan Malleson postulates that the insertion of suppositories, soap stick, and enema nozzle may be responsible for vaginismus in women. She writes, "Anyone who has witnessed this will recognize the extreme pain to which the child is subjected. The baby who is repeatedly attacked in this way will scream and stiffen at the very sight of the attacking object."* This kind of conditioning during childhood will create lasting impressions, and the individual will associate fear and pain with any attempted penetration of the body. Two results follow from the regular experience of enemas. The child contracts and tenses the muscles surrounding the anus, including those of the pelvic floor and the buttocks, as a defense against the threat of penetration; and movement while the penetration is in effect is severely restrained. Since the anus is so close to the vagina, the fear of penetration and movement extends to and embraces any act of penetration involving this organ.

The reaction to the repeated experience of enemas may take the form of resistance or submission. Vaginismus may be a form of unconscious resistance to penetration that is associated with the painful and humiliating early experience. More frequently, the child adopts an attitude of submission to the inevitable and accepts the mother's statement that it is good for the child. It is easy to see how this submissive attitude becomes transferred later to the sexual act. But while the enema may bring a feeling of relief after the bowel

*"Vaginismus: Its Management and Psychogenesis," *British Medical Journal*, 1942, p. 215.

movement that it induces, the passive and submissive attitude in sexuality ends only in frustration.

May didn't remember having enemas before the age of seven or eight. However, each time she had a baby, she experienced the preliminary enema as the "worst part" of the procedure. On two occasions, her husband tried anal intercourse with her: "I found it awful and very painful. He said he enjoyed it, but I would not let him do it again." The pervasive nature of May's unconscious fear of being penetrated anally was also shown in a different context. Doing an exercise in my office while I was standing behind her, May observed, "A fear shot through me that you might shove something up my rectum. In fact, I had the same fear the first time I was in your office. The thought of an erect penis going in passed through my mind, but I put it right out of my thoughts. I could not have told you for fear that you would take me for mad."

We are now in a position to understand one important aspect of May's personality that was revealed in her figure drawing. The sneer on the face of the female figure expressed May's contempt for the male and her feeling of superiority to him. At the same time, it also expressed her contempt for the woman who becomes involved with an inadequate man and who must, therefore, dominate the relationship. But this concept is extremely well covered up by an attitude of devotion and self-sacrifice. Despite her conscious effort to be different, May was quite similar to her domineering mother, with whom she unconsciously identified. Her contempt for the male derived also from the experience of the enema. Unconsciously, she viewed the act of sex as "pushing the penis into the rectum" (vagina), to which she submitted despite the feeling of humiliation that it engendered in her. The repression of the feeling of humiliation gave rise to contempt for herself and for the male. The complex interplay of unconscious forces in May's personality may be more comprehensible if I answer her question, "What do you want of me?" May believed that a man wanted her to mother him, to take care of him, to indulge his desires. This was certainly true of her first husband. At the same time, she expected him to want to "shove it up her ass." This is exactly what her first husband tried to do.

May could not divorce her role as mother to her husband from her attitude of sexual submission. These were complementary attitudes that balanced her feelings of inferiority (sexual object = piece of ass) and superiority (mother = protector). In the same way, her contempt for the male was reflected in her contempt for herself. Evidently, what was missing in her personality was the image of a woman who could be the wife and equal of her husband and the mother of his children. In her sexual attitude, May was the small girl submitting to an enema. May conceded that she might be sexually immature; however, she regarded herself as mature in other respects. It was difficult to make her see that she was only a little girl wearing her mother's shoes.

This analysis of May's personality is intended to explain the neurotic attitudes responsible for her inability to achieve a vaginal orgasm. Her problems were not purely psychological, for they were structured in the tensions of her body. Her passivity was reflected in an overall reduction of body motility. Muscular tensions in the lumbosacral region, in the buttocks, and in the thighs severely restricted pelvic movement. Through the identification with the male, that is, by focusing her sexual feelings on the clitoris, May denied that she was a sexual object (passive, submissive) and asserted her right to be considered the equal of man (active, aggressive). Fixation upon the clitoris is a compensation for the feeling of inferiority associated with being penetrated. In this very process, however, May's neurosis was deepened and her problems became intensified. In my clinical experience, I have never known a woman to find satisfaction and happiness in a marriage in which her only form of sexual release was obtained through clitoral stimulation. Every marriage I have studied in which this practice was routinely accepted, was characterized by feelings of conflict, frustration, and dissatisfaction.

May related that her first husband took a course on marriage at a university and that they followed the sexual practices advised in the recommended books. Since, according to these books, it was unusual for a woman to have a vaginal orgasm, her husband felt justified in concentrating on the clitoris. I had suggested to May, when I saw her, that she read Marie Robinson's *The Power of Sexual Surrender*. Her reaction to this book was, "I only wish you could have told me about it ten years ago. My sex life would have evolved very differently, I am sure."

The clitoral orgasm represents one form of orgastic impotence in the female. Another form of orgastic impotence exists when the female is incapable of reaching any climax whatsoever in the sexual act or through any form of stimulation. I would not describe such women as frigid, for many of them welcome the sexual act and find pleasure in the closeness and intimacy with men. There are others, however, who are frigid in that they experience no sensation of erotic desire from the sexual caresses of the male. In the frigid woman, the vagina is unlubricated and sexual intercourse is painful. Such cases of sexual anaesthesia were much more common in the Victorian era. Many studies were devoted to this problem, by the early psychoanalysts. Our interest, however, is in the problem of orgastic impotence, to which much less attention has been paid. To further illustrate this problem, I shall present the history and personality problems of another patient who was unable to achieve a sexual climax.

Doris had always been attracted to boys as far back as she could remember. Sexual feelings were never lacking. As a child, she used to let her panties hang down between her legs, which gave her erotic sensations in the genital area. As an adult, she was easily aroused and experienced strong desires for sexual intercourse. Her problem was rather clearly revealed in her report on a fantasy she had had after masturbating. She said, "I was half-asleep and half-awake and was thinking that I have always held something back from people. I'm afraid to give of my whole self. At this point, a mental image came into my mind of a box with a closed lid which represented what I held back. I opened it and it was empty. I was startled. It made me think that I tell myself I hold back but I'm really afraid that there isn't anything there to give—or if there is, I don't know what it is or how to reach it."

This image of emptiness is one that troubles many individuals. Patients often complain of feeling empty. Since no one is truly empty, how can we reconcile this fact with the feeling of an inner emptiness? The feeling of emptiness reflects the absence of feelings of love—love of oneself, of a person of the opposite sex, of family, neighbors, or friends. The box in Doris's fantasy referred not only to the vagina, of which it was a symbol, but also to the chest which enclosed the heart. What Doris was saying seemed to be, "I don't know if I have a heart, or if I do, I don't know what it is or how to reach it."

Doris had always been ambivalent about her femininity. In the course of therapy, she became conscious of homosexual feelings. Closeness to certain of her girl friends excited her sexually. Fortunately, Doris was able to accept this fact, and these feelings didn't trouble her. She had never engaged in any homosexual activity and was always involved sexually with men. Her homosexual feelings were part of her sexual complex, which also included strong feelings of envy toward men. Several times she expressed the feeling that she wished she were a boy and had a penis. On one occasion, she dreamed that her sister had a penis, and she remarked, "It didn't seem too strange. It was very obvious and noticeable and it fascinated me. She might have been me, or the dream may have expressed my wish that I had one." When Doris was born, her parents were disappointed that she wasn't a boy.

Fantasies and dreams are subject to multiple interpretations. The empty box in Doris's fantasy could also refer to her lack of a penis. Lacking a penis, Doris felt empty and unable to move. But while such an interpretation is valid, it would be more accurate to say that being unable to love and feeling empty, Doris associated this with the absence of a penis.

Doris suffered from two physical afflictions. She was subject to repeated attacks of asthma, and she struggled with a neurodermatitis that was so severe at one time that all she could do was lie in a starch bath for hours on end. Her asthma resembled her orgastic impotence. Asthma is an inability to let the air out, and orgastic impotence is the inability to discharge sexual feeling. Both of these conditions were cleared up by the therapy after their meaning had been elucidated in the course of analysis.

A dream that Doris reported provided some indication of the nature of her sexual problem. "I was walking down the street with C. [a small girl,]" she said. "We stopped at a corner to get a paper, and a man there leered at us. Later, C. mentioned that she knew him and that he had given her $10 for sucking on a candy cane. I knew what she meant, and I was horrified that such a thing had happened to her at so young an age and that there was no way to undo it. I was afraid that he had really contaminated her, and I was upset by her offhand way of talking about it. She had been so innocent." Doris did not question her identification with C. in the dream. She was aware that she had been exposed to adult sexuality as a young girl and that it had made her feel unclean.

One memory played a significant role in unraveling the

tangled skein of her feelings. Doris recalled that at the age of three, she and a little boy used to lie on a couch and watch her mother clean and diaper her newborn baby sister. She remembered the sexual feeling that the scene evoked in her. But she also recalled that she was very constipated at this time. She had not moved her bowels for days, and she remembered that there was a large, round, hard fecal mass stuck in her rectum. She remarked, "I used to feel it. It seemed like a part of me. I was also afraid of it, afraid to let it go, but knowing that I'd have to and that the longer I waited, the worse it would be. I knew that it would hurt and that mother would be mad or upset."

The denouement of this case proved most exciting. It occurred a short time after the above memory was recalled. The session started with Doris's statement that she felt different from other girls. She remarked that she didn't feel at ease with them. She said, "I can't make small talk. I can't look at people if I don't know them well. I'm afraid I'll reveal something or the lack of something. I feel ashamed about my skin condition. I don't want anybody to see it."

Then Doris related a fantasy that she had had since childhood: "I had the fantasy of my father coming into my room while I was asleep and making me pregnant and I wouldn't know it. It scared me very much." She added that he used to drink, and she thought that he might lose his head and come after her with an ax.

"What would he do?" I asked.

"Cut my head off," she said.

"What did that mean?" I questioned.

"He could do something to me and I wouldn't be aware of it," she answered.

My interpretation was that if her father caused Doris to lose her head, she would have relations with him and become pregnant. Such a fantasy could arise in a child, if on some level of consciousness she felt that her father was not to be trusted. Doris had to "keep her head" to guard against the possibility that her father might lose his. The need to keep her head and the desire to let go in orgasm created a personality conflict that immobilized Doris in the sexual act.

The fantasy related above could also be interpreted as an expression of Doris's childhood wish to become impregnated by her father. Here we have one of the major conflicts in her unconscious: the desire to become pregnant and the fear of it. Doris then related that in the course of her marriage, she had tried and tried to become pregnant but with no success. This discussion brought up some references to her abdomen. Doris said that her abdomen had always been a problem for her. She had always tried to hold it in, to make it small and tight, but this restriction interfered with her breathing and made her anxious. My suggestion that she let her abdomen out and not try to hold it in helped her achieve a degree of relaxation in the early stages of the therapy. She remarked, "It always looks like I'm pregnant, but I'm not. Am I afraid unconsciously that I am pregnant and that it will show?" As she lay on the couch, she cried out, "My belly!" and began to sob deeply.

In the light of this insight, it became possible to understand one function of the skin eruption on her face. It occurred to me that it might be a diversionary maneuver, so I asked her, "Why did you want your skin to break out?" Hesitatingly, she answered, "To take attention away from my belly. I'm always afraid they'll see." And she added, "All my life I've been afraid to let my belly out, afraid it will show I'm pregnant. But I'm not," she insisted.

Could this fear have some connection with her inability to achieve an orgastic release? I asked her to associate to the word "orgasm." "What does this word mean to you?"

"Letting go, pain, and mess. Loss of control and the fear that something will come out that will make me ashamed." She rubbed her eyes and said, "My eyes don't want to see something."

"What don't you want to see?" I asked.

"The mess, and I don't want anybody else to see it either," she replied.

The "mess" could have only one interpretation in view of the foregoing. It represented the large, hard, fecal mass in her rectum that she was afraid to let out. She was afraid that it would "make a mess" and that her mother would be angry and upset, and she was afraid that it might prove to be a baby. The latter would reveal her fantasied sexual transgressions with her father. The psychoanalytic concept of the identity of feces with child is well illustrated in this case. But my concern here is with the relation of feces to orgastic impotence. Orgasm, to Doris, represented letting go, letting it out. Feces equals child, which equals sexual feelings. Any disturbance in the function of bowel movement will reflect itself in a corresponding disturbance in sexual movement.

The functional unity of the alimentary canal is such that similar disturbances are found at the two ends of the tube. Thus the inability to let out may parallel an inability to take in. Doris had another difficulty that had some relation to her inability to have an orgasm. She was inhibited in both sucking and biting. I discussed this problem with her in a session. On that occasion, Doris had put her knuckle into her mouth. As she clenched it with her teeth and sucked on it vigorously, her vagina became flooded with sexual feelings. The mouth and the vagina are homologous organs in the sense that both are receptive cavities. The significance of this functional relationship in regard to sexuality was discussed in an earlier chapter. When Doris perceived the sexual feeling, she remarked, "I'm afraid to bite because once I start biting, I'll bite it off—breast, penis. Why did I have so much trouble swallowing?" She began to cry deeply and repeated her question. Then she added, "I felt something. It's my fault. Swallowing is becoming pregnant. It's like an orgasm."

Doris's deep-seated wish and fear of becoming pregnant was partly responsible for her difficulty in swallowing. The young child believes that her mother becomes pregnant by taking something into her body orally. By not swallowing, by not taking it in, the little girl thinks that she can avoid becoming pregnant. But why did Doris wish to become pregnant? To say that she wanted to be like her mother or to take her mother's place with her father explains only the psychological motivations. What were the physical needs that induced this wish? A baby is a symbol of love. The pregnant state denotes that a woman has been loved and is filled with love, that is, with the product of love. Doris's fear and concern (in her fantasy) that her box was empty, which was interpreted as a lack of love, explained her wish to be pregnant. In the adult woman as well as in the young child, pregnancy is identified with the feeling of being loved. It is one of the easiest ways to fill the inner emptiness.

The memory of another incident in her childhood came back. Doris recalled that when she was quite little, her mother had told her where babies came from. She sensed that it had required a great effort on her mother's part to be so frank. When her mother had finished, Doris remembered that she flew out of the room saying, "I don't believe it, I don't believe it!" But then she added, "I don't recall her being pregnant, though she must have had a big belly before my sister was born. All I recall is her coming home from the hospital with my baby sister when I was three."

Doris could not have been unaware of her mother's condition. If she blocked out her memory of that state, it was to deny the significance of the big, full belly. She, too, had had a full belly (anus, full of fecal matter), and she had interpreted her mother's information to mean that a child is born through the anal canal. In more ways than one, Doris's problem had been "too big and too much." She was exposed to the facts of life too early, and they were too big and too much for her. Her development became confused. Genitality was mixed with the oral longing for love and colored with anal anxiety. Her "box" was not empty but full of repressed feelings. Analysis showed that Doris's wish was to become pregnant as a means of satisfying her oral needs. But pregnancy posed dangers. It would betray the incestuous desire for the father, and it would present the seemingly insoluble problem of how to bring the child forth without "making a mess." Orality was burdened with genital feeling. Doris could not bite or swallow for fear that it would lead to pregnancy. Her difficulty in breathing expressed her fear of letting anything out. Unable to function as an adult and unable to regress to the child, Doris could react only with crying and temper tantrums. All these feelings had to be brought to the surface and released so that she could fill up with the affection that she wanted to give and to receive. Until this was accomplished, Doris was blocked by her fear of "taking in" and her fear of "letting out." Sex was for Doris a desperate attempt to find love in the maze of impulses and defenses that constituted her personality. That is, Doris was trying to reach her heart. It was no surprise that she inevitably became lost in this confused situation and was unable to find an exit (climax).

Doris's deeper feelings then emerged. She said, "I don't want sex, but to be close. I wanted to be held and to be loved, but if I went to my father, he would interpret it as a sexual desire and would push me away. My mother was aware of my feeling for my father. She tied everything up with sex. If I went to my father for love, she would make it look like sex, and he would know it and wouldn't accept me. I couldn't go to her either. Is this why I can't be free and spontaneous? I'm too preoccupied with sex. It's always in my mind, consciously or unconsciously. It enters into everything."

After the above expression of feeling, Doris's pattern of neurotic sexuality slowly broke up. She had used sex as a way to gain closeness and love, and it had failed. In doing this, she had followed the example of her parents, who confused the child's love with adult sexuality. When therapy was resumed after a summer recess, Doris recognized that she would have to give up her infantile clinging and dependence on a man if she wished to gain emotional maturity. Spontaneously, she brought up this point and made a decision to alter the nature of her relationships with men.

A recurrence of the itching dermatitis developed on parts of her body, but not on her face. This was analyzed as a displacement of infantile masturbation. As a child, Doris had not been able to touch her genital area with her hands. She would let her panties hang down as a substitute mechanism. Though she masturbated regularly as an adult, she had never achieved any climax or release. In the course of analysis, she realized that she should be able to do it for herself (give herself pleasure and satisfaction), and she wanted very much to be able to do it for herself.

Two events transpired that helped to resolve her problems. She developed a number of boils of such severity that she was hospitalized for a week. In the hospital, Doris felt free for the first time from the pressures of her job situation. She became consciously aware of her compulsive attitude toward work. She had driven herself so hard on the job that she was exhausted at the end of each day and was unable to care properly for her apartment or herself. When she returned to work following her release from the hospital, she functioned at a more normal pace, but she also became aware for the first time of feeling very tired. Her fatigue had been masked by her compulsiveness. The need to pay more attention to her physical well-being focused her energies and attention upon herself. The result was a strengthening of the feeling of self and a diminution of her overinvolvement with outside situations, men, and work. With this new sense of direction, feelings of independence appeared. And Doris reported that she had experienced a climax while masturbating.

The second event was the loss of her job, one she had held for many years. She had been thinking of leaving it, but events anticipated her move. She was discharged with very liberal severance pay and felt a great sense of release and freedom. For the time being, she had no need to work; and for once in her life, she could "let go" of herself. In the context of a new attitude toward life and a rediscovery of the self, orgastic sensations appeared in the sexual act. They were not all that could be desired, but they were a beginning. And they increased in pleasure and number as her personality matured and blossomed. For some time now, Doris has been going with a young man who is understanding but uninvolved, tender but not clinging. Their relationship has been a source of considerable pleasure to both. It has helped her to make the necessary advances toward womanhood.

Doris is a completely different person from the one I met several years ago. Her face is soft and happy looking, her eyes have a calm expression. Her body feels good to her. Having recovered her body, she now wishes to take care of it with good food, sleep, fresh air and exercise. Until recently, she had neglected this whole aspect of existence. Many problems remain, both physical and psychological, but Doris has a new confidence and a new security. Like a flower that buds slowly but opens overnight, the changes had been long in preparation. But only such slow changing, which is tantamount to growth and not a magical transformation, is dependable and enduring.

I have treated many women who have gained some measure of orgastic potency through the resolution of internal conflicts. It has never been an easy task. We should not delude ourselves that orgastic potency can be achieved by detours or manipulation. Sex is not an isolated phenomenon. The sexual function of a woman reflects her womanhood or her lack of it. If we are confronted with orgastic impotence in a woman, we must suspect the presence of deep-seated conflicts in her personality. Infantilism, immaturity, and masculinization are among the fixations that stunt a woman's personality. They undermine her sexuality and deny her sexual fulfillment. They cannot be eradicated by the whitewash of sexual sophistication. If we are to gain a deeper insight into the problem, we should inquire into the historical background of the current confusion about the feminine personality and the feminine function.

14

The Double Standard

It takes little imagination to realize that the sexual problems of women have some relation to the double standard of morality to which they have been subject for countless generations. What normal girl hasn't been brought up to guard herself against the sexual advances of men or to regard a seduction as a defeat of her personality? It is so much a part of our culture that we speak of a "fallen woman," but never of a "fallen man." The wife who steps outside her marriage to have sexual relations is condemned; the husband is merely criticized. The young woman is shamed into sexual morality; the young man is exhorted merely to be discreet. Among their peers, the seducer is acclaimed, the seduced is pitied. Until recently, the pleasure of sex has been the prerogative of the male. The emancipation of woman has culminated in her demand for equal privileges and equal satisfactions.

The harm that the double standard has inflicted on women extends beyond the restriction of her sexual activities. It has operated over the years to split her unitary nature into two opposite aspects: as a sexual object, she is an inferior being; as a devoted and sacrificing mother, she is a superior being. Sometimes the values become reversed. The woman as a sexual object may become a famous movie star, while the woman as a mother is relegated to an inferior role. The courtesan was envied and despised, the housewife approved but patronized. Now psychologists tell the modern woman that she should be sexual object and mother, courtesan and housewife, all at the same time. Unfortunately, the split in the consciousness of woman has persisted for so long that it cannot be healed by a facile denial or wished away by sexual sophistication.

The double standard reflects the relegation of woman to an inferior position in Western culture. Her person has been subject to masculine domination, and her personality has been submerged in a patriarchal culture. Simone de Beauvoir was not without justification when she described women as the "second sex." It has been a long, uphill fight for woman from the time when, under Roman law, she was her husband's chattel to her present freedom and dignity as an equal citizen. It required a great effort to open the door of education to her, and only recently has she been accorded the right to vote in democratic countries. But if her struggle for recognition has been largely won in the political and social areas, it is still in progress in the sexual area. Here, decrees and laws are of no help. The experience of the Soviet Union with prostitution illustrates the difficulty. Despite a sincere effort to end this problem through laws and reeducation centers, there are as many streetwalkers in Moscow today, according to Maryse Choisy, as there are in New York, London, or Paris.

The sexual problems of women cannot be divorced from those of men. This is illustrated in a popular witticism that states that "the reason women keep their girlish figures is to retain their boyish husbands." The double standard affects the male only slightly less than it does the female. It dissociates his tender and affectionate feelings from his sexual feelings. It may create a condition of sexual impotence in a man with respect to women of his own social standing. It was not uncommon in the years prior to World War I for a man to be impotent with his wife but seemingly potent with a prostitute. The early analysts treated many such cases. It would be a mistake, however, to believe that this problem has disappeared. The man who carries on an affair with his secretary but whose sexual relations with his wife have deteriorated is not regarded as impotent by sophisticated standards. Yet this is the same problem in another form: the dissociation of love and respect from sex. This split in the man's personality undermines his orgastic potency. To think of men, therefore, as the villains who are responsible for the double standard and woman's derogation is to take too shortsighted a view of this problem.

The double standard has its origin in the development of Western culture, which is dominated by the masculine ego and its ideal of power. It was preceded by a more primitive culture in which the feminine functions and feminine attributes determined man's relation to nature and life. This earlier stage is known as the matriarchal period in contrast to the later patriarchal period. During the matriarchy, kinship relations were derived solely from the mother. The male was viewed as an extension of the female, who was worshipped as the Great Mother, or *magna mater*. Another way of seeing the great cultural change that occurred at the dawn of history is to relate it to the dethronement of the early feminine deities and their replacement by masculine figures that later were glorified in the Judeo-Christian concept of God the Father.

The image of the Great Mother, which the primitive ego depicted in sculpture and drawing, was the hermaphroditic woman, with a beard or a penis. She combined the masculine and the feminine. In early Egyptian mythology, she was Neith, the birthgiver, "the mother who bore the sun," but who was also a goddess of war. Hathor wore a solar disk with cow's horns; she gave milk and bore the sun, but she was also a "blood-thirsty despoiler of mankind." The Great Mother was the goddess of life and death, of all nature and its manifestations. She was the personification of nature, wild and untamed; the fang of the beast as well as the song of the bird belonged to her. Her worship was associated with bloody sacrifices, both human and animal, and fertility rites involving actual or symbolic castration. The Great Mother had double aspects: "good mother" and "terrible mother," giver and taker, provider and destroyer, life and death. In this sense, she was nature as primitive man experienced it. But she was also the mother of one's infancy, who nourished and comforted but who could also abandon or hurt the child. Here, too, she had a double aspect: "good mother" and "bad mother."

The struggle that overthrew the female deities was not a fight between man and woman but a creative conflict between the forces of culture and the unconscious. It was a struggle fought in the mind and soul of primitive man and woman, as it is still fought by every individual in his ontogenetic development. It is the struggle of the conscious mind to comprehend the forces of nature and to bend them to its will. It is the struggle of the ego to make itself master of the id, and only to the degree to which this struggle is successful is civilized life possible.

The ascendancy of the male principle can be correlated with the growth of consciousness and the development of the ego. The ego develops out of consciousness as self-awareness or self-consciousness. It represents the differentiation of the individual from the group. Primitive consciousness experienced itself as identified with and as part of nature and the group in what Lucien Lévy-Bruhl called "participation mystique." The ego's experience of the self created the dichotomies of self and the other, I and the world, heaven and earth, male and female. These distinctions were always present, but they were buried in the pervading sense of mystical identification. If nature is perceived in feminine terms, the emerging and developing ego becomes identified with the masculine principle. This process, which is represented mythologically as the "separation of the world's parents," assigns to consciousness a masculine quality in both man and woman. Light, day, and heaven represent the masculine as opposed to darkness, night, and the unconscious, which have a feminine character. Unconsciousness is sleep, and sleep is a symbolic return to the womb and the earth.

A key factor in the overthrow of the matriarchal system was knowledge of the role played by the male organ in procreation. In some cultures, such as that of the Trobriand Islands, its function in conception was unknown until the twentieth century. It had been assumed that conception occurred when the spirit entered the woman's body from the water or the air. Woman's body was regarded as a vessel that contained within itself the generative principle. Its symbol was the cornucopia, which poured out the fruits of the earth. It is easy to understand the primitives' difficulty in relating sexual relations to pregnancy and birth. The infrequency of pregnancies as compared with the large number of sexual acts and the long time interval between conception and birth seemed to negate any direct connection. This knowledge was first acquired by nomadic tribesmen, whose economy depended upon the herding and raising of animals. It can be assumed that they transferred it to cultures based on agricultural pursuits. But this knowledge did not undermine the matriarchy until the appearance on the social scene of private property.

Historically, the growth of the patriarchy can be related to the cultural advance from the Stone Age to the Bronze Age, marked by the use of metal implements. The smelting of ores and the forging of metals depended on the ability to harness fire for constructive activities. Stone Age man had used fire for cooking and warmth. Its employment, however, as a means of transforming nature (ore into metal into instrument) represented a major change in man's relation to nature. It gave man the power to change nature, a power that depended on his will, in contrast to Stone Age man, whose attempt to control or influence nature depended on the use of magic and ritual. It made possible the acquisition of the power of property.

Both knowledge and property existed in the matriarchal stage. Stone Age man had accumulated certain experiences, and he was aware of certain sequences of events. But the phenomenon of natural transformation exemplified by the vegetative cycle or the birth of a child was a mystery to him. It belonged to the unknown or dark forces. The knowledge eventually gained by the ego was the knowledge of cause and effect, of relationships. It was the knowledge of good and evil. The good consisted in the power to transform nature; the evil was man's awareness of his isolation, his insecurity, and his mortality. Erich Neumann in *The Origins and History of Consciousness* makes the same observation: "Ego consciousness not only brings a sense of loneliness; it also introduces suffering, toil, trouble, evil, sickness and death into man's life as soon as these are perceived by an ego." All these negative aspects of life existed before, but they were events, not concepts; misfortunes, not threatening dangers. A whole system of security defenses had to be erected against these dangers.

The power of property is such a security defense. Property in the sense of power had its inception in the production of surplus. Surplus foodstuffs, whether animal or vegetable, are the kind of property that represent security against nature, for it makes its owner somewhat independent of the vicissitudes of nature. The stored grain in a warehouse is man's protection against the danger of lean years when food is scarce. In this connection, it cannot be ignored that the stored grain in the Pharaohs' warehouses provided the material basis for their power and control. But the dependable production of surplus foodstuffs required the use of tools superior to those of Stone Age man, that is, metal tools. Similarly, the use of metal weapons enabled the possessor of property to guard it more effectively against depredation. Thus a complex of factors, including knowledge, the use of fire, metal, and surplus food, transformed the Stone Age

culture with its matriarchal organization of society into a
culture based on power and dominated by the masculine
principle.

The difference between these two cultures relates to the
distinction between personal and impersonal power. Primitive
man had personal power in the form of skills, esoteric knowledge such as that of the medicine man, or special physical
attributes such as strength. He also had property in the form
of shelter, clothing, utensils, tools, and weapons. But his
property, like his knowledge, was part of his person. It
belonged to him as his body belonged to him and could not
be alienated. Similar property could be acquired by any other
individual. The power represented by the possession of surplus food is impersonal and absolute. It is independent of the
personality of its owner much the same way that a sword has
power independent of the person who wields it.

What has all this to do with the question of the double
standard? Is it not significant that for thousands of years, and
until recent times, the acquisition of knowledge and the
ownership of property have been regarded as the domain of
the male? Why has the female been allowed only a derivative
participation in this cultural advance? What bias exists in the
unconscious mind of man against woman? Is she still regarded as the Great Mother who threatens to castrate or destroy
the male? The answer to the last question must be yes. The
fear of woman is as deep as the fear of nature, which is
coextensive with man's fear of his own mortality.

The Pharaohs used their power not for the common good,
but to further their security defense against the awareness of
death. The art of mummification and the construction of the
Pyramids testify to their preoccupation with death and their
desire for immortality. Lewis Mumford writes beautifully on
this subject in *The Condition of Man:* "Death happens to
all living things: but man alone has created out of the
constant threat of death a will-to-endure, and out of the
desire for continuity and immortality in all their many conceivable forms, a more meaningful kind of life, in which Man
redeems the littleness of individual men." In its most basic
form, the desire for continuity and immortality is focused
upon the heir, the son who will carry on "the name and
exploits of his father." Wilhelm Reich felt that sex repression
originally stemmed from the practice of "cross-cousin marriage." This means, in effect, that the ruling classes limited
the sexuality of their children to ensure the orderly transfer

of power from one generation to the next. It is known that incest was practiced among the Pharaohs, probably for the same reason.

In the lower classes of a society, the question of legitimacy or illegitimacy is less important than among the well-to-do. In a tribal culture in which individuality has not assumed the significance it has for civilized peoples, the problem of illegitimacy does not exist. It is common knowledge that the double standard also serves to assure a man that his heirs are the offspring of his seed, not another's. The insistence upon chastity and fidelity cannot have a purely economic motive. In Normandy, among the peasant people, an illegitimate child is welcomed as a help on the farm. Psychological and religious motives underlie the demand for female chastity. In a man's mind, a woman's chastity offers some guarantee that his power will pass down to his descendants. The story of Tom Jones shows that a blood tie is often stronger than conscious affection. The man's infidelity poses no such danger to his ego. Fortunately, this situation is changing. A broader social consciousness and a more limited future horizon have combined to emphasize the importance of the here and now.

Nevertheless, the double standard has operated to split the personality of the female into two antithetical functions: sexual object and mother. Among the ancient Greeks, the female as mother or daughter was largely confined to the home. She took no part in men's affairs and occupied herself with running the household and raising the children. The confinement to this role reduced her value as a sexual partner to her husband. The gap that this situation created in the emotional life of the male resulted in erotic attachments outside the home. These took the form either of a homosexual interest in a young boy or of a liaison with a courtesan. Homosexuality in ancient Greece reflected an attitude of misogyny that is absent in Homer's writings. Robert Flaceliere in his study *Love in Ancient Greece* notes that "many of the ancient Greeks lavished all their sexually rooted affections upon boys. For they considered members of the other sex inferior beings, lacking all education and refinement, good for nothing but to insure a posterity." Greeks who were heterosexually minded could "resort to courtesans" for their pleasure.

There were two kinds of prostitution in the ancient Greek world. Religious prostitution was organized by certain cults as a service to the goddess of love. The city of Corinth boasted a "thousand dedicated prostitutes," who attracted many tourists and made the city wealthy. In addition, there were many independent prostitutes. Most hetaerae, or courtesans, were slaves or came from the poorest families. Flaceliere discounts the idea that the hetaerae were better educated than the freedwomen. Some were musically talented, but their main appeal was as sexual objects.

From the point of view of the Greek ego, woman was an object to use, either sexually or as a mother. The former is associated with prostitution, the latter with marriage. This attitude changed somewhat during the Alexandrine period, but the hierarchy of values bequeathed by the classical Greeks has persisted to the present. Consciousness, knowledge, and reason (masculine values) are regarded as superior to instinct, intuition, and feeling (feminine values). Similarly, power as a value superseded the sense of identity and mutual obligation that were the bases of earlier tribal relationships. Unfortunately, but perhaps necessarily, the growth of individuality was achieved at the expense of the human rights of other individuals: the slave in ancient times, the feudal serf, the subject of national states, and the woman.

Two forces, each the offspring of masculine consciousness, attempted to redress this uneven and unjust state of affairs. One of these great forces was the concept of Christian love. For two thousand years, it has attempted to offset the appeal of power by the ideal of brotherly love. It introduced a new dimension into the relation of man to woman, one that was foreshadowed in myth and story. In the hero's struggle with the monster, a representative of the Great Mother, he is often abetted by a friendly female figure who succors the hero in his peril and is ready to sacrifice herself for him. Neumann says of these females that "the sisterly side of the man-woman relationship is that part of it which stresses the common human element; consequently it gives man a picture of woman that is closer to his ego and more friendly to his consciousness than the sexual side." What was a vision in the myth became a reality in Christian life. The personality of the woman was thus raised to a new level.

The other force was the development known as romantic love, which also acted to ennoble the woman and enhance her value. The fair lady of the knight's dream was an object of worship, not of sexual desire. He could sing her praises and go into battle wearing her colors, but he was not allowed to possess her. In the early practice of romantic love, the lady was often the wife of another man. Marriage, at any rate, was against the rules of romantic love. The object of the knight's passion was idealized. Only in this capacity could she ignite his ardor to the point of undertaking heroic deeds. She became the inspiration of his activities, but not the fulfillment of his longing. Springing from a greater consciousness of individuality, romantic love aimed at a higher, more spiritual awareness of the woman, divorced from her sexuality.

Knowledge, power, Christian love, and romantic love are valid ideals for civilized man. The goal of a higher consciousness is a legitimate objective. An exaggerated emphasis upon consciousness may result, however, in the loss of the unity of the personality. An undue insistence upon the importance of the ego easily leads to isolation and paranoia. Knowledge insidiously turns into sophistication when feeling no longer guides its application. Mastery over nature often ends in the destruction of nature. The emancipation of woman is a hollow victory when it is obtained by the denial of her essential nature as the vessel that holds the mystery of life.

15

The Sexual Roles
of the Female

Women have four principal roles in relation to the male sex: sexual object, sister, romantic ideal, and mother. These roles do not exist on the level of instinctive behavior, which characterizes the animal function. Instinctive behavior functions without regard to conscious considerations and is therefore independent of any concept of role playing. In the primitive stage of the human condition, these aspects are undifferentiated; the female appears in her total function as the Great Mother, which combines all her implicit roles. With the emergence of the ego and the overthrow of matriarchal culture, the unity of woman's personality was dissociated into the antithetical categories of sexual object and mother. Prior to this development, women fulfilled both these roles within the total function of the Great Mother concept. The dissociation that occurred at the beginning of civilization can also be viewed as a process of crystallization whereby what was previously implicit was then explicitly recognized. Similarly, the cultural evolution that produced Christianity and courtly love revealed two more aspects of the female personality: sister figure and romantic ideal.

These four roles correspond to the four stages of her personal life: daughter, sister, sweetheart (romantic ideal), and mother. Woman's psychosexual development is a growth process that incorporates each preceding stage into her maturing personality. When she reaches the final stage of motherhood, she has passed through and successfully integrated into her being the other aspects of her nature. Motherhood is not the goal but the final step in the progression toward the fulfillment of her nature. Each stage is an outgrowth of the preceding one. A woman cannot function as a sister to a man without previously having fulfilled the role of daughter. However, if there are disturbances that fixate a girl's development at an earlier stage, her adult function will reflect this disturbance; that is, it will be dominated by this aspect of her personality.

Normally, these aspects are submerged in the living reality of the woman as a person. In a healthy marriage, a husband does not regard his wife as a sexual object, sister, romantic ideal, or mother. He responds to her biologically and thinks of her as a unique person. However, if her pattern of behavior is limited and structured to a specific role, he will become conscious of her in terms of that role. Thus, a man who visits a prostitute acts with the awareness that she has assumed the role of sexual object. If a woman's psychosexual development has been fixated in one of these stages, the man's reaction to her is limited by the specific role she has assumed. He unconsciously reacts to her in terms of this role. This is not to say that the neurotic woman doesn't attempt to fulfill the other roles, that is, to be a whole person; her ability to do this, however, is handicapped by the arrest of her psychosexual development at an incomplete level. I shall present the character structure and sexual behavior of the female whose personality is fixated upon each of these roles.

1. Arrest of development at the daughter level owing to an inability to resolve the oedipal situation fixates a woman's personality upon the role of sexual object. Such a woman will become a psychological prostitute. She may easily become a professional one. The difference is one of degree. Prostitution is not the taking of money for the use of one's body (the sacred prostitutes of Corinth gained no financial reward for their services); the term "prostitution," as I define it, consists in permitting one's body to be used sexually without any feeling for the other person. In the psychological sense, this kind of prostitution also embraces the common variety of streetwalker and call girl. The taking of money for such services adds a further insult to the male. It indicates to him that whatever feeling he has for the woman means nothing to her. Maryse Choisy states that "the prostitute who takes money from a man is castrating him." On the other hand, the giving of money to a woman can be interpreted as an expression of gratitude. It is the demand for money that reflects contempt.

Prostitutes have been studied analytically in the past decade, and the basic unconscious tendencies that motivate such behavior are known. In each case, it has been shown that there was a lack of parental love to the degree that the child felt unloved and unwanted. This basic deprivation produced a split in the child's relation to the other and to herself. Feeling unloved, the child denied her need for love and projected it upon others. Denial and projection are the basic mechanisms that the unloved child uses to protect herself against the pain of her rejection. They become the controlling forces that dominate the professional prostitute's behavior.

The immediate effect of the deprivation of love is an inability to be alone. The prostitute's neurotic reaction to her need for human warmth is the rejection of all normal social relationships in place of which she substitutes pseudorelationships: with her customer, with her pimp, with other prostitutes, and with underworld elements. The lack of love is compounded by a lack of understanding on the part of her father upon whom the child transfers her unfulfilled oral longing. This transfer, which occurs in every girl's psychosexual development, creates an exaggerated dependence on the male figure. The professional prostitute denies her dependence and projects it upon men. She feels, on one level of consciousness, that all men need and desire her. This feeling is supported by her observation that most men will respond to her as a sexual object. Her awareness of her sexual appeal emerged early in her life. In most cases, there is a history of sexual violation or overtly expressed sexual interest by older men when she was still a child. The loss of self-esteem which results from her rejection as a love object but her acceptance as a sexual object produces a revulsion against sexuality and a repression of sexual feeling in the child. Again, denial operates, and the revulsion is overcome in the interest of a pseudorelationship to the male. But the repression remains, and the professional prostitute is frigid. Her need for sexual feeling and satisfaction is projected on the male. Frustrated in her attempt to be a person, the prostitute hates men and is afraid of them. The fear is masked by contempt, and the hatred is covered by a submissive attitude.

The overall personality that emerges from this background is deficient on the ego level, devoid of a sense of self, and lacking in genital feeling. The prostitute is an immature individual with an oral character structure in which schizophrenic and paranoid tendencies are generally present. The split in her personality is reflected in an ambivalence toward men; the need for love and acceptance is directed toward the pimp, whom the prostitute fears and hates, while the customer experiences her indifference and contempt.

The professional prostitute represses her awareness of her need for love and "acts out" in antisocial behavior and rebellion her negative feelings toward men. The psychological prostitute, as distinguished from the professional, represses her rebellion and "acts out" her need for love. Since her behavior is not antisocial, its meaning can be derived only from a study of her personal history. Laura is a good example.

When I first met Laura, she was about forty years old. She felt that she had gotten nowhere in life. She had been married once, during the war, but her husband made no effort to support her and left her for another woman. A child born during her married life was given up for adoption. Following the breakup of her marriage, Laura had many affairs and lived with a number of men. Several pregnancies ended in abortion. Laura seemed unable to develop a lasting relationship with a man. Besides her marriage, which lasted three years, she had had only one other relationship with a man that had lasted for more than one year. There was no lack of men to whom she gave herself sexually. Sexuality was important to her (she was familiar with Wilhelm Reich's ideas about the function of the orgasm), yet she had never experienced an orgasm with a man or through masturbation.

I would describe Laura as a psychological prostitute. She never demanded anything from the men she slept with, and few of them gave her anything. She seemed content to give herself to a man if he expressed any desire for her. She was a girl who couldn't or didn't want to say no. Laura supported herself by working as a secretary, but she had never held a position long enough to earn a good salary or accumulate a reserve. She would quit her job, as she left her men, because it was unfulfilling. Necessarily, she lived in very modest circumstances and was often in debt. The lack of material possessions didn't seem to bother Laura, for she regarded such things as relatively unimportant. Laura was a drifter. She drifted in and out of several analytic treatments, and I was able to work with her for only a short time.

The most outstanding quality about Laura was a softness of manner and expression. Her brown eyes were like limpid pools, and they reminded me of the eyes of an animal. Her voice was soft and well modulated. Her lips were sensuous, with a tendency to pout. The expression in her face reflected the appeal in her personality. A man could easily respond to it as a direct request for love, and he would not be mistaken. Laura was of above-average height. Her body was thin and willowy but strong. She had a narrow chest, full breasts, and a small, immature pelvis. Her legs were long and straight and showed signs of varicose veins. Although forty years of age, Laura looked no more than thirty. Emotionally, she was still a girl.

Laura was the oldest child in a family of four children. She said that she had never felt close to her mother, whom she described as an emotionally weak woman, childlike in her attitude. She felt very close to her father, and she regarded herself as "daddy's little girl." Laura recalled many physical intimacies with her father such as being kissed, sitting on his lap, and having him put her to bed at night. She was aware that her father responded to her charms as a little girl and that her mother was envious of and hostile toward her. Unfortunately, Laura's father died when she was ten years old, and the children were placed in an orphanage, where Laura stayed until maturity.

It would be a reasonable deduction that Laura's promiscuous sexual activities represented a search for her lost father. Brigid Brophy, writing about the professional prostitute, says, "The male sex is a lottery in which the prostitute has bought the highest possible number of tickets. Anyone in her holding may be the winning number, the father she is seeking." Of course, the prostitute never finds him. To find the father and have sex with him is to commit incest, which even the prostitute cannot do. Is Laura doomed to spend the rest of her life searching for a lost image? Is she fated to repeat her childhood experience of having a father and losing him? If so, what are the dynamics of her character that impose this fate upon her?

Laura was fixated upon the daughter stage in her relationships with men because she was unable to find any solution to the oedipal situation. This is to say that she could not pass beyond the role of "daddy's little girl" because she could not cope with her sexual feelings for her father. Both parents were responsible for Laura's difficulty. Her father's response to her as a sexual object bound her to him in a latent sexual relationship that could not be realized. It alienated Laura from her mother, whom Laura regarded as a rival. Laura did not accept her mother and, therefore, could not achieve any conscious identification with her. She was unable to run a home properly or to manage the cooking duties. Yet Laura showed many of the traits for which she rejected her mother. Like her mother, she was emotionally weak and immature. And like her mother, who placed her in an orphanage, Laura gave up her own child for adoption.

As a child, Laura instinctively felt that she understood her father's sexual need and could satisfy him. This was not a conscious knowledge, but an awareness by the child of her feminine nature and of its significance as an acceptable sexual object for the male. This awareness creates the situation known as the oedipal problem. It corresponds to the preliminary budding of genitality that terminates the oral phase of development. If undisturbed by adult sexual reactions, it will subside to allow the further development of the child's personality. But for Laura, such a normal development was prevented. She was alienated from her mother and dependent on her father because of her hope that he would devote his life to her in return for her willingness to fulfill his needs. This understanding became the basis of Laura's relationship to all men and betrayed the infantile attitude that could envisage such a "deal." Laura never grasped the idea that love cannot be bought through service or submission.

In Laura's behavior, the positive side of the prostitute's ambivalence was dominant. Instead of denying her need for love, she accepted it; she was aware of the necessity for finding and asserting her sexuality; and she accepted her dependence on the male, whom she also feared and hated. Laura's inability to reach a climax vaginally was caused by an inadequate pelvic movement. In the sexual act, she reached forward with her pelvis as a baby does to get the breast. After the penis was inserted, she clung to it out of fear of losing it. Owing to the rigidity in her legs and pelvis, Laura's sexual movements were hesitant and insecure. The fixation of the pelvis in the forward position was so strong that it immobilized her breathing. She couldn't have an orgasm because she couldn't "let go." And she couldn't find a satisfactory husband because she couldn't say no to a man.

There is a prostitute in every woman who was her father's daughter; that is to say, every female child is intuitively aware that she has what it takes to make a man happy. She senses in some deep corner of her being that men would do things for her because of it. She knows unconsciously that the female is a sexual object for the male, and she accepts this fact. The reaction of older women to any behavior in a young girl that suggests this awareness is often extreme. Girls have been called tramps, prostitutes, and other names for dancing innocently, yet perhaps provocatively, in front of their fathers or for showing a special interest in them. Great harm is often done to the child by the adult's overreaction to such ingenuous exhibitionism. Such actions are the natural expression of the essential nature of the female. This nature will undergo transformations in its normal development if it is left undisturbed. In many ways, Laura's behavior with her lovers resembled that of the professional prostitute with her pimp.

The negative side of the ambivalence was also present in Laura's behavior, but rarely directly expressed. Her appeal for love was not without its destructive component. The seductive charm of her eyes and manner was as lethal as the Venus's-flytrap. The man who entered her was eaten or devoured, psychologically speaking. Only by swallowing the man could she fill the inner emptiness of her being. Whatever a man gave her would never be enough. Her need was insatiable, and her lovers could only feel guilty for their failure. In the end, she spit them out as worthless. Her contempt for the male was openly voiced. She remarked, "They don't know if they're getting something or nothing in sex." Laura reacted to her frustrations with a depression that isolated her in a black cloud and often dragged her lovers down into her despair.

The men who responded to Laura's appeal were looking for a mother figure. I had occasion to treat one of Laura's lovers. He was looking for a mother who would be soft and understanding, one who would not demand too much of him. Laura promised these things. She was looking for a father who would be nice to her, protect her, and love her. They were like two children playing the game of being grown-ups. It couldn't work, and it didn't.

2. The sisterly relation to a man is based on common interests and a sense of equality. It reflects the feelings of a preadolescent girl toward boys of her own age group, her brothers and their friends. A true sisterly feeling toward a boy or a true brotherly feeling toward a girl implies an acceptance of the other's rights as a person and a respect for the sexual difference. The sisterly relationship, however, is

basically asexual, since it is biologically determined by the latency period, which extends from the age of five or six to adolescence.

Many girls are arrested at this level of personality development, which does not stop them from getting married or having children. However, the fixation at the sisterly level conditions their relationship to their husbands. The marital relationship is not primarily a sexual one, but an undertaking of mutual support in the world. I had occasion to treat a man and wife who were in such a relationship. They struck me as two eleven-year-olds walking through a dark woods and holding each other's hand for protection and assurance. Actually, each was afraid to be alone, and when one threatened to leave, the other panicked. The man was thirty years old and his wife was twenty-six. Both had previously been married.

The woman in a sisterly relation to a sexual partner regards herself, above all, as his companion and his helpmate. She wants to share his life, to be at his side during his struggles, and to consult with him in his decisions. It would seem that there is nothing wrong with this attitude. Difficulties arise, however, the moment the man insists upon a life of his own. This he is bound to do sooner or later, for he will sense her attitude as binding and controlling. The sisterly woman, if I may so describe her for the purpose of this discussion, is not content to remain in the background. Her desire to be indispensable to her husband causes her to attempt to prove that she is superior to him in intelligence or worldly affairs. Thus, she is not only his companion and helpmate, but also his competitor.

It is not difficult to foresee the problems that can arise in such a relationship. Everything is shared, no feeling is personal. Every expression of mood is a reflection upon the partner. Sex is not a passion but an affirmation of a community of interests, a pledge of loyalty. After the initial excitement of breaking the incest barrier has worn off, the sexual feeling usually deteriorates rapidly. For the sisterly woman is basically afraid of sex and enters into such a relationship to avoid her sexual guilt.

How does a girl become fixated at this stage? The sisterly relationship to a man is a partial solution to the oedipal problem. The complete failure to solve this problem, as in Laura's case, leads to psychological prostitution. The sisterly relationship can be considered a defense against psychological prostitution; in other words, the sisterly woman denies that her lover is her father by asserting that he is, instead, her brother. Thus, while the sisterly woman denies her oedipal guilt, this guilt is, nevertheless, strong enough to prevent her from fully asserting her right to sexual fulfillment.

Martha could be considered a sisterly woman. There was an adolescent quality about her body, which was straight and lean, with narrow hips, a small waist, and normal shoulders. She had a small head with dainty features, which made her appear petite despite the fact that she was of average height. Martha was twenty-nine, married, and the mother of two children. She complained of feelings of depression, chronic fatigue, and a lack of sexual satisfaction. She thought that going back to work might be one answer to her difficulties, but she sensed that her difficulties were somehow connected with her relationship to her husband.

Her marriage, Martha said, had not been based on either passion or romance. She had been involved sexually with a number of men who excited her more than her husband did, but she had married her husband because he appeared to be strong, hardworking, and dependable. He was, in fact, her most persistent suitor. In the course of therapy, Martha realized that her marriage was really a "business" of living together. She observed, "The lack of physical feeling between us is frightening to me."

Why did Martha marry the man who was least exciting to her? Her premarital relationships were promiscuous, and the pleasure Martha experienced in them could not be dissociated from her feeling that she was acting like a "prostitute." In fact, her father had called her a whore on more than one occasion for staying out late. Her marriage was an opportunity to escape from her home and to free herself from the guilt of sexual indulgence. Her premarital relationships, like those of Laura, offered her no security. Her husband offered her companionship and support but no sexual excitement.

One day, Martha described her feeling toward her husband as being that of a sister. She added, "When I first met Leo, he encouraged me to be like his sister, who was boyish. He wanted me to wear slacks, to give up the use of lipstick, and cut my hair short. He felt inferior to me on the intellectual and athletic levels. He chose me for the qualities that threatened him, and now he holds it against me. I know I compete with him."

Martha could reach a climax sexually if she pushed hard

enough for it, but it was never satisfying. Her sexual activity was compulsive. To have an orgasm meant to be a woman; but she couldn't achieve it because her basic attitude toward her husband was sisterly. I have heard many versions of the same story from other women. The sisterly woman feels that her husband is unresponsive to her effort to communicate with and help him. She feels that the relationship is one-sided in that he can criticize her, but if she attempts to criticize him, he rejects it. This feeling may reflect her experience as a sister with an older brother. Actually, the sisterly attitude does not develop out of the girl's experience of being a sister, but out of the oedipal situation.

Martha grew up in a home dominated by her mother, who was an ambitious and aggressive woman. Her father was a simple, hardworking man whose main interest was to earn a good living for his family. He avoided conflict with his wife by allowing her to have her way. The relationship between mother and daughter was not close. Martha was a middle child and was expected to cause no trouble for her mother. Between father and daughter there was a bond of sympathy that was not openly acknowledged. Martha realized that any overt display of sexual feeling for her father would not be tolerated by her mother. The queen bee destroys all competitors. At the same time, she sensed that her father needed moral support and would have welcomed his daughter's affections but that he dared not accept them. In this oedipal situation, Martha repressed her sexual feelings in favor of a sympathetic understanding for her father. The ambivalence that this repression created was apparent in the following incident that she related: "My four-year-old boy was crying over some injury. Leo demanded that he stop, but the child didn't. So Leo said to him, 'I'll give you something to cry about.' He was about to hit the child, but I stopped him because I didn't think it was right. So Leo got furious with me. I was torn because I hate to start a thing in front of the children. After all, he is their father, and he's got to have some authority."

The incident and her comment revealed Martha's conflict between her feelings for her child and her sympathy for her husband. She was reluctant to diminish her husband's image and his ego. The sisterly woman feels that she has to support the man, for without her help, he is weak. This feeling is the basis for her role as helpmate. But by being sorry for him, she diminishes him. A father without authority in his own home is a poor figure, and this was the image Martha had of her own father.

In contrast to the daughter-prostitute, the sisterly woman has achieved a partial resolution of her oedipal problem. She has discovered a basis for relating to the opposite sex other than as a sexual object. By adopting a friendly asexual approach to men, she expresses her disapproval of her mother's attitude. She would build a man's ego, not destroy it; share his struggles, not just profit from them. The emphasis betrays the need for mutual support. Father and daughter become covertly allied in the struggle against the mother. This alliance against the image of the "Great Mother" makes them equals, but reduces both of them to children. The daughter becomes a sister to her father. Such cooperation, based on fear, joins them together in their anxiety and insecurity. It binds them to their helplessness and makes them despise each other.

Ambivalence characterizes the relationship of the sisterly woman to husband, father, and mother. To the degree that she feels the need to support her husband's ego, she is contemptuous of him. Similarly, her sympathy for her father covered her contempt for his inability to stand up against the mother. In her relationships to men, her father and later her husband, the contempt is repressed because of the necessity to join forces against the stronger power of the mother.

Despite her overt alliance with the male figures, the sisterly woman is unconsciously identified with her mother. Like her mother, she resents the man's weakness and feels humiliated by it. Also like her mother, she will assert her superiority over the man by insidiously dominating the relationship. Her identification with the passive male on the ego level, and with her domineering mother on the unconscious level, explains why the personality structure of the sisterly woman is described as masculine-aggressive.

The bond of need that unites the sisterly woman to her mate precludes independence and orgastic potency. Because of her identification with the man, she is generally limited to a clitoral climax. To achieve this, she requires the cooperation of her partner, and the sexual relationship takes the form of one "doing" something for the other. From what I have said earlier about homosexual attitudes in heterosexual relationships, it is obvious that the sexual attitude of the sisterly woman has this quality. Her personality has latent homosexual tendencies, and her body configuration frequently has a masculine or boyish appearance. In terms of orgastic potency, the sisterly woman is between the woman who is a sexual object and the woman who is the romantic-ideal type. Whereas the prostitute has no climactic experience in the sexual act, the sisterly woman is capable of a clitoral release. On the other hand, the sisterly woman's response is less than that of the romantic-ideal type, who is generally capable of a partial orgasm.

A mature woman can act as a helpmate and companion to her husband without becoming sisterly. This aspect of the female personality doesn't dominate the mature woman's relationship to the sexual partner as it does in the case of the sisterly woman. Consequently, she is neither competitive nor destructive. Because she is a whole woman, she can be a true friend.

3. The woman whose personality is fixated at the romantic level relates to men as a sexual person. She differs from the daughter-prostitute type who holds herself out as an impersonal sexual object. But, while her appeal to men is on the sexual level, her personality precludes the idea of her being possessed sexually, for this would reduce her to the position of sexual object. Thus, on one level of her personality, she remains a virgin. Her psychosexual development corresponds to the adolescent stage of about sixteen to eighteen years of age.

The arrest of emotional development at the stage of the virgin or romantic ideal stems from an oedipal situation which was not fully resolved. This personality structure denotes a growth beyond the "sister" level, and indicates that the girl has not repressed her sexual feelings as the other types have done. On the other hand, she has not been able to escape the conflict of her relation to her father. His acceptance of her was conditioned upon her suppression or "holding back" of sexual activity. She is the "well brought up" girl who is assured of her parents' affection and esteem as long as she does not transgress the code of sexual morality. The guardian of this code is the authoritative father whose rigidity reflects his own sexual guilts and conflicts. Sexual repression, in the case of the daughter-prostitute type, stems from a real fear in the child's mind that her father or some other adult male will respond sexually to her. In the case of the romantic ideal or virgin type, this fear is transposed into a fear of her own sexual response. She is not "daddy's little girl," as Laura described herself, but "daddy's big girl." It has been said of this female personality that "her heart belongs to daddy," unlike Laura who gave herself body and soul to her father. The romantic relationship produces a more or less conscious dissociation between the feelings of love and sexuality.

The personality structure which is determined by this conflict has been described in the psychoanalytic literature as the "hysterical female." In Freud's time, the manifestations of this conflict between love and sex were seen as hysterical reactions or hysterical crises. Freud and the early analysts treated women who were raised under a Victorian morality. These were women for whom the mention of sex was taboo, who fainted if they were unexpectedly exposed to the facts of life. The hysterical reaction was due to the sudden release of suppressed sexual feeling. Since the moral atmosphere has greatly changed, the hysterical reaction has largely disappeared, but the hysterical character structure remains the same. It is a personality determined by the inability to reconcile the romantic aspects of love with the physical expression of love in sex. But, where the Victorian female clung to her romantic ideals and inhibited her sexual activity, her modern counterpart engages more freely in sex but dissociates it from her romantic aspirations. The conflict, while still charged with considerable force, is less explosive; the hysteria is seen mostly in outbursts of crying and occasional screaming.

How does the woman who adopts this role function in real life? During courtship, when she is acting out her role as romantic ideal, her excitement temporarily fuses the feelings of sex and love. This fusion is gradually lost in the course of marriage as reality replaces illusion. The romantic ideal cannot be maintained in the face of the physical intimacy that the marital situation requires, as the romantic lovers of the fourteenth and fifteenth centuries knew. Sexual possession removes the distance or barrier that is necessary to the feeling of romantic love. The husband becomes equated with the father toward whom sexual feeling had to be repressed. This transfer of feeling from father to husband occurs because both are viewed as authoritative figures who demand conformity to a restrictive moral code. The result is that the love for the husband assumes a compulsive quality and there is a progressive loss of sexual excitement in the marriage. Since romantic excitement exists only outside the patriarchal family, the "hysterical female" becomes flirtatious with other men. The woman who is fixated in this role always has a romantic lover in her life—that is, some man for whom she is a romantic ideal. This lover can be a real person or a fantasy figure.

The "hysterical female" needs the constant stimulation of romantic love to sustain her sexual excitement. She seeks this excitement from other men and from her own children; that is, she becomes seductive. She demands that her children admire her beauty and respond to her charms. To attract other men she may overstep the bounds of acceptable behavior. These demands of her ego prevent her from giving herself fully to her children or her husband. Breast feeding, like sex, is regarded by the "hysterical female" as a denial of the romantic image in which the woman is placed on a pedestal and adored. Yet sexuality is the lure that the "hysterical woman" uses to entice others into her worship. Since it is effective only as long as the man does not possess her, it becomes a block against her full surrender of her sexual feelings. Wilhelm Reich pointed out that the "hysterical female" uses sex as a defense against genitality. Necessarily, her orgastic response is limited. She is capable of a vaginal orgasm, but her reaction is partial; it does not envelop her total being. She is left with a feeling of frustration which drives her in fantasy or reality to amorous adventures.

There are positive and negative sides to the character of the hysterical female. Her acceptance of the sexual nature of the man-woman relationship supports the man's masculinity. Her insistence that his sexual desire be subordinated to the romantic ideal denies him satisfaction in the relationship. She is a challenge to a man, which excites his passion, but she eludes his grasp and thwarts his victory. In her negative aspect, the hysterical female is the young witch, seductive and enticing but ensnaring and destroying. Like all neurotic personalities, she is under the compulsion to "act out" upon her lover the rejection she suffered at the hands of her father.

Carol described the split in her personality as follows: "All my life, whenever a man fell in love with me, I pushed him away. I could give myself to a man sexually, but I felt trapped when he wanted to possess me. How can I overcome this fear?"

Physically, the "hysterical female" has an attractive body that is well shaped and properly proportioned, clear eyes, and an alive manner. If the sexual repression is more severe, a dulling of expression occurs. Her conflict is manifested either in rigidity or in a flexible armor that I described in *The Physical Dynamics of Character Structure*. The degree of rigidity is in direct proportion to the severity of the sexual rejection by her father. On the psychological level it is expressed in an exaggerated pride that says, "I shall hold myself back so that you cannot reject me again." On the physical level, the rigidity is associated with muscle tensions in the neck, shoulders, back, and legs.

Carol showed these rigidities to an unusual degree. Despite an extremely active athletic life, her legs were as rigid as sticks. She was able to relate this rigidity in her legs to an inordinate need to be independent, that is, to stand on her own feet under all circumstances. The tension in her legs was associated with a stiffness in her lower back which almost immobilized her pelvis. This pelvic tension represented an inhibition of sexual surrender, for surrender meant the loss of independence. Carol was able to explain her tensions in terms of her relation to her father. He had insisted upon an attitude of courage and daring as the price for his approval. Father and daughter had been close companions in many physical activities, but Carol's need for tenderness and affectionate support by her father were ignored. Her father idolized her in his image, which denied her sexuality. In turn, she idealized her father at the expense of her sexual feelings.

Carol searched all her life for a man who would be soft and tender, yet strong and fearless; that is, she looked for a knight-hero. The romantic lover or knight-hero is an idealized father figure, the father seen through the eyes of a three-year-old girl when these qualities characterize his attitude toward her. But while these qualities are not inconsistent, real men are not ideal figures. Carol had been married twice, each time to a man who looked strong and dependable, but who proved to be possessive, insecure, and immature. Carol was surprised when I told her that she would never find her knight-hero. Her vision of a romantic lover was a defense against her inability to give herself fully in love to a man. The therapeutic task was to heal the split in her personality.

In the early part of therapy a considerable effort was made to relax the tense muscles in Carol's legs and feet. Bending and kicking exercises produced some improvement. During these exercises, Carol realized that the tensions in her legs were tied to an immobility of the pelvis and that the total rigidity of the lower half of her body served as a defense against the surrender to strong sexual feelings. When such feelings were allowed to come through, Carol experienced a remission of the headaches from which she suffered and an amelioration of her mood of irritability and frustration. These remissions were only temporary. The deeper block against sexual surrender had not been overcome. The repressed hostility against the male had to be released. This was partially accomplished by having her physically express her anger—for example, by having her hit the couch. In this way she could release the feelings of hostility toward her father for his rejection of her need for closeness and physical contact. Two years of this work slowly transformed Carol from a rigid, frightened, hysterical female into a woman who could be soft and tender, yet strong and secure. In the latter part of therapy, she alternated between rigidity and softness, withdrawal and yielding, fear and surrender.

The persistence of her headaches, though their frequency had greatly diminished, indicated that Carol had not fully resolved the conflicts within her personality. One day, Carol came into my office feeling tense. She complained that she had suffered from a headache that was so severe that it nearly blinded her. Patients who have been in therapy for some time generally gain sufficient insight to understand why a symptom appears. I asked Carol whether she knew what had provoked her headache. Her answer was in the negative.

"What emotion do you associate with blindness or the inability to see?" I asked her.

"You mean 'blind with rage'?" Carol responded.

"Perhaps your headache resulted from the suppression of feelings of anger. Did anything happen to make you angry?" I asked.

"The night before the headache, I had to wrestle my way out of the embraces of a persistent date. It left me exhausted. Do you think the headache resulted from the tension of that evening?"

"It could very well have developed from the suppression of your anger," I replied. "If you had gotten angry and been firmer in your rebuff, I think you might have avoided the headache."

This dialogue led to a discussion of Carol's relation to men. She said that she didn't get angry because she was afraid to displease the man. She was afraid of his reaction, and she felt that she might need him. In the past, under these circumstances, she would either have been submissive or have become hysterical. Now she could resist, but she was still unable to express her anger when pressured. At this point, I gave Carol a tennis racquet to hold as we talked. Holding the racquet, she said, made her feel less impotent, less helpless. "It feels like a penis in my hand, and it makes me feel strong," she remarked. Saying this, Carol realized that she associated femininity with the condition of being weak and helpless in the face of the powerful male, who possessed a penis. This male figure was a symbol of her father, of whom she was afraid and to whom she dared not express sexual desire.

A therapeutic session that provides such an important insight helps to clarify a patient's problems. It enabled Carol to understand that her rigidity and her withdrawal were defenses against the threat of the supposedly superior power of the male. While hitting the couch with the tennis racquet, Carol felt the strength of her anger as a force that could be used for self-defense in place of the passive resistance she had previously employed. The acceptance of her anger allowed her to yield more fully to her sexual impulses without feeling threatened by her surrender. It provided a means of releasing tension that would otherwise be converted into hysterical symptoms such as her headaches. Her subsequent progress proved that for Carol, as for any hysterical female, sexual satisfaction is inseparable from the ability to feel and express anger toward the male sex. The expression of anger releases the frustration that was experienced in the oedipal situation. The existence of this frustration results in tension that is manifested in a hysterical symptom or a hysterical reaction.

It is extremely difficult for a disturbed neurotic person to comprehend the negative effect of behavior that is regarded by the ego as self-protective. The child-woman does not see the rejection of the male as implicit in her personality. The sisterly woman blinds herself to the fact that in her role as companion and helpmate, she negates the man's sexual interest in her. The hysterical female accepts this interest but unconsciously feels that it cannot be associated with love. The denial of the negative feeling results in its projection upon the sexual partner. In the mind of the woman, it is the man who insists upon her playing these roles. Necessarily, men are chosen who so insist.

4. The insidious interplay of neurotic tendencies in mar-

riage is most clearly revealed in the marital problems of
women who play a mother role toward the man. I was
consulted by a young woman who was despondent over the
threatened breakup of her marriage. Shortly afterward, I saw
her husband, who claimed that he had never truly loved his
wife and that now he was in love with another woman. To
support his position, he said that during the past five years of
his marriage, he had had affairs with a number of women
and that his wife knew this. The tragedy of this situation was
not only the wife's feeling of loss and betrayal, but the hurt
to two children, both girls, who were attached to their
father. Ruth, who became my patient, did not understand
how her husband could abandon his responsibilities to his
family or why he wanted to leave her, since she had been so
devoted to him. Ruth felt that her husband needed her. He
was, she said, immature and did not know his own mind. His
salvation, she believed, lay in his commitment to the marriage and to the family.

Ruth was sensitive, intelligent, and not unattractive. Her
appearance, however, was not a matter of great importance
to her, since she based her appeal to men on her good nature
rather than on her sexuality. Ruth had not had any sexual
relations before marriage, although she was no wallflower.
Sex after marriage never resulted in an orgasm for Ruth, but
she enjoyed the intimacy. Her sexual response to her husband
improved after she learned of his extramarital affairs. Despite
this knowledge, she claimed that she loved her husband
deeply. He didn't seem to appreciate this devotion. He felt
that Ruth was too dependent on him and not attractive
enough physically. Ruth accepted his criticism of her clinging
and determined to stand on her own feet. Her first attempt
was admirable. It gave her a new view of herself as a person
and a new outlook on life. Unfortunately, it collapsed after
two months.

The collapse of this first feeling of independence and
maturity indicated the necessity for a deeper analysis of
Ruth's personality. I pointed out that she was a mother figure
for her husband: she felt mature in relation to his immaturity, she undertook to help and support him, and she permitted
him sexual freedom as long as he returned to her. Ruth
accepted this interpretation of her attitude. She was aware
that her appearance tended to be matronly, although she was
only thirty years old. Ruth didn't understand how she had

become a mother figure, since her relation to her father had always been "very good."

"My father," she said, "has always been somewhat of an idol to me. Every night, I sat in his lap as a child to read the funnies, and I guess I always felt safest there. He's always adored me, and I him. I could usually get what I wanted from him within reason. He is a very warm person. He may appear weak to some men, but he is quietly strong. Mother would try to run things, but if Daddy put his foot down, it stuck and no one argued."

The close relationship between father and daughter continued into adult life. Ruth remarked, "Even today, we stand and hold each other closely. But to this day, I can't put my arms around my mother. I don't feel any physical warmth for her."

Ruth related two early memories that indicate the difference in her relation to her parents: "My earliest memory is jumping from the top of the porch railing into my father's arms below. I must have been about two. I loved it. I was not frightened. The next thing I remember is having my mouth washed out with soap for talking back to my mother. I was taught at a very young age not to talk back to adults. It stuck." It is apparent that from earliest childhood, Ruth was devoted to her father and antagonistic to her mother. The oedipal problem that arose in this situation could not be easily resolved.

As a young girl, there were two qualities about Ruth that impressed people: a mature behavior and an awkward physical appearance. Ruth remarked that people always said, "I was dependable beyond my years. While no one criticized my behavior, they did find fault with my appearance. I was the perfect example of 'that awkward age.' My mother always told saleswomen that she didn't think I would ever outgrow that awful stage. The whole family bemoaned the fact that I had my father's legs and mouth, both big."

It is not unreasonable to assume that Ruth's awkward appearance had some relation to her precocious maturity. Did she become a mother figure in order to avoid the sexual implications of her relationship to her father? Or did she mature too quickly in order to displace her mother as her father's love object? Ruth never developed the bodily grace that is characteristic of girls who are conscious of their erotic feelings for their father.

When Ruth was thirteen, a sister was born. Her mother

went back to work a week after her return from the hospital
and hemorrhaged. So Ruth undertook the 2 A.M. feeding of
the baby. "Don't get me wrong," she said. "I asked for it. It
made me feel important. But as a result, I was required to
come home every day after school to take care of the baby."
Ruth's lack of protest against this burden, which continued
through her high-school years, indicates the degree to which
she was willing to assume her mother's role.

To break through therapeutically to the unresolved oedipal
problem necessitated some awareness on Ruth's part of her
sexual feelings for her father. Her idolization of him constituted a strong resistance to this perception. Ruth suspected
that her father was not all she pictured him to be, but the
key to his personality and her difficulty was missing.

Then, shortly after her divorce, Ruth had an experience
that opened her eyes. She had met another man whose
personality showed the same characteristics as her husband's.
She felt sexually attracted to him, but she realized that he
was a "misunderstood, overgrown little boy" who needed
understanding and mothering. She said, "I was always attracted to men like that. It was safe because these men didn't
need sex from me. So while I got excited, I felt safe. My
approach to men was, 'Tell Ruth your troubles.' Getting
involved with a real man scares me."

This time, however, Ruth abandoned the "safe" position
and had sexual relations. She said:

> "It was very good. I reached a climax vaginally, but
> when he left, I began to shake and sob violently. I found
> myself saying, 'Daddy, Daddy.' I felt like a little girl.
> Did I want my daddy to come and protect me? I felt so
> utterly alone and abandoned. I felt I wanted to go back
> and be a little girl and not face the responsibility for
> what I had done. Why did I call for my daddy?
>
> "I recognized that it was my father I wanted. My
> father has always been able to reach me on a very deep
> level where I am completely vulnerable. I used to 'snug-
> gle' with my father in bed. Was I afraid that if I allowed
> any sexual feelings to come through to him, he would
> reject me and abandon me?
>
> "My father could also be described as a misunder-
> stood, overgrown little boy. I feel that all the women in
> his life took advantage of him and used him. His father
> died when he was four years old. His mother was a

strong, domineering type who played on his sympathies. She demanded that he take care of her. My mother hated her, but she was very much like her. She also dominated him in a very subtle way. Did I lose respect for my father because of his overgrown-boy attitude? My mother was so wrapped up in the world of money that all of us children felt we were secondary to money in her life. She was ambitious. I tried to mother my own father as a child, to take care of his needs. I felt sorry for him."

The mother role may also be described as the mother-martyr role, for self-denial is typical of this personality structure. This attitude differs from that of the "sister" type who regards herself as an equal to the man and expects his support and protection. Psychologically, the mother-martyr woman shows dominant masochistic tendencies in her personality. However, there are also masochistic elements in the sister personality, and these roles are not always clearly distinguished in practice. But where the sister role implies an active attitude, the mother role imposes a passive-submissive attitude. The submissiveness covers a feeling of superiority to the male, who is relegated by her role playing into the inferior position of son. It also covers her contempt and hostility toward the male. And, if she is superficially submissive in her relation to her husband, surreptitiously she attempts to dominate him through her martyrdom. Ruth's self-sacrifice for her husband was in marked contrast to her mother's domineering behavior. The conflict in this personality is between submission and dominance.

The asexual approach to a man represented by the mother-martyr role covers an attitude of sexual submission which is similar to that of the daughter-prostitute. The mother role may be viewed therefore as a defense against the position of sexual object. To maintain this defense, the woman's activities are focused upon her role as mother; food becomes more important than pleasure and children more important than the self. Usually, she produces a large family which is a perfect excuse for her lack of interest in herself as a person.

This history of the mother type includes the stages of daughter, sister, and an attempt at the position of the romantic ideal. The inability of her father to respond to her femininity and to support her against her mother forces her to retreat into an asexual role. This development produces a maturity, as in Ruth's case, which is precocious and self-negating. She ends up as a woman, not a child, but she is unable to assert her right to sexual fulfillment. Unlike the sister figure, her personality has few masculine elements. If her masochistic tendencies are overcome, her sexual feelings will emerge in strength. Otherwise, sex will be an unrewarding experience without orgastic release or emotional satisfaction.

The four roles I have described above represent neurotic solutions of the oedipal situation. The final form of a girl's relationship to her father determines the pattern of her relationship to all men. This pattern is set by a specific conflict in each case. For the mother type the conflict is between submission and dominance in her relation to the male. Submission denotes relegation to the daughter role, as sexual object. Dominance in the role of mother is an assertion of worth as a person, on an asexual basis. The mother who dominates the family becomes a sexual object in the genital relationship.

The conflict in the daughter role is between rejection and acceptance of herself. The prostitute rejects herself as a person, but accepts herself as a sexual object in terms of the male's need of her. Because of this need for her, the prostitute often regards herself, unconsciously, as the giving, holding, and sheltering mother of all men who seek her services.

The conflict of the romantic ideal type is between surrender and resistance to the male. Surrender implies being possessed by the male, which in the eyes of the hysterical female reduces her to a sexual object. In her unconscious, therefore, the hysterical female must remain a virgin. Her resistance to surrender is expressed in her characterological rigidity, and in her insistence that the man worship her.

In the case of a sister type, the conflict is between passivity and aggression. Passivity is associated with weakness and inferiority, both of which are equated with the feminine by the sister type. She regards aggression as an attribute of masculine superiority. For the sister type, equality means being "like" a man.

The four aspects of a woman's personality are psychological constructs to describe patterns of behavior. In reality there are no pure types, and roles are often intermingled. The roles of mother and daughter are often combined in different degrees. Similarly, the roles of sister and romantic ideal may be enacted by the same individual. The woman who is a romantic ideal type also wants to be companion and helpmate to the man. The woman who adopts the sister role is very disappointed when her husband fails to view her as a romantic figure.

In the normal relationship, woman is all things to a man. She is daughter, sister, romantic ideal, and mother at one and the same time. Her changing functions in the course of even a single day will reveal all aspects of her complex personality. For example, as the person who prepares breakfast, runs the home, and cares for the children, she is a mother. At the concert or theater and in their cultural exchange, she is a companion. She is the helpmate with whom the man discusses his business or professional affairs. In the evening, beside a fire or at a party, she becomes romanticized. And, of course, in bed, she is a sexual partner. A woman doesn't change her personality to fit these roles—that would be like changing her body to fit the clothes she wears. She can fulfill these roles as the situation requires because they are part of her nature. But such a statement leaves unanswered the mystery of that nature.

A man can find companionship and help in another man. He can engage someone to keep his house and look after his children. But only a woman who accepts all the aspects of the feminine personality can be a totally satisfying sexual partner for a man. If she fulfills these other roles because she is his sexual partner, they become expressions of her total love for the man. Divorced from her sexual feeling, her other functions are neurotic substitutes for her inability to surrender herself sexually. Through the different aspects of her personality, the sexuality of a woman is made to shine with all the brilliance of a well-cut diamond. At the heart of her nature lies the magic of her sexual appeal.

The double standard began as the antithesis of ego and body, creating the concept of higher values and lower values. It is operative in our culture as the dissociation of love and sex. This dissociation splits the basic unity of the female into fragments: sexual object, sister, competitor, romantic ideal, seductive witch, mother, and old witch. Regardless of which aspect is dominant, it can be shown that the fragmentation results from a rejection of the sexual feelings of the young girl.

In every case history, the problem of the woman relates

back to her relationship to her father. To him the young girl transfers the unfulfilled longing for oral gratification and body contact and upon him she projects the image of sexual satisfaction and happiness. The former is a real need, the latter is part of the child's playful preparation for life. Their union in the girl's attitude and feeling makes it impossible for the father to treat one casually and the other seriously, even if he can distinguish between them. If he responds positively to her oral needs, he risks overinvolving the girl sexually and creating an insuperable oedipal problem. But the failure to respond to the real need is taken as a sexual rejection. There is, as I see it, no way out of this difficulty for the father. The problem of unfulfilled oral needs should not arise in the first place. If it does not arise, the girl's sexual feelings for her father can be dealt with normally.

Throughout this book, I have emphasized the close connection between orality and genitality. The failure of women to breast-feed is, in my opinion, the most important reason for unfulfilled oral desires. I believe that an adequate period of breast feeding is three years. How many women have the patience or the strength to provide this kind of oral gratification to a child? Not the daughter type or the sister type or the hysterical female or even the woman who plays a mother role to a man has what it takes to fulfill her children. Thus the sexual problems of one generation are visited upon the next. The circle cannot be broken until the double standard that divides a man into a thinking being (*Homo sapiens*) and an animal body is fully discarded by both woman and man.

16

The Sexual Roles
of the Male

The double standard distorts the sexual function of the male as much as it does that of the female. As a moral code, it splits the unity of his response to the female into respect for and fear of the mother figure and desire and contempt for the sexual object. To neither can he give himself fully. The effect is to diminish his sexual passion and to decrease his orgastic potency. He feels guilty toward his wife for withholding from her his physical affection, and he feels guilty toward his paramour for denying to her his respect and love. His guilt leads to a reactive compulsiveness in both relations.

The double standard also creates two opposing sets of values, masculine and feminine. The masculine values—consciousness, the ego, and power—are regarded as superior to the feminine values—the unconscious, the body, and the object. This superiority is related to the assumption that the function of the phallus represents a higher sexual principle than that of the vagina. The phallus derives its assumed superiority from its role as the active organ in the sexual process. It becomes a representative of the fertilizing power of the sun god, with whom man identifies himself. Woman as a representative of the earth becomes an object to be acted upon by man. But all these values are part of man's own nature. He is conscious and unconscious, an ego and a body, actor and object. Thus, the nature of man is divided into two antithetical aspects.

In his masculine aspect, man is the possessor of the power to fecundate the woman. The conscious knowledge of this function creates the category of father and reduces the woman to the roles of sexual object and mother. In his feminine

289

aspects, man belongs to the woman. Early consciousness regarded the Great Mother as all-inclusive—the masculine elements in nature were her offspring, not her equals. On this level, man is still her son.

The double standard doesn't eliminate the Great Mother. Her functions are subject to the power of the father principle, but only to the extent that this principle or power can control and dictate her responses. Man can fecundate woman and plant the seed, but thereafter the male power is impotent to affect the transformation that the seed undergoes in the body of the Great Mother to become the child or the corn. The reproductive process is separated into the masculine function of fertilization and the feminine functions of containment, transformation, and birth. When a man dominates a relationship with a woman through the conscious use of power, he is a father figure. If the relationship is dominated by the woman, the man is reduced to the role of a son.

The historical unfolding of the male's personality parallels that of the female. The cultural developments that introduced the aspects of woman as sister and romantic ideal determined the corresponding roles of brother and knight for the man. In his role as brother, man is the protector and friend of the woman. His power is shared with her, or, rather, the two combine their common resources against the Great Mother and the father. Ideally, brother and sister support each other's emerging personality. Actually, they may become competitors in an extension of the earlier sibling rivalry between them. Man in his role as knight-hero is dedicated to the rescue of the fair maiden. She is always the captive of the dark forces, that is, of the unconscious. She is the sleeping beauty who has to be awakened to the excitement and romance of love. She has to be freed from her subservience to the Great Mother and from the possession and control of the father. The knight affirms the sexual appeal of the female as a person.

The different functions that man can fulfill in his relationship to woman are related to the stages of his own life history. In his personal growth, he will be successively son, brother, knight, and father. Each stage is progressively integrated into his developing manhood. The father position is not the goal, but rather the last stage in his experience of self-realization. A man whose psychosexual growth and development have proceeded normally includes in his relationship to the female these four aspects of his personality.

The sexual difficulties that arise when the normal development is arrested or disturbed are reflected in a man's attitude toward power. Many times they are more clearly apparent in this area than they are in either his sexual function or his personal relationship to a woman. How a man handles money, for example, is a good indication of how he functions sexually. Money is abstract power, and power is a symbol of sexual potency. It has been pointed out that money is a masculine invention. In our culture, it is a real source of power. It confers upon its possessor personal prestige and social position. It has supplanted the hereditary title as a symbol of rank and status. It can be anticipated that the man who is fixated in the role of the son will be unable to accumulate money, while the father role will be associated with the possession or management of money and power. I shall discuss the character structure and sexual behavior of the male whose personality is fixated upon each of the masculine roles: son-lover, brother-protector, knight-hero, and authoritative father.

As in the case of the female, fixation upon each of these roles is determined by the neurotic resolution of the oedipal situation. Fixation results from the persistence of a basic conflict in each case. The conflict of the son-lover is between acceptance and rejection of himself. He accepts himself on the infantile level of omnipotence but rejects his right to possess either the female or money.

The brother-protector's conflict is between aggression and passivity. His aggression is for the benefit of the woman, while his passivity denotes his inability to satisfy his own needs. Since he cannot use aggression on his own behalf, he is forced into a passive position with respect to the female with whom he identifies. His passivity is also expressed in his attitude toward money and power.

The conflict in the case of a knight-hero is between surrender and resistance to the female. Surrender to love implies submission and dependence on the female as the Great Mother. He resists being reduced to the level of the son-lover. His inability to surrender prevents him from forming a mature relationship with the female, and he is arrested at an adolescent stage. The result is an adolescent attitude toward sex and money, both of which are used to glorify his ego.

In the father role the conflict is between dominance and submission. The authoritative father dominates and controls his family. His behavior, however, is compulsive, and reflects

his submission to the sexual morality of his own father with
whose authority he identifies. He is submissive to those above
him in power, while he dominates those below him.

1. A good example of the personality that develops when
emotional growth is arrested at the level of the son is seen in
the individual known as the playboy. Formerly, this type of
personality was called a spendthrift or, in another context, a
prodigal son. The term "playboy" is more appropriate in that
it carries an implication of immaturity that is well merited.
The playboy dissipates not only his money, but also his sexual
energies. There is a common expression that describes this
type of behavior. The individual who squanders his money in
the search for sensual pleasure is said to "piss it away." This
expression indicates that the playboy's need is to get rid of a
tension rather than to obtain satisfaction and fulfillment. He
gets rid of his sexual feeling in the same way. Sexual intercourse when one is under the influence of alcohol and has no
personal feeling for the sexual partner partakes of this quality. The discharge of semen takes place as a continuous flow,
like the act of micturition, instead of in the form of the
characteristic pulsatory ejaculation. Such sexual activity is
indiscriminate, promiscuous, and leaves the sexual partner
with the feeling of being used.

The playboy attitude is not the exclusive property of the
so-called international jet set. Many men, some of them
married, squander or waste their money in drink with a
profligacy that approaches that of the playboy. When the
money is spent on alcohol, it is literally being "pissed away."
Seen in this light, the problem of alcoholism cannot be
divorced from the inability to hold money or to use it
constructively. It is this inability that characterizes the spendthrift, whether the money is used for drink, lost in gambling,
or spent in foolish ventures.

It is not merely fortuitous that the expression "piss it
away" came to be associated with this behavior. There is
some underlying connection between the inability to hold and
contain the excitation of money or sexual feeling and the
inability to contain urine. This connection seems to be that of
sexual guilt, particularly guilt about masturbation. Frequent
urination, especially in boys, is a substitute means of making
genital contact in the face of masturbatory guilt. Adults often
urinate as a means of relieving sexual tension. The close
connection between the sensation of a full bladder and sexual

feeling is manifested in the confusion that surrounds the phenomenon of the morning erection, to which reference was made in Chapter 2. This erection has been falsely attributed to the pressure of a full bladder, since it disappears after micturition. It is now recognized to be a true expression of sexual feeling. Sexual guilt is also reflected in the neurotic fear of voiding while having intercourse.

The relation between micturition and infantile masturbation is revealed in the following memories that a patient recalled during therapy. A young man remembered that at the age of five, his father severely reprimanded him for holding his penis in his hand. The next day, he said, he urinated on the floor of the apartment while his parents were away. He had the distinct feeling that he did it to get even with his father for the reprimand. It is conceivable that the playboy is similarly getting back at his father by squandering the money he has inherited.

I have found that strong feelings of guilt about masturbation are characteristic of men who have become fixated at the son level of development. Masturbation is the rational behavior of a person who has a strong sexual urge in circumstances where no other satisfactory outlet is available. It provides release and satisfaction at the same time that it furthers identification with the body as a source of pleasure. In masturbation, the feeling is reinvested in the self. This is precisely what the playboy cannot do with his money. He cannot use it constructively. He cannot employ it for self-advancement because this is too closely related to self-gratification. Sexual guilt attaches to the money as a symbol of sexual feeling. Money "burns a hole in his pocket." He squanders it to be free of this feeling of guilt, just as he urinates symbolically whenever he is sexually excited.

The arrest of a child's development at the level of the son-lover cannot be explained solely on the basis of infantile guilt over masturbation. Characterologically, the son type is an oral personality who has not been able to resolve his oedipal problem. He is still bound to his mother and afraid of his father. He feels that the world owes him something to make up for the deprivation he suffered as a child. He may even find a woman who is willing to support him and be the mother he is seeking. Some of the sexual problems of the son type are illustrated by the following case of a thirty-year-old man who consulted me about his sexual preoccupations. He was obsessed by fantasies of rape, and ideas of incest. One day he asked me:

> "Am I a mother fucker? All week I sensed my preoccupation with this thought. I felt I was dangerous. I had rape ideas.
>
> "With older women the desire is so strong that it overwhelms me. My head and neck feel like they are going to explode. I feel that I want to fuck them sadistically, but I am afraid to hurt them. Then I get to feel I just want to die from despair.
>
> "When the sexual charge is very strong in me, I feel as big as life. I used to feel impotent. Now there is some feeling of omnipotence if I sense that I can have my way with a woman. Power is the ability to make another person feel sexually alive and responsive. If I can excite a woman, that is my dream. But the moment she is excited, I realize I am in trouble. Then I have to reject her out of fear of failure. I am afraid that I'll come too quickly and she will be unsatisfied. In my first sexual experience, when the girl couldn't have an orgasm, I felt responsible. So I resorted to cunnilingus."

Cunnilingus is an oral activity that is displaced from the breast to the genitals. This displacement is provoked by fear of the mother who reacted negatively to the infant's desire for oral erotic gratification. The sadistic feelings that this patient expressed were derived from repressed impulses to bite the breast. In cunnilingus, the man fulfills two desires. Consciously, he feels that he satisfies the woman. Unconsciously, he satisfies his feeling of revenge by assuring himself that he has bitten off her penis and that it can no longer threaten him.

This patient described his mother as a seductive woman who sought to bind him to her in a dependent relationship. At the same time, he was afraid of his father, who, he said, used to beat him regularly. Under these conditions a conscious identification with his father was impossible, and the boy was thrown back into a dependence on and fear of the mother, who unconsciously became the terrible Great Mother of antiquity. Such a situation prevents the normal ego development of the boy and fixates his personality at the primitive son-lover stage. He will alternately rebel against his subservience, then sacrifice himself to please the mother, and this pattern will characterize all his relations to women. Since he cannot fight the woman with a masculine ego, he will resort to the magic of sexual power, the power to excite her and thereby transform her into the "good mother" who will fulfill his oral needs. His actions recall the primitive use of fertility magic to ensure a good crop. Cunnilingus represents the sexual approach of a man who dares not possess the woman.

The son-lover has no interest in money. Money is real power, not infantile omnipotence or primitive magic. It represents the power to possess the woman, which power belongs to the father.

Since the woman is always a mother figure for the son-lover, success in terms of money is tantamount to incest. His failure in life is self-determined. Psychologically, the son-lover has an oral character structure in which schizoid and psychopathic tendencies conflict. He is obsessed with the idea of power, but unable to do anything about it. He is always orgastically impotent and often erectively impotent. His erective potency depends on his ability to subdue the woman and reduce her to the level of a sexual object. If she retains her power as a mother figure in his mind, he will suffer a symbolic castration by the loss of his erection. But his failure will be followed by rebellion and rage, and a further attempt to overthrow the Great Mother. A normal marital relationship is not possible with such conflicts.

2. The brother role is an asexual approach to a woman. The man whose personality is determined by this stage of development is capable of earning money, since it will not be used to gain power over the female. For the same reason, he will never make the kind of money that represents such power. If he is a good "brother," his money will be shared with his wife to further her growth and development. If he is competitive, he will use it to prove his superiority. In the latter case, he verges on the behavior of the father figure.

The problem of the brother personality is the lack of sexual satisfaction. He attributes this lack to the inadequate sexual response of his wife. While he may complain of his wife's unresponsiveness, his identification with her generally prevents any move to obtain sexual fulfillment elsewhere. His interest is in helping her as a "big brother" should. Little does he realize that it is his big-brother attitude that is partly responsible for her unresponsiveness.

Robert was a big brother to his wife. He could be considered a good husband who was deeply concerned about his wife's difficulties. He was kind, sympathetic, and understand-

ing, not only to his wife but to other men and women in
trouble. Robert had thought at one time that he would like to
go into the ministry because he had a strong urge to help
people. Yet his own problems were such that he had all he
could do to handle them.

One day, Robert told me:

> "I have come to the realization that I have a money
> problem. I seem to equate money with dirt. This goes
> way back to my childhood. In my family, money and
> politics were considered symbols of dirty, nasty behav-
> ior. My family never had money. As soon as my father
> got any money, it disappeared. My mother was a good
> manager, but she didn't pass any of it on to me. I don't
> want to touch money. I let my wife handle all the
> money affairs, and I shut my eyes to what goes on. But
> then I am upset when I see how much we have spent
> and how little we have to show for it. I feel that I am
> shirking my responsibility somehow."

After making this statement, Robert remarked that his
mind was cloudy and that he could go no further with the
analysis of the problem. However, a few minutes later, he
added, "I like to make money. This is a big improvement,
because there was a time when I talked myself out of a big
raise. I used to take a raise in pay with mixed feelings."

In our further discussion of this problem, Robert revealed
that he rarely spent money on himself to satisfy his wants
despite a good income. He carried a minimum amount of
money on his person so that he would not be tempted to
spend any. By turning his money over to his wife, he gave
her the responsibility for satisfying his desires. Robert's inability to spend money on himself reflected his guilt about
self-indulgence and masturbation. In an early interview, I
asked Robert whether he masturbated. He told me that he
did, but that he felt guilty about it.

Robert not only gave his wife the responsibility for satisfying his material needs, he also handed her the obligation of
satisfying his sexual needs. This was the basis for his complaint about her sexual unresponsiveness. Thus, in one respect, he was the big brother who earned the money and
protected his wife; while in another, he was the little brother
who looked to her to provide for his needs and desires. In
surrendering his power, he renounced his manhood and be-

came the little brother. How could his wife become sexually excited at the prospect of relations with her little brother? Only by asserting his manhood could Robert achieve the kind of sexual relationship he desired.

It is not generally appreciated to what extent power or money enhances the sexual attractiveness of a man to a woman. Formerly, this kind of sexual attractiveness was an attribute of men who held positions of nobility or rank. It is probably related to the fact that, in general, the leaders of a group are its most outstanding individuals. Any form of power is a symbol of superiority, whether the power is personal, such as physical strength, or impersonal, such as wealth. Sexuality is a form of power in a biological sense. It represents the power to excite a woman, to impregnate her, and to fulfill her. The son-lover personality exaggerates this feeling of sexual power to the point of omnipotence. But the knowledge of this power is indispensable to a man if he is to be sexually aggressive toward a woman. This is what is missing in the brother type, and without it he is weak and hesitant.

What factors fixate a boy at the level of the brother relationship? Robert indicated his lack of conscious identification with his father. He had been very much afraid of his father, who had a violent temper. As a boy, Robert was never able to challenge his father, and so he retreated into a passive attitude. His remarks show a sympathy and understanding for the position of his mother, who had to manage without much money. Robert felt sorry for his mother and consciously identified with her against his father. He was thereby able to find a partial solution to his oedipal situation on the basis of an asexual relationship to the female. The determining factors in this kind of character structure are very similar to those which fixate the girl at the sister level. By joining forces with his mother against the tyranny of his father, the boy adopts a brother role toward his mother which is later transferred to all women.

The character structure of the brother type fits the analytic description of the passive-feminine male. The physical structure of the passive-feminine male shows certain feminine characteristics. There is a visible tendency to roundness and softness of the body outline, especially evident about the hips. His voice is typically soft and modulated. His movements are limited in range and not very aggressive. While the resemblance to the feminine is striking in the adult male, a more accurate interpretation of these features is that they are boyish. The boyishness of the passive-feminine male is a direct expression of a lack of aggressiveness owing to the inhibition of sexual feelings in the oedipal situation.

3. The personality structure that emerges at the next stage of development is known analytically as the phallic-narcissistic male. The name indicates that this male type is obsessed with the idea of sexual prowess. But he is also the knight-hero whose ego is preoccupied with romantic illusions. The phallic-narcissistic male is sexually oriented toward a woman and aggressive in his approach. He derives his feeling of power from his identification with his penis. In this respect, he is similar to the oral character, though he lacks the latter's feeling of infantile omnipotence which collapses in the face of reality. For the oral character, the penis is a symbolic nipple and not a genital organ. The phallic male differs from the passive-feminine type, who shuns the idea of sexual power. But the weakness in the personality of the phallic character is that he is afraid to possess the female, who is a mother figure. He has not advanced to the stage of the father role.

The so-called great lovers are men with this type of personality structure. Their achievement is measured in terms of sexual conquest. Casanova and Frank Harris are good examples of personalities fixated at this stage of psychosexual development. The primary interest of the phallic male is the seduction of the female. In its extreme form, the seduction is aimed at the virgin, who, in the psyche of the seducer, is the captive princess. Casanova regarded himself as a hero when he achieved the seduction and defeated the forces who guarded the virgin, her mother and father. He felt like an adventurer who, having stormed the fortress of social morality, claimed his prize. But his victory was short-lived. His exploits had meaning only in terms of his ego. Neither physically nor realistically did he gain any satisfaction or advantage from his exploits. The circumstances of his sexual adventures denied him the possibility of orgastic fulfillment. He was afraid to lose his heart to the female. The experience of love escaped him. In the end, Casanova, like Frank Harris, died alone and penniless.

The phallic male is the counterpart of the hysterical female. He cannot unite the feelings of love and sex for the same person. The woman he loves becomes a mother figure who loses her appeal as a sexual person. The girl he seduces is the stranger. The act of seduction proclaims that he is not a "mother fucker," since he is not emotionally involved with the sexual object. To further his defense against incest, he will choose as sexual objects young girls, preferably virgins. The virgin could not possibly be his mother. But his defense betrays his anxiety. He has incestuous feelings for his mother that have to be repressed through fear, fear of castration at the hands of his father.

The amorous pursuits of the phallic male can be explained by his castration anxiety. Each conquest is proof to his ego that he is still potent. This potency would disappear if the woman did not present herself as a challenge. Unconsciously, the phallic male views himself as the challenger to the authority of the father. But he must always challenge, never win. To win would require a life-and-death struggle with the father, who is viewed by the adolescent psyche of the phallic male as the stronger figure. To lose is to be castrated. One can always remain the challenger on a hit-and-run basis. Since all women are his father's property, each conquest must be followed by a withdrawal of interest. Emotionally, the phallic male is a perpetual adolescent.

Why does the potency of the phallic male diminish when he takes possession of the sexual object? In other words, why does this type of personality suffer a reduction of sexual feeling after marriage? At this point, it can be assumed that the fear of the father has decreased considerably. What remains is a deeper fear of the mother. Marriage is looked upon as a victory for the woman. He has been "hooked" or "lumbered," as Littlechap discovers in *Stop the World, I Want to Get Off!* His freedom has been abrogated, and his egoistic pride in his adolescent manhood suffers a sharp decline. By "hooking" him, the woman has proved herself to be the stronger person, and the phallic male is reduced to a position of subservience to the Great Mother. In this situation, the hero, if he is one, can mature to become a father figure or regress to the role of the brother. Or, what is more likely, he can continue his sexual exploits, using the concept of the double standard as a justification. The hysterical female maintains her illusions by dreaming of a romantic lover outside the marriage. In the same position, the phallic male persists in his pursuit of the elusive virgin.

Virgins are the most elusive creatures. As soon as they are possessed by a male, they lose this quality and become sexual objects. The importance of virginity lies in the fact that the virgin is not the mother. Once penetration has been accomplished, this illusion is lost, so a new adventure must be undertaken. The search for the virgin is a quest for eternal youth.

Money is never the prime objective of the phallic male, and for this reason he never becomes very rich. It is indispensable to him, however, in his need for independence of action. The phallic male handles money in the same way in which he treats his sexual feeling. It is to be spent, not accumulated. And he spends it in furtherance of the ego image he has of himself as a handsome, daring, and romantic figure. He can also earn money, since his aggressive outlook on life provides the means for its acquisition. In the eyes of his contemporaries, he appears to be a social success. Fate in the form of character catches up with him as he grows older; and as the years pass, his adventures show up as frustrated attempts to be a man.

In reality character types are not uniform, and there is no pure type. The neurotic tendencies that determine patterned behavior vary among individuals. Some phallic males are fairly healthy persons who are able to mature into positive father figures following the experience of fatherhood. In others, the romantic picture of the knight on horseback becomes a caricature, the leather-jacketed hoodlum on his motorcycle.

Physically, the phallic male has a well-shaped body that is distinctly masculine, good muscle tone and posture, and a quick and lively manner of expression. The weakness in his body structure is its rigidity, most evident in the muscles of the back, the neck, and the legs. This rigidity is a defense against collapse and surrender, which are synonymous to the phallic male. Falling in love is viewed unconsciously as a surrender to the female and a collapse of independence. The physical rigidity and the psychological fear of surrender inhibit his "giving in to" the strong orgastic sensations and produce a degree of prematurity of ejaculation, which yields only a partial orgasm. His sexual conquests are a compensation for his orgastic impotence.

A young man becomes a knight-hero when he is viewed in this light by his mother. Her investment of libidinal feeling in her son creates his feeling of attractiveness to women. But if this investment is made at the cost of her relationship to the father, it will create an unconscious antagonism on the father's part toward his son, and it will jeopardize the son's security in relation to his father. The latent incestuous nature of the mother's feeling for the son fixates him at the level of knight-hero, just as the latent incestuous relationship between father and daughter determines her role as virgin—romantic ideal.

4. The progressive integration of the different stages of male development results in a man, not a father figure. The father type is a neurotic compromise of an oedipal situation. He corresponds to the mother type in the female and represents an asexual attitude toward the opposite sex. The father type acts as a father to his wife and, not infrequently, as a tyrant to his children. His ambition is power, in the form of either money or, lacking money, authority and control. The character structure of this personality is anal sadistic, whereas the mother type is masochistic. Thus the father type to be considered here is a neurotic male whose goal is power, generally in the form of money, but also including power over his wife and over his children. The possession of power gives him the status of father.

The picture of the father figure I shall describe is rather old-fashioned. He is the stern disciplinarian who rules his home with an iron hand. In his petty domain, he acts as king, but without the largess that is also an attribute of royalty. He is hardworking and industrious, and he saves his money religiously. In extreme cases, he is a petty dictator and a miser. The pleasure functions in life are relatively unimportant in his scheme of life. Productivity and the accumulation of money dominate his world outlook. This type of personality is relatively rare today. The authority of the father has diminished in respect both to his wife and to his children. The concept of strict obedience to authority in the home and in the school has been replaced by the progressive ideals of permissiveness and self-expression. Of even greater importance in the disappearance of this figure is the loss of family unity and single-minded devotion to principle that formed the background of his personality. Nevertheless, it is important to analyze the dynamics of this character structure to appreciate the factors that created the father figure in the past and, to some extent, still do in the present. The changes which have developed in this role will be discussed later.

The role of father represents an approach to the woman, in terms of his financial power, which is a symbol of sexual virility and a guarantee of his ability to provide for the woman and her offspring. The relationship that develops is not one of equality. The personality of the woman is split by this masculine attitude into the antithetical aspects of sexual object and mother. As sexual object, the woman is placed in an inferior and submissive position, while as mother she exercises a subtle authority that is not overtly recognized. The female's rebellion against this situation contributed to the downfall of this kind of dynasty.

A man develops this kind of neurotic personality by resolving his oedipal conflict according to the strict code of patriarchal morality. He doesn't challenge the authority of his father as the phallic male does. Instead, he consciously identifies with his father and accepts his authority. The father of the budding father type was usually a strict disciplinarian, rigid in his attitude and frightening in his might to the young boy. His discipline was not enforced by the spoken word alone. Physical punishments in the form of spankings emphasized his power and ensured the child's obedience. "Spare the rod and spoil the child" is the guiding principle in the upbringing of most males who become father types. A boy will not challenge the authority of his father if his mother respects that authority. This respect informs the boy that if he would possess a woman, it is necessary for him to gain power equal to that of his father. The boy must repress his desire for his mother in favor of hard work and ambition. He must suppress his inclination to pleasure and erotic gratification in favor of money and power. If he fails to do this, he becomes the prodigal son. Success enables him to play the father role.

The sexual prohibitions that lead to the father role are directed against self-gratification as well as the child's sexual feelings for the mother. Satisfactory masturbation in a boy or young man promotes self-identity and independence and prevents neurotic identification with the father. In furtherance of neurotic identification with the father, a sexual outlet is often provided for the young man that does not violate the code of patriarchal morality. In Victorian days, it was not unusual for a father to initiate his son into the mysteries of sexual life by bringing him in to a prostitute. A good proportion of the patrons of brothels were drawn from the ranks of respectable fathers. The operation of the double standard in this way ensured that the young man would marry a girl of good family and increase or safeguard the father's property interests.

Characterologically, the father type is a rigid and compulsive individual. His rigidity stems from the inhibition of his sexual feelings; his compulsion, from his drive for power. In contrast to the playboy, who has a urinary problem, the father type has an anal fixation. Psychoanalytic theory relates compulsiveness to anality. In 1908, Freud published a paper that associated parsimony, obstinacy, and orderliness with anal retentive tendencies. This triad of traits, to which pedantry was added later, characterizes the neurotic father type. "Orderly," Freud writes, "comprises both bodily cleanliness and reliability and conscientiousness in the performance of petty duties." Freud uses a number of observations to support his idea of a connection between money and defecation. He mentions the story, which he claims is well known, that the money that the devil gives his paramours turns to excrement after his departure. The identification of gold with feces is supported by myths that describe gold as "the excrement of hell," by their similar color, and by such figures as the *gelt-scheisserle,* the excretor of gold coins. In Germany, a candy copy of this figure is often given to children on holidays.

It is assumed that the compulsive character holds on to money out of anal spite just as earlier he refused to part with his "productions" when this was demanded of him by his mother or nurse. It is not difficult to see how a severe training in excremental cleanliness can result in an exaggerated tendency to orderliness and parsimony. It is more difficult to understand the relation of obstinacy to bowel training. Psychoanalytic investigations have shown that at first the child was defiant and resisted parental demands for anal control. When this defiance was subdued, it went underground and became transformed into a generalized attitude of obstinacy. The means employed to accomplish this subjugation were particularly appropriate to ensure the child's subjection to the father. Freud notes that "painful stimuli to the skin of the buttocks [spankings] ... are instruments in the education of the child designed to break his self-will and make him submissive." Spanking is the one form of punishment that will make a boy submissive to male authority, since it constitutes a direct homosexual humiliation. In a more extreme form, such as caning, it was the ultimate authority in the training of the English upper-class young man for a military career.

The identity of money and gold with feces does not explain the association of money with sexual power. It does not

account for the emergence of the father figure as a positive
force in the organization of society. Freud's analysis is based
upon the neurotic exaggeration of this identity. Its roots go
deep into the cultural history of man. Human and animal
excrement were the first fertilizers that man discovered and
still are the best. It is conceivable that an agricultural economy that depended for its survival upon the cultivation of
limited areas of arable land would regard feces as real
wealth. In Switzerland, as late as 1950, I saw a peasant
farmer run out into the road to gather up the droppings of a
passing horse. The use of fertilizing agents to enrich and
fructify the earth represents an advance from the primitives'
use of "fertility magic" based on sacrifice and sexuality. This
view of man's cultural development eliminates the apparent
irrationality of the identity of money and gold with excrement.

The equation of money with sexual power bypasses the
intermediate step of their relation to the fertilizing power of
excrement. The full sequence of relationships is as follows:
sexuality was the primitive fertilizing power used in magic
rites. It was replaced by the fertilizing power of excrement,
which later became identified in man's psyche with gold and
money. The equating of money with sexual power enables me
to develop my concepts more fully. Thus, a miser who is
afraid to spend money cannot "spend" himself. The word
"spend" has a definite sexual connotation. A man is spent
ofter orgasm or ejaculation. The fear of spending oneself is a
neurotic factor that inhibits the surrender to full orgasm.
Many patients have reported that their early adolescent masturbation was accompanied by attempts to prevent or hold
back the ejaculation. The loss of the semen was viewed as a
depletion and experienced as a weakening of the body and
the personality. In other words, it was conceived by the
unconscious as a loss of power. The Biblical story of Onan
supports this idea, for the sin of Onan lay not in his masturbation per se, but in his refusal to use his semen to fertilize
his brother's widow according to Hebrew law. He, therefore,
wasted the power of his seed. Prior to the sexual enlighten-
ment of the past forty years, it was a common belief that
frequent masturbation or sexual activity reduced one's power
to beget a child.

The father-type man is obsessed with productivity in terms
of both children and wealth. His obsessive attitude reduces
his children to objects or things that he possesses. It had

previously reduced his wife to a possession. With the loss of the personal meaning of relationships, there is a corresponding loss of pleasure and joy. The compensation for the loss of pleasure is the ego satisfaction of increased productivity or greater wealth. This personality structure is not infrequently very successful in the world of affairs. He may become quite rich and gain considerable power despite an underlying sexual guilt. His success does not violate the incest barrier, since it is achieved by the repression of sexual feeling. When he finally possesses his mother (wife), she will have lost her significance as a sexual object for him. He will have become his father.

Although the old-fashioned father type is relatively rare now, the emphasis upon productivity and wealth as goals of living has increased. The father type of today is a man for whom sexual pleasure and joy in living are subordinate to these goals. For him, sex is only a biological need, like eating, sleeping, and having a bowel movement. His erection is merely an indication of a tension that has to be released so that he can get back to the business of making money. He plays golf because this is the manly way, but this activity, too, often takes on a compulsive quality. Achievement becomes an end that displaces the physical pleasure of activity. In desperation, he seeks some measure of personal pleasure in an affair with his secretary or he becomes dependent on the call girl. The double standard defeats his attempt at self-realization.

On the superficial level, the double standard operates differently in the mind of the man than it does in that of the woman. Consciously, man doesn't reject his sexuality. Quite the contrary. Since his masculine sexuality is proof of his superior nature (manhood, logical being, and so on), he could hardly be expected to deny this mark of his superiority. A man doesn't base his claim to superiority upon his intellect, his ego, or his greater strength. To found his claim upon these grounds could prove quite dangerous. How can he be sure that there isn't a woman who is more intelligent, more logical, more certain of herself, or even physically stronger than he is? There was such a woman in his life once, his mother. She was superior to him in every way, but she was a woman. She didn't possess a penis, the symbol of superiority. Of course, no man would make a public assertion of superiority over the female on this basis. He rationalizes it on the

ground of his superior intellect. But his attitude toward sex
reflects the true basis for his feeling.

A man can approach the sexual function from two different directions. He can approach it instinctually, that is,
through his feelings, in which case, his relationship to a
woman is determined by their "participation mystique" in the
natural phenomenon of sexual excitation and discharge. In
this situation, the personal element in the sexual relationship
is subordinate to the transpersonal or instinctive factor in the
sexual drive. The other approach is a conscious one, an
awareness of the meaning of the sex act in terms of his
relationship to a woman. In the conscious approach, man
becomes the power who does something to a woman that
transforms her. He takes possession of her ("has her"),
impregnates her, and fulfills her. In the ego of man the actor,
woman is an object to be acted upon as he acts upon the
earth and nature. The ego bases its right to act thus upon its
assumption of possession and its assertion of power.

No man approaches the sexual act through feeling or
conscious awareness alone. Every man combines feeling and
awareness, instinct and knowledge in his relation to woman.
If I draw distinctions between these two directions, it is in
order to better understand the differences that characterize
the behavior of different men, differences that are quantita-
tive rather than qualitative. If the sexual advance is motivated primarily by feeling (love, passion, or lust), the man's
sexual behavior is more spontaneous. Since a woman's response under these conditions is determined by her feelings,
man and woman meet as equals. To the degree that the ego
intrudes itself into the sexual relationship, the sexual act
becomes an expression of possession and power over the
woman. The man undertakes to perform, and the serpent of
sexual failure raises its head in what was paradise. No man in
our culture can dissociate his ego from his sexual function or
renounce his inner feeling of superiority. That is, no man can
escape his cultural upbringing.

Where a double standard operates in a woman to create the
dissociation of love and sex, its effect on the man is to oppose
the idea of power to that of sexuality. Power requires control; sexuality demands surrender. Power imposes obligations;
sexuality discharges tensions. Power creates inequalities, subject and object; sexuality is the interaction of equals. Power
is a function of the ego and the mind; sexuality is a function
of the body. Power leads to action; sexuality is a giving and a

sharing. On a deeper level, this dissociation is merely another aspect of the neurotic conflict between love and sex. The masculine ego identifies itself with sex interpreted as power to oppose the demands of love. This peculiar twist distorted the biological meaning of sexuality and created the double standard. Man's sexual function is viewed as possession of the woman, while her response is regarded as submission.

A double standard also prevails in a man's relation to his work. If he is an employer, he may be torn between his natural desire to gain as much profit as possible and his human concern for the well-being of his employees and customers. As an employee, a man's obligation to his employer may easily run counter to his personal interest. It is not easy to reconcile the drive for money and power with one's feelings as a sympathetic and sensitive person. It often happens that one of the values is sacrificed by the pressure of neurotic familial forces beyond the individual's control. If money and power become the dominant value, a person may develop psychopathic tendencies. In the psychopath, the ego is more important than the self; that is, the image masks and dwarfs the person. If the desire for money and power is repressed, schizoid tendencies may appear. The individual may withdraw into an inner world of meditation and self-preoccupation, with a corresponding diminution of the total personality.

I could give many examples of the conflicts produced by double standards. A man's relation to his children reflects the conflict resulting from one such set of values. Every sensitive father is uncertain about how to reconcile the need to punish and discipline his child with his feelings of affection and protection. There was no such problem in primitive matriarchal cultures. Authority in the family was exercised by the child's maternal uncle. The true father was a friend to whom the child could relate without fear. But such social orders required very little discipline or training compared with that which is required to bring up a child in civilized cultures.

Another example of the operation of a double standard is reflected in man's inability to form a unified concept that would embrace religion and scientific thinking, business and social responsibility. One copes with these conflicts by compartmentalizing life. Religion is for Sundays or church, while science governs all secular activities. Business is for money-making, while personal interest in one's fellow man finds expression in works of charity and benevolence. Double standards are cultural phenomena that arise from the antitheses of body and mind, spirit and matter, reason and instinct. Unlike the animal, man's instinctive reactions are controlled and modified to conform to socially accepted ideals of behavior. But how much control, what modifications, and for what reasons are questions that cannot easily be answered in a particular case. This is especially true of the sexual function. How much morality is consistent with healthy sexuality is a question to which only experience can provide an answer.

The process of antithesis and dissociation acts to create a polar tension that heightens consciousness if the ego function of synthesis acts normally. In this process, all functions of the organism are raised to a higher level of intensity: pleasure is increased, sexual orgasm is more vividly experienced, and life becomes more enjoyable. It is also possible for the antithesis to result in heightened conflict. If a constructive synthesis fails to occur, the tension cannot be resolved. In this situation, the result is illness, not health; neurosis or psychosis, not sanity; unhappiness, not joy. The problem in its simplest terms is how to adjust the conflicting demands of nature and culture.

While a problem can be stated in its simplest terms, it cannot be worked out in those terms. The practical solution of neurotic difficulties requires a knowledge of the complex factors involved. Even when that knowledge is acquired, its application to a specific situation, social or individual, poses another set of problems. This difficulty reminds one of the story of the bear who went over the mountain to see what he could find. He found another mountain. But the immensity of the task need not deter us from climbing the mountain. A part of our being, the unconscious, tells us that on the other side of the mountain is a fertile plain. This inner feeling is as valid as the cold logic that recognizes the difficulties in realizing that vision.

17

The Truth of the Body

The breakdown of the old sexual morality associated with patriarchal authority has challenged the attention and thinking of all serious persons. In a cover story on the subject of "Sex in the U.S.: Mores and Morality," January, 1964, *Time* magazine reviewed the current confusion about sexual values. The article noted as progress the disappearance of the double standard of sexual behavior, the greater acceptance of sexual fulfillment as a legitimate desire, and the increase in open-mindedness toward sexual problems. At the same time, it deplored the lack of spiritual meaning in the sophisticated view of sexuality.

No easy solution can be anticipated for this problem—the crisis goes to the very roots of our culture. In a world that has become increasingly industrialized, standardized, and dehumanized, sexuality seems to many the only force that is capable of uniting man with his instinctive, unconscious, and animal nature. The *Time* article notes this attitude: "There is also a tendency to see in sex not only personal but social salvation—the last area of freedom in an industrialized society, the last frontier." But this area is also being rapidly exploited commercially in man's greed for money and power. Even this frontier may disappear in a so-called scientific objectivism that will reduce the sexual function to a technique. If this last great mystery of life is translated into a formula, man will become an automaton, completely dominated by his ego and stripped of all passion and lust. In the name of progress, productivity replaces inspiration, and spontaneity gives way to compulsion. Today one can readily discern a compulsive attitude in work, play, and sex. The

only hope lies in man's growing dissatisfaction with his
present way of life and his realization that the joy of living,
which finds its highest expression in sexual orgasm, may be
escaping him.

It is easy to make a fetish of orgasm, and Wilhelm Reich
has been accused of fostering a cult based on this concept.
This charge appeared in a magazine article entitled "The Cult
of Sex and Anarchy," published in *Harper's Magazine* in
1945. From personal experience with Reich, I can deny this
accusation. The fact remains, however, that such an attitude
did develop around Reich's teachings. His ideas were seized
by many "rebels" to justify their antisocial feelings and their
isolation from the social effort. Rollo May believes that a
preoccupation with orgasm may lead to a new form of
neurosis. I am in accord with May on the possibility of this
danger. But the significance of orgasm cannot be ignored.
The full orgasm, as I described it, is an index of emotional
health, since it represents the ability of an individual to unite
consciousness and unconsciousness, ego and body, affection
and aggression in a total response. Precisely because this
unity is lacking in modern man is he incapable of full
orgastic experience in the sexual act. However, orgasm is the
result of, not the *means* to, a complete life. It is a mistake to
regard orgasm as having some mystical power to resolve
personal problems. The emphasis of a rational approach to
emotional illness should be upon the conflicts and schisms
that rend the unity of the modern personality and not upon
orgasm or orgastic potency.

The basic conflict is between man's rational nature and his
animal nature. It is the conflict between the ego and sexuality, in which the ego stands for consciousness of self, knowledge, and power, while sexuality represents the unconscious
forces operating in the body. These unconscious forces must
be recognized and accorded a status equal to that which is
assigned to the "higher" functions of the mind. Knowledge,
power, and wealth are meaningless unless they contribute to
the general well-being of the individual and to the welfare of
society. But they cannot do this if they ignore the claims of
the body for expression and fulfillment. So far, I am sure all
will agree, but many voices will be raised in protest if I insist
that in our culture the claims of the body are denied.

I commented in several places on the physical rigidity and
immobility that many patients show. Few of them were
aware of the physical tensions that paralleled and structured

their emotional problems. The prevailing idea, to which they subscribed, is that emotional difficulties are purely psychic and reside somewhere in one's "head." Popular thinking regards the body and the mind as two separate entities. If this kind of thinking is allowed to persist in the course of analytic therapy, it creates a gulf between what the patient learns and how he functions. It permits the illusion to continue that knowledge is a substitute for feeling. It encourages the avoidance of the truth that the sexual function of the individual is an expression of his unity of body and mind.

I have shown that sexual difficulties are intimately bound to physical disturbances in the form of muscular tensions, pelvic rigidities, spasticities of the leg musculature, and restricted respiration. Sex is a physical function that depends upon the grace and coordination of the body for its pleasure and satisfaction. We are naïve if we think that all that is needed for enjoyable sex is a willing partner. It is pure sexual sophistication to believe that sexual freedom is an attitude of the mind. Is one free to enjoy sex if his body doesn't move rhythmically? What kind of sexual freedom is gained through the use of obscene language or the indulgence in sensuality? Only an egoist would confuse license with freedom.

The overvaluation of the ego and the intellect has negated the truth of the body. To the ego, the body is an object to control. The ego develops through its control of bodily functions. But when one goes so far as to regard the body as a machine, one risks losing the one reality that can sustain sanity in this confused time. Carl Jung states this problem clearly: "If we are still caught by the old idea of an antithesis between mind and matter, the present state of affairs means an unbearable contradiction; it may even divide us against ourselves. But if we can reconcile ourselves with the mysterious truth that spirit is the living body seen from within, and the body the outer manifestation of the living spirit—the two being really one—then we can understand why it is that the attempt to transcend the present level of consciousness must give its due to the body."

The truth of the body refers to an awareness of the expression, the attitude, and the state of the body. The phrase is meaningful only in terms of awareness. To know the truth of the body is to be aware of its movements, its impulses, and its restraints, that is, to feel what goes on in the body. If an individual doesn't *feel* the tensions, rigidities, or anxieties of his body, he is, in this sense, denying the truth of his body. This denial takes place on the unconscious level as a loss of perception of the bodily condition. It is frequently accompanied by the expression of the opposite state or feeling. For example, patients often mask a feeling of sadness by compulsive smiling, with the result that they are unaware of the feeling of sadness. Other patients cover up the hostility manifested in cold, hard eyes and a set jaw by an exaggerated politeness and formality. The truth of the body may be concealed by rationalizations or intellectualizations. A patient may rationalize his inability to express anger by saying that anger is not an appropriate reaction. The truth for this patient may be that he cannot mobilize or sustain a feeling of anger because of chronic muscular tensions in the shoulder girdle. Orgasm is a feeling of the body that expresses love for the sexual partner. Orgastic impotence indicates a fear of love on a sexually mature level. How many persons are aware of this simple truth of the body?

The feeling that the heart "opens" to love is a truth of the body. It may not accord with the scientific view to relate the heart to love. But, then, science is not interested in feelings, only in mechanics. When people speak of love without any bodily sensation of that emotion, they are talking of images, not feelings. Some persons find it difficult to say "I love you" because they lack this specific feeling. Others use words without regard to the bodily feelings they imply. In a similar way, people speak of sexual desire without having a strong sexual urge. What they mean is that they want a sexual contact to make them feel alive and excited. This dissociation of loving words from sexual feeling is characteristic of sensuality as described in Chapter 10. The expression "I love you" often means "I need you," and it is a request for love rather than a declaration of a body feeling.

The idea that the heart is the seat of love is pertinent to the question of orgastic potency. In all neurotic individuals, one finds that the chest wall is extremely tense. In addition, the diaphragm is contracted, the belly is sucked in, and the shoulders are unyielding. The heart is literally encased in muscular armor which protects it but also isolates it from the feeling in the genital area. This "armoring" explains why the sexual sensations are limited to the genital organs and do not extend to the total body in a full orgastic reaction.

Another physical condition that interferes with orgastic potency is a flat, sucked in belly and tight, tucked in buttocks. In a man, a flat belly is supposed to be a sign of masculinity.

The ideal of manly posture has been and is the West Point carriage: belly in, chest out, shoulders squared. But if such posture is called for in soldiers, it makes no sense in terms of sexuality. It is a posture that denotes control, restraint, order, and, perhaps, command. It emphasizes the ego values, but it inhibits the surrender to the unconscious and to the feelings necessary for orgastic discharge. It reduces the body to an instrument of the will, and it decreases orgastic potency. The contraction of the belly prevents feeling from invading the pelvis. It cuts off the genital organ from the rest of the body and transforms it into a tool. The tight buttocks further limit sexual feeling. They give the pelvic thrust a sadistic quality by making the movements hard and driving. The penis is transformed into a weapon. This posture can claim to be masculine only in that it denies the feminine side of man's nature. The soft "full-bodied" sexual feelings are regarded by the ego as aspects of the feminine.

It is difficult to understand why women often adopt standards of masculine attractiveness as their own. A recent department store advertisement illustrated this new value humorously and dramatically. It showed in side view a young woman whose appearance—she was dressed in slacks, flat-chested, had no belly and no hips—caused one boy to ask another in the copy of the ad, "Who's your kid brother?" This new value, the boyish physique, is an unconscious denial of female sexuality. It indicates the degree to which the masculine ethos has permeated female thinking. One can only conclude that the superficial disappearance of the double standard is owing to its replacement by a single one—the masculine standard.

While any lessening of the double standard is not to be regretted, this recent development has been accompanied by a deterioration of morals, of values, of love, and of the physical body. The poor physical condition of so many men in our culture has become an object of concern of and study by a presidential committee. But all exhortations, programs, and projects seem helpless to deal with this chaotic situation. Cut off by the power of his rational mind from the mystical ties that bound his ancestors to nature and to life, modern man has also rejected the ideals and beliefs that sustained his father—among them, the double standard of sexual behavior. As an individual alone, he can look only to himself for a code of behavior that gives meaning to his life. In the truth of his body and in his sexual feelings, man has a guide to moral and ethical conduct that can fulfill his being and satisfy his nature.

Reich, in *The Function of the Orgasm,* proposed a morality based upon the concept of genital self-regulation. This concept developed out of his observation that when patients gained the capacity for full genital surrender, the whole personality of the patient changed radically. Compulsive attitudes toward work and sex disappeared. Sexual promiscuity ended, not because of any moral compulsion, but because such behavior failed to yield the satisfaction that the patient wanted. The "genital character," as Reich described the individual who had attained this capacity, had the ability to combine sex with love or love with sex: "It was as if the moral agencies disappeared completely and were replaced by better and more tenable safeguards against anti-sociality, safeguards which were not at variance with natural needs, but were, on the contrary, based on the principle that *life is to be enjoyed.*" The genital character is not hedonistic, as this statement might imply, but rational. He has the power of choice: when and how to seek the satisfaction of his desire. It would be a rational choice because there would be no internal conflict with repressed desires. For example, a man with a genital character structure would not seduce a girl. It would go against his feelings. He would look for a girl who would respond spontaneously to him. Sex for the individual with a genital character structure is a meaningful and enjoyable experience. For the neurotic individual, "the sexual act is essentially a demonstration of 'potency.'"

Reich's analysis of the differences between compulsive morality and natural self-regulation impresses one with its logic. The sexual chaos of the twentieth century seems to prove that such self-regulation is necessary. Having arrived at the conviction that self-regulation is possible, that it does exist naturally, and that it might conceivably become universal, Reich devoted his life to the problem of making this concept a social reality. It is not pertinent here to go into the history of Reich's life and work and its culmination in the fiasco of his imprisonment and death. In bitterness and frustration, Reich finally came to believe that the mass of the people were not ready to accept and fight for this ideal. He concluded that thousands of years of sexual repression and compulsive morality had created in modern man a fear of freedom and sexual pleasure.

Reich posed the question: "Why has the concept of a

sharp antithesis of nature and culture, instinct and morals, body and mind, devil and God, love and work, become one of the outstanding features of our culture and *Weltanschauung?*" His answers, however, were predominantly on the negative side: "In order to be able to exist in the world, they had to fight and destroy in themselves that which was most true, most beautiful, most their own," and, "Money-making as the content and goal of life contradicts every feeling." These answers are fundamentally true. The human tragedy that results from these contradictions in human nature is apparent to all. But Reich had not explored the history of human consciousness as Jung and Neumann had done. The struggle for consciousness, individuality, and culture was a difficult one. The price, as we see it now, may have been too high, but it has not often been questioned before except by a few great thinkers. Arnold Toynbee compares the state of civilized man to the plight of a mountain climber on a steep face who is perched on a small ledge. Below on the plain is the primitive condition. Above lies the mountaintop to which civilized man aspires. But the ascent is perilous and most difficult. To fall is death, to hold on and struggle until he is ready to attempt the ascent is painful, even torturous. But what other choice does man have?

The vision of the height is not enough to justify a desperate all-out effort to scale the precipice. Reich tried and failed. We must gain more knowledge, find new ways, develop techniques we do not yet possess. The concept of self-regulation founded on full orgastic potency is a vision, not a skill; an ideal, not a path. It has not proved applicable as a therapeutic tool, as Reich reluctantly admitted in his later years. Consequently, we cannot fully accept Norman Mailer's interpretation of Reich's concept, namely that the orgasm frees the individual's possibilities for a creative life. It has to be stated in reverse: a free individual (free from neurotic conflict) can explore his possibilities for creative living, one of which, perhaps the key one, is the capacity of full orgastic surrender in the sexual act.

The problem is not sex, but sexuality. And sexuality is a function of the body, not only of the genital apparatus. Reich made a serious slip when he contrasted "neurotic" character with "genital" character. Every adult is a "genital" character to the degree that he carries on a sex life. He could reasonably claim that since sex is important to him, he is functioning "genitally." The term "neurotic" can be contrasted only

with its opposite, "healthy." Neurotic and healthy are opposite ends of a spectrum in which health means the capacity to
enjoy life and neurosis the incapacity for that enjoyment.
These are subjective criteria. Objectively, health must represent a state of the *body*, that is, a body that is vital, alive,
free from chronic muscular tensions, coordinated in its movements, harmonious in its parts—a body with which the personality is fully identified. In other words, health cannot be
divorced from the attributes of beauty, grace, and truthful-
ness. Such a body is sexually alive.

The problem is not genitality, but sexuality. I stated in an
earlier chapter that the homosexual has genital feelings but
that the rest of his body is comparatively "dead." This is true
to a different degree of all neurotic individuals, and it accounts for their incapacity to have a total bodily response in
the sexual climax. In fact, when a strong genital excitation
develops that is dissociated from the feeling in the rest of the
body, it is experienced as unpleasant. Homosexual activity
arises from the need to "get rid of" this unpleasant feeling.
But the homosexual is caught in his perversity because he
believes that genital feeling is the way to life. It is a belief
based on a lack of knowledge of the truth—the truth that his
body is frozen, immobile, and unresponsive. Only this truth
can free him, since only through the mobilization of body
feeling can he overcome the fears that prevent a relaxed
approach to a woman.

We are not accustomed to thinking in terms of the truth of
the body. For too long, Western thought has regarded the
body as a mechanism, an instrument of the will, or a repository of the spirit. Modern medicine, for all its advances, still
holds to this view. We do not take our bodies seriously
except when something goes wrong. Then we run to a "re-
pairman." We have not yet accepted Jung's simple hypothesis: "Since there is a form of body as well as of behavior or
mind, a general characterology must teach the significance of
both physical and psychic features." Here, again, it is Reich's
genius that laid the foundation for such a characterology.

I would offer the hypothesis that the individual who is in
touch with his body and in contact with his feelings doesn't
lie. He doesn't lie because it makes him "feel wrong." Children don't like to lie; they say that it makes them "feel bad."
If one misrepresents himself, one creates an internal conflict
between the projected image and the reality of the self. This
conflict is experienced as a physical tension by healthy per-

sons. It results from the attempt of the body to conform to the image, which it cannot do. But if a person has no contact with his bodily feelings, he doesn't perceive this tension. When stating an untruth, he may not even be aware that he is lying.

Such lying is typical of the psychopathic personality. This type of individual is considered to be without conscience by almost all psychiatrists. My experience with a number of such cases is that they have almost no feeling of their bodies. In common language, we may say of such a person that he "talks through his hat." There are several classic examples of this kind of behavior. We all have seen the comedy skit in which one person is arguing loudly, excitedly, and angrily. His partner asks, "What are you excited about?" and in an obviously hysterical and excited tone, the answer comes back, "Who's excited?"

A similar split often appears in the sexual behavior of a man. It is rare for a man who loses his erection either before or during intercourse to face this response honestly. The common remarks, as girls report them, are: "This never happened to me before," "I don't understand it," or, "It will be all right next time." The truth, as the body expresses it, is that he has lost his desire for the girl. This may happen because of anxiety, guilt, or fear. He may be uncomfortable in the situation, afraid that the girl may expect a lasting relationship, anxious about his ability to satisfy the female, and so on. I am sure that each man in this situation senses his real feelings on some level of awareness. If he can accept them and express them, the conflict can be resolved and his potency will return. If we are afraid to face the truth of our body or its feelings, we prevaricate, dissemble, and adopt a pose.

I could offer a good argument for the proposition that all forms of lying and deceit represent a running away from the truth of the self or of the body. Certainly body and self cannot be two separate entities. However, it is not fully relevant to argue this proposition here. I would like to suggest that an inner morality and set of values can be founded on the principles of self-knowledge and self-acceptance, in which the truth of the body is incorporated. This would not lead to egotism or narrow self-interest. The self does not exist in a vacuum. Nor is this such a simplistic view as Ernest Hemingway's one-sentence manifesto: "What is moral is what you feel good after, and what is immoral is what you feel bad after." In the present state of affairs, most persons do not experience such clear-cut feelings. One may feel good and bad about an activity or good at one moment, then bad the next as deeper feelings emerge. Not until one is fully in touch with one's body, fully aware of its feelings, its tensions, its qualities, is one capable of making moral judgments, even though they are limited to one's own behavior. Rather than formulating codes, we should look for a "way." The way to a richer life is certainly through a fuller experience of the body and its sexuality. I shall not insist that it is the only "way," but it is a valid way of life, one that synthesizes the antithetical functions of man's personality.

I have stressed that sexual maturity is not a goal, but a way of life. The sexually mature person has the courage to face the truth of his body, as a result of which he respects his feelings and himself. He also respects his sexual partner, people in general, and the phenomenon of life in whatever form it manifests itself. His self-acceptance embraces that which he has in common with all human beings: life, liberty, and the sexual impulse. The person who hates himself, hates his body and the bodies of other people. In asserting his right to sexual happiness, the mature person accords others the same right. He has what I call an "open heart." Because his heart is open and not closed, the sexually mature person gives himself fully to those he loves. In return, everyone loves and respects the individual with an open heart. He is wholehearted in his activities and wholly fulfilled and satisfied by their results. He is, of course, orgastically potent. I have known such persons, and they have enriched my life. They justify my faith in people.

The individual with a "closed heart" is afraid to love. In the final analysis, it is this fear that makes him act in a neurotic way. He knows the meaning of love, and he is aware of his need to love, but he cannot open his heart to the feeling of love. Certainly he wasn't born that way. I see such persons constantly in my practice. In each case, there is a history of disappointment in love at a very early age. Patients recall how as babies they cried for a parent who didn't respond. Sometimes this is confirmed by a parent. During a time when behaviorism as a psychological doctrine was in vogue, several mothers told me that they were advised by their doctors not to pick up their crying babies lest they spoil them. Other patients recall that their longing to be nursed often went unsatisfied. Some recollect the image of a "bad mother" whose irritation at the seemingly endless demands of the infant manifested itself in a harsh or hostile manner. The combination of repeated disappointments and fear produces a defense against further hurt. This defense takes the form of an "armoring" expressed physically in a chronic rigidity of the chest musculature. The heart becomes "closed" by being imprisoned in a rigid thoracic cage, which in turn limits respiration and inhibits feeling. Every neurotic patient suffers from a disturbance of respiration resulting from chronic tensions in the chest wall and in the diaphragm. Psychologically, the "closed heart" is expressed in the attitude, "I'll love you if you love me." Conditions are denials. The neurotic individual can't love but projects his inability onto others.

There is no quick and simple method to overcome neurotic disturbances. In order to achieve an "open heart," a person must feel secure enough within himself to risk disappointment and strong enough to face the fear of being alone. He must resolve all the neurotic conflicts, which split the sense of self and block his full identification with his body. And he must overcome the cultural tendency to dissociate the ego from the body and love from sex. This is not easily done; analysis is a long, arduous procedure and is not always fully successful. But health and happiness are worth the effort.

I can offer no simple prescription for a satisfactory and healthy sexual life. The sexual crisis that confronts this age will require for its resolution some major changes in thinking and attitude. A new personal and social order based on an appreciation of the truth of the body must emerge. Man's awe in the face of the seemingly unlimited potentialities of the human mind should not make him lose respect for the infinite wisdom of the body. Scientific sexology, if it is to be helpful, must not be blind to the mystery of love that lies at the heart of the sexual act.